The Coloniality of Catastrophe in Caribbean Theater and Performance

Camilla Stevens · Jon D. Rossini
Editors

The Coloniality of Catastrophe in Caribbean Theater and Performance

palgrave
macmillan

Editors
Camilla Stevens
Rutgers, the State University of New Jersey
New Brunswick, NJ, USA

Jon D. Rossini
University of California
Davis, CA, USA

ISBN 978-3-031-85790-4   ISBN 978-3-031-85791-1   (eBook)
https://doi.org/10.1007/978-3-031-85791-1

© The Editor(s) (if applicable) and The Author(s), under exclusive license to Springer Nature Switzerland AG 2025

This work is subject to copyright. All rights are solely and exclusively licensed by the Publisher, whether the whole or part of the material is concerned, specifically the rights of translation, reprinting, reuse of illustrations, recitation, broadcasting, reproduction on microfilms or in any other physical way, and transmission or information storage and retrieval, electronic adaptation, computer software, or by similar or dissimilar methodology now known or hereafter developed.
The use of general descriptive names, registered names, trademarks, service marks, etc. in this publication does not imply, even in the absence of a specific statement, that such names are exempt from the relevant protective laws and regulations and therefore free for general use.
The publisher, the authors and the editors are safe to assume that the advice and information in this book are believed to be true and accurate at the date of publication. Neither the publisher nor the authors or the editors give a warranty, expressed or implied, with respect to the material contained herein or for any errors or omissions that may have been made. The publisher remains neutral with regard to jurisdictional claims in published maps and institutional affiliations.

Cover credit: Cover art photograph by Deborah Jack. *waterfront* (2002) from her *Imagined Spaces series* (2006)

This Palgrave Macmillan imprint is published by the registered company Springer Nature Switzerland AG
The registered company address is: Gewerbestrasse 11, 6330 Cham, Switzerland

If disposing of this product, please recycle the paper.

This book is dedicated to all of the artists and scholars who engage counter catastrophic strategies in the Caribbean.

Acknowledgments

This book of essays has its roots in the fall of 2022 at the American Society for Theatre Research (ASTR) meeting in New Orleans, where we co-convened a working group on the coloniality of catastrophe in Caribbean theater and performance. We thank ASTR for the support it provides for scholars in the field of theater and performance studies, and we thank our working group participants, whose perspectives helped lay some of the conceptual groundwork and formulate some of the central questions of this volume. In addition, for Camilla, annual meetings hosted by the Caribbean Studies Association have been an important space for seeking more cross-cultural dialogue on Caribbean performance cultures. We would also like to thank the Digital Library of the Caribbean (dLOC) and the Repeating Islands blog for posting our call for papers, for we surely reached a wider pool of scholars thanks to them. Many thanks to each of our contributors for entrusting their work to us and for their receptiveness during the process of revisions. We express deep gratitude to Deborah Jack, the artist of our stunning cover art, and her studio manager Patricia Chevez, for their responsiveness and generosity. It was a pleasure working with Isis Sadek, our copy editor, and we are appreciative of her careful editing and gracious suggestions for our authors. Finally, Camilla would like to thank the School of Arts and Sciences of Rutgers University-New Brunswick, for its steady research funding, and Jon would like to thank Paula for her patience and support.

Contents

1	**Introduction** Camilla Stevens and Jon D. Rossini	1
2	**Guy Régis Jr's Post-earthquake Vigil: Keeping Watch on Catastrophe in *De toute la terre le grand effarement*** Emily Sahakian	29
3	**"We Must Face Haiti": Rawle Gibbons's 1993 Production of *The Black Jacobins*** Raj Chetty	49
4	**Staging the Païdeuma: Nature and Insurrection in Aimé Césaire's *Une tempête*** Eren Jaye	67
5	**The Coloniality of *Naufragio* and Utopia in Teatro Buendía's *Otra tempestad*** Eric Mayer-García	85
6	**Making Theater in the Face of the Storm: Shakespeare in Paradise, Healing, and Theater** Nicolette Bethel	107
7	**Drowning in the Wake** Ian A. Bethell Bennett	127

8	"No More Drumming. Nor Sticks": The Colonial Catastrophe that Conditioned Caribbean Performance Shrabani Basu	145
9	Interrogating Disaster Through Apocalyptic Narratives in Dominican Theater José Emilio Bencosme Zayas	163
10	Sensing Catastrophic Realities in Diasporic Puerto Rican Theater Megan Bailon	179
11	PROMESA, Anti-colonial Drag, and Diasporic Puerto Rican Trans Revolution Lawrence La Fountain-Stokes	197
12	Beyond Catastrophe: Teresa Hernández and the Puerto Rican Performative Body in the New Millennium Priscilla Meléndez	219
13	Catastrophe, Theater, Performance: Praxes of Re/Making the Caribbean With/Out Coloniality, A Conversation with Eliézer Guérismé, Judith G. Miller, Gaël Octavia, and Gina Athena Ulysse Christian Flaugh	241
Index		269

Notes on Contributors

Megan Bailon is a Lecturer in Chicanx and Latinx Studies at the University of Wisconsin-Madison. She holds a Ph.D. in Latin American Literature and her pedagogy and research focus on contemporary Caribbean theater and performance as well as embodied explorations of labor, solidarity, and belonging in Latinx cultural expression.

Shrabani Basu is an Assistant Professor of English at Deshabandhu Mahavidyalaya, Chittaranjan, India. She has worked on cultural hybridity, marginalization, and performance in the Caribbean anglophone context. Her article "The Foil and the Quicksand: the Image of the 'Veil' and the Failure of Abjection in Iranian Diasporic Horror" was published in *Cinema: Journal of Philosophy and the Moving Image*. Her book on the gendered representation of Caribbean performance was published in 2022 (Palgrave Macmillan, Singapore).

José Emilio Bencosme Zayas is an independent researcher, theater artist, writer, and translator from the Dominican Republic. As a Caribbean citizen, he addresses questions of colonialism, memory, identity, cultural, and political production in the region and its diasporas. He holds an M.A. in Theatre and Performance Studies from Queen Mary University of London.

Nicolette Bethel was born and raised in Nassau, Bahamas. She has lived, studied, and worked in the UK and Canada. She is a playwright, poet, fiction writer, and scholar. She is also a theater producer and director and is the Festival Director of the Shakespeare in Paradise theater festival. She serves as Chair of the Dundas Centre for the Performing Arts in Nassau, Bahamas. She blogs occasionally at http://nicobethel.com.

Ian A. Bethell Bennett is an Associate Professor and former Dean of Liberal and Fine Arts at the University of the Bahamas. He holds degrees in Trade Policy, Cultural Studies, English, and Spanish. His research interests include gender in development and migration, and his recent publications focus on tourism and unequal development in the Caribbean, particularly in The Bahamas and Puerto Rico. He also researches Haitian and Cuban migration to and through The Bahamas and is currently working on a project on statelessness in The Bahamas.

Raj Chetty is an Associate Professor of Caribbean literature at St. John's University. His work appears in *Small Axe*, *Palimpsest*, *Meridional*, *Afro-Hispanic Review*, and *Callaloo*. His collaborative projects include "Dominican Black Studies" (a special issue of *The Black Scholar*); Ethnic Studies Rise!; and establishing the *Journal of Critical Race and Ethnic Studies*. He is working on two books, one on Black literary and expressive arts in the Dominican Republic, another on performance legacies of C. L. R. James's Haitian Revolution plays.

Christian Flaugh is an Associate Professor in the Department of Romance Languages and Literatures (SUNY-University at Buffalo). At UB, he co-founded and co-coordinates the Humanities Institute Performance Research Workshop. Flaugh is the author of *Operation Freak: Narrative, Identity, and the Spectrum of Bodily Abilities* (McGill-Queen's 2012), and co-editor of *Marie Vieux Chauvet's Theatres: Thought, Form, and Performance of Revolt* (Brill, 2018). He has published in *Cultural Dynamics*, *L'Esprit Créateur*, *Francosphères*, *Journal of Haitian Studies*, *The Methuen Drama Handbook of Gender and Theater* and *Theatre Topics*.

Eren Jaye is a Ph.D. candidate in the Department of French at the University of Virginia, where she is an Interdisciplinary Doctoral Fellow in Caribbean Literature, Arts, and Culture. She is completing a dissertation on the role of environment in francophone Caribbean theater. Her interests include the history of the Atlantic world, ecopoetics, theater, and folklore in a postcolonial context. Before returning to the United States, Eren lived in France where she taught at L'Institut catholique de Paris.

Lawrence La Fountain-Stokes is a Professor of American Culture, Romance Languages and Literatures, and Women's and Gender Studies at the University of Michigan, Ann Arbor. He is author of *Queer Ricans: Cultures and Sexualities in the Diaspora* (2009), *Escenas transcaribeñas: ensayos sobre teatro, performance y cultura* (2018), and *Translocas: The Politics of Puerto Rican Drag and Trans Performance* (2021). Larry performs in drag as Lola von Miramar and has appeared in several episodes of the YouTube series *Cooking with Drag Queens*.

Eric Mayer-García is an Assistant Professor of Theatre, Drama, and Contemporary Dance at Indiana University, Bloomington. Mayer-García's first book project retraces the embodied transmission of experimental theater practices across borders in the Americas from 1965 to 2000. Mayer-García has published research on vanguard theater, latinidad, and theater historiography in *Theatre Survey, The Journal of American Folklore, Atlantic Studies, Theatre History Studies, Chiricú Journal: Latina/o Literatures, Arts and Cultures, Theatre Journal,* and various edited collections in Theater and Performance Studies.

Priscilla Meléndez is a Professor of Hispanic Studies at Trinity College. She specializes in Spanish American theater of the twentieth and twenty-first centuries and centers her research on Mexican, Argentine, and Caribbean theater and performance. Meléndez is the author of *La dramaturgia hispanoamericana contemporánea: Teatralidad y autoconciencia* (1990), *The Politics of Farce in Contemporary Spanish American Theater* (2006), and *Asaltos al escenario: Humor, género e historia en el teatro de Sabina Berman* (2021). Her essays have appeared in *Hispanic Review, MLN,* and *Modern Drama* among others.

Jon D. Rossini is a Professor in the Department of Theatre and Dance and the Graduate Group in Performance Studies at the University of California, Davis, and has been an invited international lecturer at Francisco José de Caldas Universidad Distrital in Bogotá, Colombia. He is the author of *Contemporary Latina/o Theater: Wrighting Ethnicity* (Southern Illinois, 2008) and *Pragmatic Liberation and the Politics of Puerto Rican Diasporic Drama* (Michigan, 2024) and more than 25 articles and chapters on Latine theater and other subjects.

Emily Sahakian is an Associate Professor in the Departments of Theatre and Film Studies and Romance Languages at the University of Georgia.

She is the author of *Staging Creolization: Women's Theater and Performance from the French Caribbean* (University of Virginia Press, 2017) and co-author of a translation and critical edition of *Tale of Black Histories* by Édouard Glissant.

Camilla Stevens is a Professor in the Departments of Spanish and Portuguese and Latino and Caribbean Studies at Rutgers University-New Brunswick. She specializes in Latinx, Latin American, and Caribbean theater and performance studies. Along with articles on race, migration, and cultural identity in Caribbean theater and edited play anthologies, she has authored *Family and Identity in Contemporary Cuban and Puerto Rican Drama* (Florida, 2004) and *Aquí and Allá: Transnational Dominican Theater and Performance* (Pittsburgh, 2019).

List of Images

Image 4.1	Corrie Green as Ariel and Tevin Davis as Caliban in Aimé Césaire's *Une tempête* (*Photo Credit* Anna Kariel)	81
Image 6.1	Shakespeare in Paradise's 2016 production of *You Can Lead a Horse to Water*, directed by Philip A. Burrows. L-R: Jonico Pratt as Son, Valene Rolle as Mother, and Gabriel Hudson as Old Fool. Photograph by Peter Ramsay	112
Image 11.1	Christine Carmela as Lolita in the Soho Rep production of Mara Vélez Meléndez's *Notes on Killing Seven Oversight, Management and Economic Stability Board Members*, New York City, 2022 (Image courtesy of Soho Rep)	201
Image 11.2	Christine Carmela as Lolita and Samora la Perdida as the Receptionist in the Soho Rep production of Mara Vélez Meléndez's *Notes on Killing Seven Oversight, Management and Economic Stability Board Members*, New York City, 2022 (Image courtesy of Soho Rep)	208
Image 12.1	Teresa Hernández as El mime in *Mimeologías* (*Photo Credit* Antonio Ramírez)	224
Image 12.2	Teresa Hernández as El mime in *Mimeologías* (*Photo Credit* Antonio Ramírez)	225

CHAPTER 1

Introduction

Camilla Stevens and Jon D. Rossini

STORMY WEATHER: COLONIALITY AND CATASTROPHE IN THE CARIBBEAN

It is impossible to resist introducing a volume on theater and catastrophe in the Caribbean without referencing the iconic opening scene of William Shakespeare's *The Tempest*, wherein humans struggle with the elements and each other as they navigate a storm that shipwrecks them in the New World. Indeed, three of the essays in this volume address Shakespeare's play and its Caribbean adaptations as a sort of urtext for addressing the catastrophe of colonialism in the Caribbean. Bahamian scholar and theater practitioner Nicolette Bethel, moreover, notes that the ecological and imperial power struggles depicted in Shakespeare's play are all too familiar to Caribbean audiences today (Bethel, 107). As we write this

---

C. Stevens (✉)
Rutgers, the State University of New Jersey, New Brunswick, NJ, USA
e-mail: camilla.stevens@rutgers.edu

J. D. Rossini
University of California, Davis, CA, USA
e-mail: jdrossini@ucdavis.edu

© The Author(s), under exclusive license to Springer Nature Switzerland AG 2025
C. Stevens and J. D. Rossini (eds.), *The Coloniality of Catastrophe in Caribbean Theater and Performance*,
https://doi.org/10.1007/978-3-031-85791-1_1

introduction, Hurricane Beryl, the earliest Category 4 Atlantic hurricane on record, threatens islanders across the Eastern Caribbean. The hurricane season has extended due to climate change, and the time, energy, and resources expended under hurricane watches, warnings, impacts, and post disaster rebuilding now occupies an alarming portion of the lived experience of the region's peoples. Furthermore, following Naomi Klein's formulation of disaster capitalism, natural disasters have been used to justify political, material, and social post disaster recovery interventions that, under the guise of assistance or transformation, have typically been in the service of sustaining, reinforcing, or restructuring forms of neocolonialism (Klein 2018). The Caribbean continues to be marked by European and US colonial practices, as well as the ongoing socioeconomic crises created by neoliberal economic policies, debt, and the refusal of meaningful and consistent engagement toward liberatory futures.

While a meteorological hurricane watch indicates the existence of a potential, imminent threat as predicted by human-centered perception and analysis, Jamaican poet laureate Olive Senior's poem "Hurricane Watch" offers a different point of view:

> Every year we are forced to reinvent ourselves, growing
> shabbier. Perhaps uncertainty comes from the shifty
> breath of Hurricanes, their unlocked eyes revolving
> always counter-clockwise. Watchful. Unmaking us. (Senior 2022, 420)

Senior's poem evokes surveillance and the sense of threat by the personified "shifty breath" and "eye" of the hurricane that "watches" humans as it moves across the Caribbean archipelago. By shifting perspective, Senior centers the hurricane and highlights the ubiquity of stormy weather in Caribbean life. She captures the anxiety of living under the continual threat of hurricanes that have the power to "unmake" human worlds. Like Senior, writers and visual artists across the circum-Caribbean have produced in their works powerful narratives and images about natural disasters ranging from the 1902 Mount Pelée volcanic eruption in Martinique, the 2010 earthquake in Haiti, and hurricanes Katrina (New Orleans 2005), Maria (Puerto Rico 2017), and Dorian (The Bahamas 2019) to name a few twentieth- and twenty-first-century examples.[1] Catastrophes on the order of political upheaval, armed conflict, economic hardship, refugee and migrant crises, gender violence, and public health emergencies also inform Caribbean cultural production and have had disastrous effects on Caribbean societies. In this context, what possibilities exist to survive, adapt, rebuild, and reimagine? Caught in a relentless cycle of natural disasters, Senior notes that the Caribbean and its peoples grow "shabbier" after each iteration, offering a pointedly visual marker of the danger of the discourse of resiliency as repetition results in degradation without radical change. Senior's verses crystallize in poetic form the slow decline that develops from having to repeatedly respond to disaster in a framework of the legacies of colonialism, neoliberal austerity, the governmentality of debt, and climate injustice.

This recognition of cyclical decline foregrounds the ongoing impact of catastrophes that are too often misrepresented and oversimplified as discrete ruptures. Anthropologist Anthony Oliver-Smith argues that "a disaster is made inevitable by the historically produced pattern of vulnerability, evidenced in the location, infrastructure, sociopolitical structure, production patterns and ideology" (Oliver-Smith 2010, 33). Catastrophes have a past, present, and future; they are embedded in history, in Europe's first contact with the Americas, and in built environments emphasizing capitalist economic interests over indigenous and Afro-Caribbean epistemologies that offer different models for human relationality with the world. Aníbal Quijano's term "coloniality" also has a temporal quality recognizing both the historical past and the unfinished and ongoing structures and enduring legacies of European colonialism (Quijano 2000). Thus, both colonialism and catastrophes have sustained consequences often obscured by the focus on singular events. The arrival of Shakespeare's ship full of Europeans is a catalytic example of decolonial philosopher Nelson Maldonado-Torres's understanding of the colonial encounter as a "metaphysical, demographic, and environmental catastrophe, that is, as a major 'downturn' in the definition of peoples, the environment, and the very basic coordinates of what constitutes a human world" (Maldonado-Torres 2019, 338). Colonialism kick started a catastrophic human and non-human decline, which has included:

> genocide, displacement, and enslavement of indigenous and African peoples; the disruption, destruction, and reconfiguration of local ecologies, economies, and governments; and the establishment and maintenance of racial capitalism as the dominant socioeconomic system structuring the

exploitation of labor and the extraction of natural resources on the island, in the region, and beyond. (Joos et al. 2023b, 4)

In addition to these legacies of colonialism, the title of our volume, *The Coloniality of Catastrophe in Caribbean Theater and Performance*, references what political anthropologist Yarimar Bonilla calls the "coloniality of disaster" and what sociologist Mimi Sheller calls the "coloniality of climate." Bonilla frames her analysis of Hurricane Maria by asking what disasters reveal, arguing that the crisis served to "lay bare the forms of structural violence and racio-colonial governance that had been operating in Puerto Rico for centuries" (Bonilla 2020, 2). Bonilla's crucial question is a pointed invocation to think past the present moment to engage the larger social, political, and economic structural forces that shape environmental conditions in the Caribbean. For her part, sociologist Mimi Sheller's analysis of Haiti's post-earthquake recovery notes the "pervasive influence of colonialism, capitalism, military power, economic domination and racialized mobility control in creating intertwined catastrophes of coloniality and climate change" (Sheller 2020, 6). She characterizes perennial and socially produced "natural" disasters as "the outcome of the coloniality of climate, the deadly logics of a racial capitalism, and the persistence of an anti-Black racism globally as a denial and foreshortening of Black life" (Sheller 2020, 166).

Many forms of artistic production engage with complex experiences of catastrophe and the often-problematic narratives that accompany them; in our view, it is crucial and deeply fruitful to delve into the specificity of theater and performance as a communal site of understanding and engagement, resistance, remaking, and transformation. The essays included in this volume take special note of the unique interventions of theater and performance from the English-, French-, and Spanish-speaking Caribbean as they engage audiences in exploring modes of survival and innovative world making. While the watchful hurricane in Senior's poem has the power to destroy the material world of the Caribbean, the aim of this volume is to consider theatrical responses to catastrophe as empowering acts that ask for spectators to accompany theater artists in reinventing and remaking worlds. In the theater, iteration is agency and renewal, a rehearsal for "getting it right," whether that be perfecting a stage performance or imagining or modeling alternatives to the real world. By employing a specific focus on the alternative possibilities inherent in performance, the essays call attention to the ways in which performance reveals the deliberately constructed roots of catastrophe and offers strategies to live and imagine otherwise. The cultural work of theater explored in this volume thus offers "counter-catastrophic" responses that produce "decolonial thinking and decolonial aesthetics and poetics," (Maldonado-Torres 2019, 340) potentially unsettling the normalization of catastrophe.

Theater and Catastrophe: Watchful Gathering

Let us return to Senior's "Hurricane Watch" to consider the human agency in watching a piece a theater, contrary to the immobility and vulnerability produced by being subject to the eye of the approaching hurricane threat. The Greek and Latin etymologies of theater (a place for viewing) and auditorium (a place for hearing) remind us that the theater is a site where live bodies are called upon to watch and listen to performers onstage.[2] In what follows, we suggest that the temporal properties of theater and catastrophes, such as iteration and suspension, and the theater's specific call for embodied co-presence demands particular qualities of attention that in themselves might offer tools for thinking otherwise in the context of catastrophe.

The time of theater is very specific and yet it is never fixed. One of the challenges historically of the tension between drama and performance was precisely the ways in which methods of analysis relied on the fixity of an object, and yet the performance turn in the social sciences and the prevalence of post-structural thinking has resulted in a widespread recognition of cultural objects as always contingently in process. The reality of this condition is evident in the doubled condition of theater, where productions are embedded in the cultural histories of the work, the history of the performance, and the intentional choice to devote resources to producing in this time and place. As such, theater is eminently conscious of its situatedness at the same time artistic choices enable potentially radical shifts. Unlike a novel or a piece of visual art, for example, whose fixed public form tends to be reinterpreted more than resituated, theater's meaning is both inextricably tied to its local conditions, even as its textual form and performance histories exceed the specific moment of performance.

Catastrophes evoke and impose multiple experiences of time. As we have noted, they are rooted in a particular history, create an unnaturally extended present, and force a future that must be remade (to Senior's point, a more tattered and less hopeful future in each iteration). In *The*

Power of the Story: Writing Disasters in Haiti and the Circum-Caribbean the authors drive home the notion that "Disasters are not one-off events. They compound and lead to a state of permanent and global catastrophe" (Joos et al. 2023a, 190). They argue that cultural production, "the power of the story," disrupts the repetitive cycle of disaster and forces a kind of contemplation that goes beyond a crisis response, which "enables us to capture new temporalities, to shed light on new relations between humans, nature, and the spiritual realm" (Joos et al. 2023a, 190). "Island futures," as Sheller puts it, will depend on "repair, care, and reparations. We need to ask: Who is responsible, who is harmed and who should be accountable?" (Sheller 2020, 166). Looking to community-based disaster risk management and radical Caribbean traditions of the past may be another solution (Sheller 2020, 24, 166). Akin to the unnatural state of perpetual crisis, Bonilla notes the expanded and stalled quality of time in the context of catastrophe she calls the "wait of disaster," a temporal logic of state subjugation and forced resiliency whereby Puerto Ricans were suspended in time waiting for an effective government response that never came (Bonilla 2020, 3). In the face of state abandonment, Puerto Ricans turned toward *autogestión*, various modes of autonomous organizing (Bonilla 2020, 9). So, while resiliency can be coopted in service of a neoliberal recovery, it can also be the site for producing new visions of post disaster/post-colonial recovery, and theater can function as an effective strategy in this process.

The efficaciousness of the theater—its aesthetic, affective, and sociopolitical impact—partly lies in its situatedness, its iterative quality, and its special arrangement of time. While the street in itself is a stage where abundant performances of everyday Caribbean life and folk customs take place, theatrical performances provide a framing that facilitates critical reflection. As Martinican writer and philosopher Édouard Glissant has argued, the particular organization of time and space created by the theater event enables a community able to reflect, to criticize, and to take shape: "Theater involves moving beyond lived experience (dramatic time takes us out of the ordinary so that we can better understand the ordinary and the everyday)" (Glissant 1989, 196). By structuring a forum of public address in which people interact through speech and gesture in the active roles of actors and observers, plays in performance demand attention and set in motion memory and imagination, which serve to stimulate and rehearse individual and collective thinking and action. Furthermore, just as memory and imagination are associated with different temporalities, the theater represents a multi-temporal space; performances take place in the present, but the stories staged often serve to examine the past and as a laboratory that experiments with envisioning an alternative present or future. A bracketed space where "the slate is wiped clean all the time" (Brook 1968, 140), the theater evades chronological time and thrives on repetition. This ritual reconstitution of ephemeral communities comprised of the creator(s) of the work, the production, and the spectators represents an intervention that interrupts the suspension of time that catastrophes produce.

In *Reading the Material Theatre* scholar and dramaturg Ric Knowles reminds us that

> Theatrical productions take place in history and, *as* cultural productions, are inextricably connected to the material, historical, and cultural contexts from which they emerge and to which they speak. Productions mean differently in different geographical, architectural, historical, and cultural contexts. They change meaning as the world in and through which they are produced and received changes. (Knowles 2004, 202)

We see a prime example of the mutually enriching interchange between theatrical productions and the world in which they are situated in the post-hurricane Maria Puerto Rican theater project *¡Ay María!*. In the same vein as Knowles's emphasis on the situated and material qualities of theater, literary scholar Arcadio Díaz-Quiñones argues that performances of *¡Ay María!* "show[s] how vulnerabilities and hopes are embedded in a distinctive political and cultural context in which, beliefs, music, and dance can mobilize the community" (Díaz-Quiñones 2019, vii).

The play was envisioned conceptually by producer Mariana Carbonell, who enlisted director Maritza Pérez Otero to help create a short work that could tour all 78 towns on the main island. Insisting on self-sufficiency, the troupe toured their interactive Theater of the Oppressed style work in an RV quixotically named Rocinante. These material conditions clearly reflect the unique power of theater to establish a collective space for affective and communal transformation in diverse spaces and with a minimum of resources beyond human ingenuity. From the first rehearsals which served less as "brainstorming" and "something more like group therapy" for the five actors who came to help (Carbonnell et al. 2019, 40), the affective power of theater was clear. The creative process and the subsequent tour and comprehensive sharing across the island created moments of watchful gathering, of small assemblages offering a moment of respite from recovery efforts, while drawing attention to the need to call out shared experiences and struggles collectively.

Situating the hurricane within the larger framework of economic, environmental, and gubernatorial catastrophe on the island, *¡Ay María!* traces in comedic and poignant terms the human experience of weathering the storm, from the "resigned" purchase of a six pack of beer as emergency rations in the face of depleted grocery stores, to the grueling aftermath of negotiating with various forms of failed government response. Using gesture and quick shifts in character they move through a series of vignettes—frustrated attempts to get help and the difficult but necessary choice to become climate refugees among the deadly governmental failures—and resolve that the federal and territorial government must "stand up" to support the people who are already doing the hard work of surviving through mutual aid and shared labor.

The bringing together of performers and communities, explicitly illustrated in the text's invitation to the audience to share their own location when the hurricane struck, generates a moment of embodied co-presence outside the immediate crisis of everyday survival. This allows for the communication of fear and frustration and reminds all participants of their collective experience, enabling them to acknowledge their given circumstances, a crucial element of Rossini's concept of pragmatic liberation (Rossini 2024). The broad circulation of this event, beyond the 78 towns of Puerto Rico to Florida and even an academic conference in New Jersey serves as testimony and reminder of the power of dissemination, communication, enabled by collective watching, which Emily Sahakian in this volume explores in the context of the wake. This sense of watchful gathering is for us a vital element of Caribbean theater, in which the political function of the theatrical work gains poignancy as it moves through specific cultural moments and historical locations.

Theater *Rasanblaj*

Broadly speaking, the theater practitioners examined in this book are not in conversation with one another, which reflects realities and boundaries fostered by different colonial legacies, histories of resistance, languages, and cultures. Tellingly, in this volume, in response to Christian Flaugh's interview question regarding "the re/making of the Caribbean through theater and performance," Haitian director Eliézer Guérismé reveals, "Before having read this question, I had never thought of the possibility of building a theater of identity, intimately woven to the future of Caribbean people" (Flaugh, 256). One of the aims of this book is to foster a pan-Caribbean view of theater and to identify shared tropes and theatrical strategies that illustrate the unique ways in which theatrical performance contributes to our understanding of the coloniality of catastrophe in the region.

In a sense, this is a renewed call for a regional approach to Caribbean theater studies. As Stevens has examined in her scholarship, both Trinidadian Errol Hill and St. Lucian Derek Walcott dedicated a large part of their creative lives in pursuit of a dramatic tradition in which professional companies would stage stories written, directed, and enacted in a uniquely Caribbean style (Stevens 2014). Their project to develop a national theater movement in the 1950s, building on efforts initiated in the 1930s, represents a vital contribution to decolonization and nation building often underrepresented in Caribbean literary studies. Hill and Walcott, along with playwrights such as Martinican Aimé Césaire, Puerto Rican Francisco Arriví, and Cuban Virgilio Piñera, all reflect a post-colonial perspective in their integration of autochthonous culture and customs with Western dramatic tropes and aesthetics in the creation of a unique national theater tradition and style of performance. Hill's 1976 anthology *A Time and A Season… 8 Caribbean Plays* stands out as an attempt to think of Caribbean theater through a cross-cultural lens and includes playwrights from across the hispanophone and anglophone Caribbean. In the introduction, Hill insists that "The language barrier, a legacy of metropolitan conquest that has for so long seemed insurmountable, can no longer be allowed to obstruct the acceptance of a common destiny as the only realistic salvation of peoples in and around the Caribbean Sea who substantially share a common past and seek similar objectives" (Hill 1976, vii). The urgency for understanding a "common destiny" undeniably resonates today, and the idea that unity and a regionally driven response must be one strategy for the "salvation" of the Caribbean is surely relevant in today's increasingly climate-driven crises.

Recent scholarship on Caribbean theater continues to underscore the post-colonial process of creating a national theater but relatively little space seems to be dedicated to seeking a cross-cultural understanding of the region's theater practices.[3] Jamaican scholar and writer Jason Allen-Paisant observes in his essay "Towards a National Theatre" that "concern with spirit has been fundamental in anglophone and francophone Caribbean theatre from the 1930s–1970s as it addresses the foremost concerns of memory and its relationship to the lived body in the context of a singularly traumatic history" (Allen-Paisant 2021, 78), yet the essays in this volume show that ritual performance and Afro-Caribbean spirituality is central to Puerto Rican, Dominican, and Cuban theater as well. The scope of Justine McConnell's essay "Caribbean Drama and Performance" (McConnell 2021) similarly includes anglophone and francophone theater makers. Our collection of essays, however, suggests that the categories McConnell offers for framing Caribbean theater studies—the syncretization of Caribbean and European elements; works that explore a global political perspective, like Afrocentrism and independent Caribbean identity; plays that examine gender and class in local political contexts; and works developed in the diaspora—are equally relevant to the Spanish-speaking islands as well (McConnell 2021, 133). A truly global approach to theater in the Caribbean and its diaspora might be impossible—our call for papers did not yield any essays on the Dutch Caribbean, and we cannot claim expertise in all linguistic areas of the region. Yet, it is the "what if" of the theatrical imagination that compels us to ask what we might learn from a more expansive pan-Caribbean conversation about theater and performance.

In "Failed Stages: Postcolonial Public Spheres and the Search for Caribbean Theatre" Christoper Balme examines the tensions between Walcott's palpably pan-Caribbean orientation in his play *Drums and Colours*, written in celebration of the West Indian Federation (1958–1962), as well as his Trinidad Theatre Workshop project, along with Hill's call for a national theater based on local folk traditions. While theater indisputably has been an important tool in imagining post-colonial national identities in the Caribbean, the failure Balme refers to is lack "of a national theater supported by the state, boasting an ensemble and a repertoire of national and international works" (Balme 2014, 240). Looking at theater production in other linguistic areas of the Caribbean—Cuba, for example—might show a different story. The anglophone focus therefore limits a fuller discussion of the development of national theater in post-colonial Caribbean. That being said, Balme's concluding insight harmonizes with our desire to create new, transnational approaches for Caribbean theater studies:

the incompatibility between a pan-Caribbean outlook and nationalist political agendas should encourage us to look at our own theaters in terms of transnational perspectives. It is all very well to emphasize the local, but we seem to be moving in all areas toward global and transnational forms of communication. In this respect, the failed stages of a Caribbean National Theatre may provide us with new perspectives to rethink theatre in transnational rather than national or local terms. (Balme 2014, 255)

While extending expertise to a multilingual region is a challenging and perhaps even untenable demand, the singular, yet expansive topic of catastrophe is our attempt to think about Caribbean theater transnationally. We follow recent invocations of artistic forms of assemblage as a means of creating a more sustained conversation on theater in the Caribbean. The approach we rehearse in this essay crosses linguistic and geopolitical borders so as to place texts and performances in relation. Following Glissant, a root identity is linguistically monolithic and rooted in a territory whereas an identity of relation is characterized by a rhizomatic branching that places cultures in contact (Glissant 1997, 143–144). If we were to claim that a field such as Caribbean theater studies exists, we propose that a strategy of relation would productively examine plays and performances from islands across colonial heritages and geopolitical borders.

Our act of curating a collection of essays on cross-cultural Caribbean theater and performance has been inspired in part by the many ways in which artists and scholars have imagined the connectedness of the region. Art historian Tatiana Flores and literary scholar Michelle Stephens write that "A vision of the archipelago as assemblage centers the insular Caribbean not as exclusive, isolated, bounded sited, but rather as unique vantage points from which to view relational patterns that extend outward in multiple directions, horizontally linking island to island, island to continental mainland, island to ocean and sea, and islanders to each other across far-flung waters and shores" (Flores and Stephens 2017, 28). For Flores and Stephens, using the archipelago as an analytical framework in visual art works to bridge the region's linguistic and cultural differences (Flores and Stephens 2017, 15).[4] Metaphors such as the Anancy spider web (Williams 2017), the rhizome (Glissant 1997), the "spiral chaos" of the Milky Way (Benítez-Rojo 1992), and the reassembled broken vase (Walcott 1970) all point to assemblage and relation, but never sameness or simple unity.

In line with these connective approaches, the recent three-volume *Caribbean Literature in Transition* (2021) provides new frameworks for critical Caribbean literary studies since the 1800s. Alison Donnell and Ronald Cummings point out shifts and transitions in Caribbean literature that are not linear itineraries: "There are, of course, no straight lines or direct trajectories between past, present and future in these 'repeating islands' of the Caribbean. Rather, as we have suggested, these historiographical articulations should be understood in terms of assemblages, 'a series of dispersed but mutually implicated and messy networks […]'" (Cummings and Donnell 2021, 10–11). In their expansive view of literary culture, Cummings and Donnell mention anthologies, competitions, and cultural festivals as important spaces for documenting Caribbean literary cultures (Cummings and Donnell 2021, 7); the collection of essays included here similarly show that the theater, like live festivals, constitutes a uniquely visible and concrete gathering point for exploring embodied Caribbean experiences. In this vein, Gina Athena Ulysse's use of the Kreyòl term *rasanblaj* is particularly compelling for thinking about a volume focused on theater. Defined as "assembly, compilation, enlisting, regrouping, (of ideas, things, people, spirits. For example, *fè yon rasanblaj*, do a gathering, a ceremony, a protest)" (Ulysse 2015), *rasanblaj* invokes the ritual quality of live performance. Performance and *rasanblaj* are intentional, embodied, and require presence. *Rasanblaj* also invokes potential for transformation and has subversive roots since African slaves were prohibited from gathering (Ulysse 2015). *Rasanblaj* thus invokes the tension and anticipation of the watchful gathering that the theater event embodies and its potentiality in producing thought and action. In contrast to the historical tendency to examine the playwrights like the ones examined in this volume in their national literary canon, this volume's *rasanblaj* of theater makers and performances gathers onstage projects under the trope of catastrophe and unveils commonalities that justify a pan-Caribbean approach.

Mapping Caribbean Theater Currents

Our call for a *rasanblaj* of essays about theater, catastrophe, and colonialism has yielded analyses of plays and performances from across the Caribbean—from Cuba, the Bahamas, Haiti, the Dominican Republic, Puerto Rico, Martinique, to Trinidad and Tobago. A good number of the essays address twenty-first-century theater works that center on "natural" disasters such as earthquakes, hurricanes, and floods specifically, while numerous others look at plays from the mid-twentieth century that engage the catastrophic effects of colonialism more broadly. We have deliberately chosen to present the essays without formal chronological, thematic or linguistic divisions; we prefer to organize our collection of texts in a more fluid notion of "currents," which are points of contact that can be made in multiple ways and can flow in different directions. In its basic usage in an oceanic context, "current" as the product of both wind and tidal forces suggests a different modality of complex relational connectivity than the archipelagic, which follows along more fixed national and transnational configurations of land masses. Currents are deliberately employed through human agency to facilitate movement, but they are also moments of drift; our arrangement of the texts is therefore meant to suggest multidirectional ways to trace the surface and subsurface intersections in the use of embodied stories as a means of witnessing the catastrophe of colonialism and the creativity generated in its aftermath.

We begin with two essays that invite us to keep watch on perhaps the most unrelenting and compounded space of catastrophes in the Caribbean, Haiti, and to think about the fundamental act of watchful gathering that theater requires. The stories of catastrophe staged in plays analyzed in this volume position readers/spectators as ethical witnesses in the face of the ongoing power asymmetries of coloniality. In Chapter 2, Emily Sahakian frames her analysis of Guy Régis's play about the 2010 Haitian earthquake, *And the Whole World Quakes, Chronicle of a Slaughter Foretold*, around the practice of watching and the communal watchfulness of the wake. Building on Christina Sharpe's polyvalent hermeneutic of the wake—the watery traces of the slave ship as a metaphor for the aftermath of slavery, mourning and commemorating the dead, and a consciousness of Black being (Sharpe 2016, 3–13)—Sahakian's reading highlights the playwright's invitation "to keep watch on the catastrophe of the earthquake and its aftermath, and on the humanity of the real people who experienced it" (Sahakian, 29). This is a powerful starting point for thinking about Caribbean theater because it incites our ethical responsibility as witnesses, and it attends to the aftermath, a crucial space where coloniality might be interrupted. The theater event is ultimately a collaboratively realized vision and communal vigil. As Sahakian puts it, "Theater cultivates a 'collective vigil' insofar as it facilitates the acknowledgement of differently positioned humans who together bear witness to truths that have been obscured and wake both to these truths and their own (and shared) humanness" (Sahakian, 37). In the play, two women, sex workers left homeless by the earthquake, account for the lives lost in the disaster, pointedly return the gaze on the international colonialist "humanitarian" response, and grapple with finding modes of human relation, intimate and otherwise, outside of the structures of coloniality. It is important to acknowledge, as Sahakian does, that as white, US-based academics, we are outsiders in our witnessing. It is our hope, however, that theater criticism is generative by exposing the ongoing and deliberate choices and dynamics of power that foster and enable inequity, and by demonstrating the ways theater and performance constitute a mode of seeing and thinking that shifts away from habitual practices informed by a cycle of colonial violence.

Chapter 3, Raj Chetty's contribution to the volume, takes up and expands the question of "keeping watch" on Haiti. Like the critique in Sahakian's piece of the opportunistic "international solidarity" interventions after the earthquake, in his analysis of adaptations of C.L.R. James's Haitian Revolution play *The Black Jacobins*, Chetty registers Gina Athena Ulysse's observation that Haiti is only featured in international press coverage after disasters, and he characterizes reporting on current political crises as "but another in a series of aftershocks that can be traced back to the racist, colonial coverage of the Haitian Revolution as it unfolded" (Chetty, 50). Richly complex theatrical engagements with Haiti counter problematic media representations and contextualize Haiti's recurrent socioeconomic and political catastrophes in the resistance against colonialism of the longue durée. As Chetty shows, Rawle Gibbons's 1993 restaging of *The Black Jacobins* in Trinidad is a response to Haiti's contemporary and ongoing struggle for sovereignty after the 1991 overthrow of Haiti's first democratically elected president, Jean-Bertrand Aristide. The directorial decision to end the historical play in the second act, leaving out Haiti's move to independence, Chetty argues, links the past and the present: "because of both internal military control and the threat/promise of external military occupation/aid, Haitian independence and democracy can't be staged. What is performed instead is a call to rally behind both the return of Haitian democracy, embodied in Aristide's return, and its independence" (Chetty, 60). To engage audience members Gibbons deliberately staged the production in a marginalized venue to draw habitual theatergoers out of their regular milieu, and he injected the play with interactive engagement to incite audience response in support of Aristide. Gibbons also breaks with the original script to directly address the audience on a problem that has remained from the origins of colonialism, sexual violence against Black women, an intersectional reality of structural oppression also touched upon in Régis's 2011 play.

For Chetty, adaptations of *The Black Jacobins* capture the shifting parameters and locations of colonialism and highlight how theatrical productions evolve to carefully document the longer histories of coloniality (as opposed to the quick snapshot proffered by the media). Gibbons's work embodies the cross-cultural thinking we believe is crucial for confronting the coloniality of catastrophe. Chetty's interview with the Trinidadian theater practitioner merits reproducing here, for it underscores the centrality of Haiti in charting a decolonial future for the Caribbean: "My own belief is as a region we don't move forward until we deal with Haiti. We must face, must come to terms with Haiti. This is how you become a region" (Chetty, 62). His artistic practice, and arguably that of all the theater practitioners highlighted in this volume, constitutes a call to witnessing, an insistence on engagement to both preserve humanity and to creatively imagine alternatives to the coloniality of catastrophe.

Chetty's study on the theatrical afterlives of *The Black Jacobins* underscores the contingency of theater productions, and the play's revisions point to the topic of adaptation and intertextual dialogue seen in the Martinican, Cuban, and Bahamian reconfigurations of Shakespeare's *The Tempest* analyzed in the following three essays. In the Caribbean adaptations, the catastrophe is not the tempest that causes the shipwreck; it is the ensuing colonization that disastrously impacts the native inhabitants and their natural world. In each case, the Caribbean appropriations of Shakespeare's famous text are subversively decolonial in nature, but they are more nuanced than a simple post-colonial inversion of power roles, thus avoiding the risk of reifying colonialist paradigms. Metatheater, masking, intertextuality, and the use of characters and rituals from Afro-Caribbean spiritual traditions create a theater that exceeds a binary autochthonous/European framework. The plays reflect a uniquely Caribbean, syncretic theater described in analogous ways by theater practitioners from across the Caribbean. Derek Walcott, for example, sought to fashion a unique style of West Indian performance and wrote plays that draw on Caribbean popular culture, as well as Western, Asian, and African forms. His works embody what he terms a hybrid "mulatto" aesthetic that deconstructs Eurocentric and nativist oppositions, but at the same time avoids promoting a definitive and unproblematic syncretic Caribbean identity. Similarly, as commented by Shrabani Basu in this volume, Rawle Gibbons proposes that the region's "first theatre" evolved from practices linked to enslaved and indentured populations, its "second theatre" employed Western performance forms, and the indigenization of these elements created a Caribbean "third theatre" (Gibbons 2023). Finally, also very much in line with the vision of a hybrid Caribbean theater, Eric Mayer-García cites Cuban theater maker Raquel Carrió, who describes Teatro Buendía's adaption of *The Tempest* in the following terms: "the play goes beyond negating the colonizer's language in search of a third language, another culture produced through syncretism" (Mayer-Garcia, 86).

As Césaire commented in the 1960s, his play, translated as *A Tempest*, decenters the story told in Shakespeare's *The Tempest* by acknowledging the multiplicity of liberation movements against colonialism, much like the revival stagings of *The Black Jacobins* show how the struggle for liberation resonates beyond the Haitian Revolution. In Chapter 4 Eren Jaye contextualizes her reading of *Une tempête* with Suzanne Césaire's writings about the relationship between nature, culture, and civilization in Martinique, which were influenced by Leo Frobenius's theory of the essence or soul of a culture he called *païdeuma*. Putting the play into conversation with these nascent eco-critical approaches enables Jaye to underscore how in the 2022 production of *Une tempête* at the Blackfriars Playhouse "resistance against colonization is not a mere human endeavor, as more-than-human meteorologic, geologic, and spiritual forces join Caliban in dismantling Prospero's order of civilization in a shared impulse to restore balance distorted by colonial, human relation" (Jaye, 79). The directorial decision to literalize what in Césaire's text is Caliban's vocal threat to destroy the island is suggestive of beginning anew, creating through a catastrophic event a decolonial relation among humans and with their environment. In their tandem staging of Shakespeare's original play, the actors and director of the company also opted to alter the ending of the story, "making Shakespeare speak back to Césaire" (Jaye, 80). The multidirectional intertextual theoretical and theatrical dialogues illuminated in Jaye's study show how Caribbean thinkers decenter resistance and counter discourse.

In a subversion of what she suggestively calls the "perhaps extractive dynamic of conventional spectatorship," (Jaye, 69) Jaye notes the use of masks, the interpolation of the audience into the fiction of the play, and the creation of a heightened ritualized theater space in *Une tempête*, which is specific to global theater trends during the time of the play's creation but are also techniques we see in numerous Caribbean plays addressed in this volume. In Chapter 5, Eric Mayer-Garcia highlights how Teatro Buendía's 1997 production *Otra tempestad* (translated by him as *An/Other Tempest*) similarly demands active audience reception in making meaning of its opaque cultural amalgam of signs and narratives by bombarding the spectator with a continually shifting mixture of Shakespearean texts (among others) and Afro-Cuban orishas and myths, physical movement, light, and sound. In what Mayer-García calls "a ritual unraveling of representational practices and colonial ideology," Shakespeare's famous text is "overtaken in an onslaught of intertexts and associations that produce new meanings and reveal hidden ones" (Mayer-Garcia, 87–88).

Mayer-García frames his analysis of the play with the colonial narratives of *naufragio* [shipwreck] and utopia that helped produce European modernity. Shipwreck narratives served to justify European colonialism in their depictions of the wondrous new lands and the uncivilized, godless, and racialized monstrous people that inhabited them. Hardly a utopia, colonizers nevertheless imagined this space as a blank slate from which an ideal republic could be created. Thus "imaginaries of utopia and *naufragio* grow out of and into one another as the extreme ends of the same project" (Mayer-Garcia, 95) and continue to resonate in the context of twentieth-century Cuba's utopian revolutionary project. In vivid detail, Mayer-García interprets the company's performance of the renowned shipwreck scene, the creation of Próspero's utopia, and a ritualized orgy and cannibalistic feast carried out by Shakespearean characters. Teatro Buendía's unique aesthetic approach engages the violence of colonialism affectively and intellectually in a way that deconstructs motifs of conquest and domination and "opens up alternative possibilities to the historical violence that transpired" (Mayer-Garcia, 87).

The violence of colonialism plays out as capitalist exploitation in a 2009 production of *The Tempest* performed at the Shakespeare in Paradise Festival in The Bahamas. Nicolette Bethel reports in Chapter 6 that despite the general lack of familiarity of the actors and spectators with Shakespeare, this adaptation in which Prospero is from a resort-owning family and Ariel is a chickcharney, a half-human, half-bird from Bahamian mythology, was the top selling production of the festival. Bethel cautions that we should not take the festival title "Shakespeare in Paradise" at face value, since naming it after "the quintessential icon of British intellectual colonialism" and invoking paradise, "one of the most destructive tropes in Caribbean socio-political realities" is meant to interrogate what it means to make theater in a neocolonial context and to remake Shakespeare for twenty-first-century audiences who have not made theatergoing a habitual cultural practice (Bethel 2017, 330).

Shakespeare in Paradise was therefore "founded to empower audiences, build Bahamians' confidence in engaging with Shakespeare, celebrate and enhance Bahamian theatre, expand the Bahamian economy beyond the sun/sand/sea triumvirate, and train Bahamian actors" (Bethel, 121). By center staging Bahamian creativity alongside Shakespeare's work theater becomes a site of counter-catastrophic contestation and reparation. Through the cultivation of empathy, the festival plays "tackle the self-loathing that results from centuries of colonial and post-colonial oppression and to give audiences a new way to see—and honor—themselves" (Bethel, 121). The performances mentioned by Bethel engage with the disastrous effects of hurricanes, global capitalism, violence and homicide, and the COVID-19 pandemic. Coming together to rehearse in the wake of hurricanes even as rescue efforts were taking place had a reparative, therapeutic effect, as did the first live, indoor performance after the COVID-19 pandemic lockdown (of a play that critiqued the erosion of democracy under emergency orders). Whether hermetic and aesthetically dense, or direct and didactic, staged stories in response to catastrophe from across the Caribbean have the potential to "provoke catharsis and, ultimately, healing on both sides—for performances and audiences alike" (Bethel, 119).

Another identifiable current in Caribbean theater is the catastrophe of anti-blackness that results from colonialism. In Chapter 7, Ian A. Bethell Bennett's reading of one of Nicolette Bethel's own plays (*The Children's Teeth*), along with another by Ian Strachan (*Diary of Souls*) extends Bethel's survey of contemporary theater activity in The Bahamas, while with Shrabani Basu's essay (Chapter 8) we return to the figure of Rawle Gibbons, but this time in his role as playwright. Bethell Bennett posits that Bahamians are "drowning in the wake," whether this be the literal drowning of Haitian migrants, the socioeconomic fall out from Hurricane Dorian, or "the structural violence of coloniality that views all Black bodies as less than and slowly erodes their ability to breathe. It is drowning in the wake of the wave as much as it is dry land drowning, where structures oppress and undermine" (Bethell Bennett, 128). The creativity and complexity of the human conflicts—gendered, generational, economic, racial—in Bethel and Strachan's twenty-first-century plays stand out from "the pervasive media-controlled reductive and threatening misrepresentations of blackness and its destructive forms of othering that permeate Bahamian culture" (Bethell Bennett, 132). The plays reveal the cultural geography of the post-independence Bahamas as a space of catastrophic slow violence enacted through power asymmetries (humans/hurricanes, rich/poor, Haitian migrants/Bahamian natives, men/women, military/civilians), spatial injustices (development/decay, geographically safe/unsafe, displacement/migration), and extractive racial capitalism (global economy, tourism industry).

The theater of Rawle Gibbons also addresses anti-blackness by staging stories that are acts of memory. His *Love Trilogy* takes up the history of repressing Afro-Caribbean cultural practices and regulating the spaces in which they take place. In Chapter 8 Basu presents instances of colonial bans or restrictive policy changes impacting Afro-Caribbean cultural traditions, such as Carnival in *I Lawah* and Baptist mourning rituals in *Sheperd*. According to Basu, "Gibbons's plays are commentaries on how the enforced middle-class propriety changed the ethical fiber of the performance (both cultural and religious) in popular perception, with any deviation from colonial policies of respectability, strictly persecuted" (Basu, 160). The plays capture different forms and rhythms of resistance and resilience against the catastrophic consequences of colonial cultural erasure, along with the creole culture produced by the contact among cultures brought about by colonialism. At the same time, Gibbons's theater is a quintessential example of a "third theatre" that hybridizes different cultural traditions. Caribbean theater is thus a cultural practice that serves as both archive and repertoire that documents and embodies the paradoxically catastrophic and generative cultural impact of colonialism.

As the essays we have been discussing suggest, whether a performance is an immediate response to process a crisis, a revival or an adaptation to address a new context, or an instance of collective memory, the temporality of theater and catastrophe is compound. Here we identify a current where plays intersect in their portrayal of the everyday affects and engagement with present-day crises informed by neocolonialism and neoliberalism. Both essays look at theater through the lessons of disaster capitalism learned through Hurricane Maria; in Chapter 9 José Emilio Bencosme Zayas examines apocalyptic scenarios—natural disasters and war—in plays from the Dominican Republic, while in Chapter 10

Megan Bailon examines how Puerto Rican diasporic theater reframes the "migration crisis" story. Each piece illuminates the systemic and structural roots of catastrophe in the neoliberal era, which exceed the acute moment of crisis, and the aesthetic work of the theater in uncovering them, including the incorporation of syncretic Afro-Caribbean religious iconography that sustain and shape the identities of the subaltern (also seen in plays analyzed by Sahakian, Jaye, Mayer-García, and Basu).

Bencosme Zayas pairs Manuel García-Cartagena's *Siete días antes del tsunami* and Frank Disla's *Un romance andaluz* because they both portray fictional doomsday scenarios; the former focuses on an impending tsunami while the latter picks up after the apocalyptic end of the world. As the tempest nears, García-Catagena's play exposes, in the context of neoliberal state abandonment, a fragmented society characterized by exploitative interactions (among humans and also instigated by Yoruba deities) and a search for salvation through migration and religion. Bencosme Zayas writes, "As in global warming, humanity triggers its own demise which comes through an external, non-human environmental force" (Bencosme Zayas, 176). By contrast, "*Un romance andaluz* tells us the other side of the story in which the conflict between peoples produces total annihilation. In both cases, the failure to organize collective responses is what enables damnation" (Bencosme Zayas, 176). Each play contains striking moments of direct audience address that encourage spectators to consider the utility of theater in encouraging community building and fomenting imagination. Through apocalyptic narratives, the plays "operate in via negativa to motivate action and question the current world order that could allow these catastrophes" (Bencosme Zayas, 165).

Bailon highlights how diasporic works *La otra orilla* (1996) by New York's Teatro Pregones and *Yemaya's Belly* (2004) by Pulitzer-prize-winning playwright Quiara Alegría Hudes employ ambiguous plots and stimulating aesthetic choices to question the framing of migration by sea as a sudden, temporary, and solvable crisis. Her essay contextualizes the stories in the repeat, perilous boat migration exoduses of the 1990s involving Cubans, Haitians, and Dominicans and argues that the plays "use a multi-sensory aesthetic approach that relies on both Caribbean poetics and Yoruba cosmology to denaturalize the Western temporal, spatial, and epistemological confines of the 'crises' they depict as they stage (im)migration stories as catastrophes that are entangled in the colonial legacies of the Caribbean" (Bailon, 181). Indeed, we might see migration not as crisis but as a manufactured catastrophe that has evolved over time from the coloniality of disaster, the coloniality of climate, colonial extractivism, and the policies of neoliberalism. By engaging the audience in the sensorial reality (visual and auditory, but also tactile and gustatory) of colonialism and neoliberalism, Bailon argues that the embodied experience of the theater "shifts thinking from how to restore the progress disrupted by a moment of crisis and toward the ritualized and sustained everyday actions necessary to address a catastrophic reality" (Bailon, 192).

The current catastrophic reality of Puerto Rico is examined in more detail in essays by Lawrence La Fountain-Stokes (Chapter 11) and Priscilla Meléndez (Chapter 12). The parodic tone of the performances examined in these essays form our final Caribbean theater current; both essays mock US-proposed solutions to the Puerto Rican debt crisis, which is "a symptom of a much deeper economic and political malaise stemming from its unresolved colonial status" (Bonilla and LeBrón 2019, 6). The fragility of the economy was heightened by a series of crises that occurred in quick succession—hurricanes Irma and Maria in 2017, Governor Ricardo Rosselló's corruption scandal in 2019, earthquakes in 2020, and the COVID-19 pandemic. Puerto Rican artists and activists have confronted these disastrous circumstances with protest and creativity, including the performances commented on by La Fountain-Stokes and Meléndez that posit "queer," irreverent, and even violent responses to the almost dystopian twenty-first-century social, economic, political, and ecological daily realities faced by Puerto Ricans.

La Fountain-Stokes demonstrates how transgender New York-based Puerto Rican playwright Mara Vélez Meléndez's *Notes on Killing Seven Oversight, Management and Economic Stability Board Members* (2022) "combines a trenchant critique of the coloniality of catastrophe" with "the history of feminist, queer, and trans resistance" (La Fountain-Stokes, 204). In the play, the protagonist, Lolita, a Puerto Rican transgender character inspired by the Puerto Rican revolutionary Lolita Lebrón, together with the Receptionist, a Nuyorican gay, cisgender character, stage seven campy drag performances in which they rehearse killing the board members of the Puerto Rico Oversight, Management and Economic Stability Board who control Puerto Rico's economic policies thanks to the enactment of the PROMESA bill in 2016. La Fountain-Stokes reads this darkly comic political play in conversation with absurdist theater, camp and queer theatrical and performance traditions, and Hannah Arendt's *On Revolution*, and argues that by attending to brown trans subjects, the play "offers parallels between a national revolution of self-determination... and an individual revolution regarding gender identity" (La Fountain-Stokes, 205–206). Moreover, by bridging the Puerto Rican archipelago and the diaspora along with cisgender and trans differences, the play offers "a collective, utopian, radical vision" (La Fountain-Stokes, 212) to counter the effects of the coloniality of catastrophe.

The work of island-based artist Teresa Hernández pushes against binarism and normativity in other ways, through the transdisciplinarity of her methods as a solo performer, writer, dancer, video producer, and cultural activist. Meléndez examines iterations spanning fifteen years of Hernández's eccentric embodiment of a *mime*, a sand fly or gnat, in her *Mimeologías* solo performance series. The lone performing body proposes a poetics of the micro, which plays with notions of visibility, audibility, and fugacity. On one level, the smallness and perhaps the annoying quality of the *mime* evokes Hernández's position of alterity in relation to the island's theater establishment, given the hybridity that makes her experimental work challenging to characterize. On another level, by critiquing Puerto Rico's colonial status, class struggles, racism, machismo and sexism, and environmental harm, Hernández becomes the proverbial flea in your ear, that, if heard, amplified, and repeated, can, despite its microscopic size, "make audible and visible the common struggles among the castaways that literally and metaphorically populate the Caribbean waters and islands" (Meléndez, 223). The different iterations of the *mime* character within certain pieces and over time transforms a single voice into many voices, representing "a polyphony of anti-establishment views that aim to confront crisis and catastrophe in an island that has experienced plenty of these" (Meléndez, 231). Meléndez extends the engagement with singularity and multiplicity in Hernández's work to parallel to tension sameness and difference that defines the Caribbean and its diaspora, "a conglomerate of continental and insular peoples with diverse cultural, ethnic, linguistic, and political roots" (Meléndez, 221).

Chapter 13 concludes the book in the form of a *rasanblaj* of francophone Caribbean theater makers convened by Christian Flaugh. The English-French bilingual conversation brings together theater makers from the francophone Caribbean, Europe, and North America, in their varied roles as playwright, performer, translator, director, and scholar, to help us to understand the creative potential of remaking—of responding to but not being bound by the coloniality of catastrophe—through

Caribbean theater and performance. In line with our desire to identify the counter-catastrophic potential of theater and performance, Flaugh beautifully concludes that "Theater and performance as alternative—as re/making—burn in the hearts of many theater and performance creatives, who have not forgotten but will not be branded by the broad, brutal reach of colonial-catastrophe" (Flaugh, 265). Judith Miller and Gaël Octavia's responses to Flaugh's questions emphasize the imagination, resilience, and hope involved in remaking worlds both within and beyond the frame of the theater. Miller notes that the francophone Caribbean plays she has translated are not tragedies, but rather lyrical songs "to the spirit of people capable of surmounting terrible odds and imagining a better future" (Flaugh, 251). Octavia suggests the catalytic force of catastrophe might bring about change and highlights the paradoxical quality of coloniality in the francophone Caribbean, where Haiti is an independent republic, while Guadeloupe, Martinique, and other islands remain tied to France. Coloniality in Martinique, then, "is the absence of a large-scale catastrophe. We long for a catastrophe (from the mathematical sense of catastrophe theory) that breaks with continuity" (Flaugh, 249–250). Since this has not come to pass, Octavia must invent stories that allegorically break with dependency, much like Vélez Meléndez's play imagines a violent end to the US-imposed economic policies in Puerto Rico. Another approach to confronting coloniality is seen in intersectional approaches to Caribbean identity. Flaugh notes that much recent criticism focuses on deconstructing gendered cultural traditions and myths, such as works by Aimé Césaire's daughter, playwright and ethnologist Ina Césaire, and Octavia, both of whom employ theater to remake cultural traditions and myths associated with female archetypes.

The interview is also revealing for its frank recognition of the lack of connectivity among Caribbean theater practitioners, which is precisely why we think the exercise of gathering research on the engagement of theater and performance with the coloniality of catastrophe can strengthen awareness of the field and help identify what we have been calling currents, or trends in theater making across the region. This is most apparent in the comments made by Haitian theater director Eliézer Guérismé, who acknowledges the region's common heritage of colonialism but notes that Haitian creolophone and francophone speakers tend to "to turn more and more toward metropolitan centers [where both languages live due to migration], than toward the other Caribbean islands which don't have that linguistic similarity" (Flaugh, 246). However, despite the barriers that impede dialogues among theater institutions across the Caribbean Guérismé suggests, "we could move from being a divided Caribbean to a united Caribbean, a multicultural people with a shared but diversified project. Separate but still united" (Flaugh, 254). This is what our book endeavors to intensify through linking the common vectors of coloniality and catastrophe from across the region and the diaspora.

This introduction establishes an overarching current of continuous, directed movement for reading the essays that registers the multiplicity of performance responses to catastrophes largely engineered by human design. But like oceanic currents, this flow is changeable and represents one of many possible ways of reading the scholarship on Caribbean theater and performance included here. Given the engagement with Afro-Caribbean aesthetics and belief systems that underpins much of the work our contributors examine, we concur with Allen-Paisant that Caribbean theater "enlist[s] the resources of spirit to translate a sense of absent presence, tracing the outlines of memory in an effort to reshape the future and contextualize the past (Allen-Paisant 2021, 68). Similarly, Ulysse writes that "the conditions of the so-called New World remain characterized by its past. Work that recognizes this intersection demands that our expressions are not determined by our conditions no matter how damning and limiting" (Ulysse in Flaugh, 259). Her performance practice, therefore, "seeks to look inward to explore the hidden depths of the imagination as source of connectivity primarily with the unseen" (Ulysse in Flaugh, 255). Futurity for the Caribbean relies on looking inwards and "bridging the hidden sea of ancestral solidarity that unites these archipelagoes, is the only one possible at this crossroads in history" (Sheller 2020, 170). This both inward and outward, forward and backward reparation-seeking gaze is paramount in addressing the catastrophe of coloniality. As we have seen repeatedly in the works highlighted in this volume, the watchful gathering that characterizes performance "mobilizes commemoration, grief, and action to disrupt ways of living, thinking, and governing that normalize a state of permanent catastrophe" (Joos et al. 2023a, 191). We hope to have shown that theatrical performance, an embodied site of collective remembrance where futures can be imagined, constitutes a powerful critical and creative intervention in the discourses of catastrophe and colonialism in the Caribbean.

Notes

1. We are thrilled to include on our book cover Caribbean artwork that captures the multiple valences of catastrophe. The book's cover art is a piece titled *waterfront* by Deborah Jack, a New Jersey-based visual artist and poet born in the Netherlands and raised in Sint Maarten, the Dutch half of the island of Saint Martin. The photograph forms part of her 2006 *Imagined Spaces* photograph series which dialogues with Toni Morrison's concept of "blood memories" (https://www.deborahjack.com/works-1/imagined-spaces). For us, the haunting orange image simultaneously evokes the bloody legacy of slavery and colonialism and a post disaster hurricane landscape. The image seems to suggest that while the hurricane winds are destructive, the human hand in environmental degradation may be even stronger. We thank the generosity of the artist in allowing us to feature her work.
2. Theater derives from the Greek *theatron*, "a place for viewing," *theasthai*, "to view," and from *thea* "action of seeing, sight, view" (https://www.merriam-webster.com/dictionary/theater).
3. It is laudable that the 2017 *Caribbean Quarterly* special issue dedicated to Caribbean theater includes articles on Èdouard Glissant (Martinique) and Eugenio Hernández Espinosa (Cuba) among a majority of pieces that focus on the anglophone Caribbean. However, none of the essays examine Caribbean performance traditions from a cross-cultural approach. We acknowledge, too, that in this volume the call for papers yielded essays focused on one linguistic tradition.
4. See Martínez-San Miguel and Stephens (2020), and Stratford et al. (2011), for in-depth accounts of archipelagic studies.

Works Cited

Allen-Paisant, Jason. 2021. Towards a National Theatre. In *Caribbean Literature in Transition, 1920–1970*, ed. Raphael Dalleo and Curdella Forbes, 68–81. Cambridge: Cambridge University Press.

Balme, Christopher. 2014. Failed Stages: Postcolonial Public Spheres and the Search for a Caribbean Theatre. In *The Politics of Interweaving Performance Cultures: Beyond Postcolonialism*, ed. Erika Fischer-Lichte, Torsten Jost, and Saskya Iris Jain. New York: Routledge.

Benítez-Rojo, Antonio. 1992. *The Repeating Island: The Caribbean and the Postmodern Perspective*. Durham: Duke University Press.

Bethel, Nicolette. 2017. Culturally Industrious: The Making of a Theatre Festival in Nassau, Bahamas. *Caribbean Quarterly* 63 (2/3): 304–338.

Bonilla, Yarimar. 2020. The Coloniality of Disaster: Race, Empire, and the Temporal Logics of Emergency in Puerto Rico, USA. *Political Geography* 78: 102181. https://doi.org/10.1016/j.polgeo.2020.102181.

Bonilla, Yarimar, and Marisol LeBrón. 2019. *Aftershocks of Disaster: Puerto Rico before and after the Storm*. Chicago: Haymarket Books.

Brook, Peter. 1968. *The Empty Stage*. Atheneum.

Carbonnell, Mariana, Marisa Gómez Cuevas, José Luis Gutiérrez, José Eugenio Hernández, Mickey Negrón, Maritza Pérez Otero, and Bryan Villarini. 2019. ¡Ay Maria! In *Aftershocks of Disaster*, ed. Y. Bonilla and M. LeBrón, 38–60. Playscript translated by Carina del Valle Schorske.

Caribbean Quarterly. 63 (2/3): Special Issue: The Caribbean Stage.

Cummings, Ronald, and Alison Donnell. 2021. Introduction: Caribbean Assemblages, 1970s–2020. In *Caribbean Literature in Transition, 1970–2020*, ed. Ronald Cummings and Alison Donnell, 1–18. Cambridge: Cambridge University Press. https://doi.org/10.1017/9781108564274.001.

Díaz-Quiñones, Arcadio. 2019. Forward. In *The Aftershocks of Disaster*, ed. Bonilla and LeBrón, ix–xiii.

Flores, Tatiana, and Michelle Stephens. 2017. *Relational Undercurrents: Contemporary Art of the Caribbean Archipelago*. Long Beach, CA: Museum of Latin American Art.

Gibbons, Rawle. 2023. *Ritual Enactments of Trinidad: Towards a Third Theatre*. Canboulay Productions.

Glissant, Édouard. 1989. *Caribbean Discourse: Selected Essays*. Charlottesville: University Press of Virginia.

Glissant, Édouard. 1997. *Poetics of Relation*. Ann Arbor: University of Michigan Press.

Hill, Errol. 1976. *A Time and a Season: 8 Caribbean Plays*. Trinidad: School of Continuing Studies, University of the West Indies.

Joos, Vincent, Martin Munro, and John Ribó, eds. 2023a. Epilogue. In *The Power of the Story: Writing Disasters in Haiti and the Circum-Caribbean*, 188–193. New York: Berghahn Books.

Joos, Vincent, Martin Munro, and John Ribó, eds. 2023b. Introduction. In *The Power of the Story: Writing Disasters in Haiti and the Circum-Caribbean*, 1–26. New York: Berghahn Books.

Klein, Naomi. 2018. *The Battle for Paradise: Puerto Rico Takes on Disaster Capitalism*. Chicago: Haymarket Books.

Knowles, Ric. 2004. *Reading the Material Theatre*. Cambridge: Cambridge University Press.

Maldonado-Torres, Nelson. 2019. Afterward: Critique and Decoloniality in the Face of Crisis, Disaster and Catastrophe. In *The Aftershocks of Disaster*, ed. Bonilla and LeBrón, 332–342.

Martínez-San Miguel, Yolanda, and Michelle Ann Stephens, eds. 2020. *Contemporary Archipelagic Thinking: Towards New Comparative Methodologies and Disciplinary Formations*. Lanham, Maryland: Rowman & Littlefield.

McConnell, Justine. 2021. Caribbean Drama and Performance. In *Caribbean Literature in Transition, 1970–2020*, ed. Ronald Cummings and Alison Donnell, 132–147. Cambridge: Cambridge University Press.

Oliver-Smith, Anthony. 2010. Haiti and the Historical Construction of Disasters. *NACLA Report on the Americas* 43 (4): 32–36. https://doi.org/10.1080/10714839.2010.11725505.

Quijano, Aníbal. 2000. Coloniality of Power and Eurocentrism in Latin America. *International Sociology* 15 (2): 215–32. https://doi.org/10.1177/0268580900015002005.

Rossini, Jon D. 2024. *Pragmatic Liberation and the Politics of Puerto Rican Diasporic Drama*. Ann Arbor: University of Michigan Press.

Senior, Olive. 2022. *Hurricane Watch: New and Collected Poems*. Great Britain: Carcanet Poetry.

Sharpe, Christina Elizabeth. 2016. *In the Wake: On Blackness and Being*. Durham: Duke University Press. https://doi.org/10.1515/9780822373452.

Sheller, Mimi. 2020. *Island Futures: Caribbean Survival in the Anthropocene*. Durham: Duke University Press. https://doi.org/10.1515/9781478012733.

Stevens, Camilla. 2014. Caribbean Drama: A Stage for Cross-Cultural Poetics. In *Re-imagining the Caribbean: Teaching Creole, French, and Spanish Caribbean Literature*, ed. Valérie Orlando and Sandra Cypess, 85–102. Lexington Books.

Stratford, Elaine, Godrey Baldacchino, Elizabeth McMahon, Carol Fairbanks, and Andrew Harwood. 2011. Envisioning the Archipelago. *Island Studies Journal* 6 (2): 113–130.

Ulysse, Gina Athena. 2015. Introduction. Caribbean Rasanblaj. *Emisférica* 12 (1). https://hemisphericinstitute.org/en/emisferica-121-caribbean-rasanblaj/121-introduction.

Walcott, Derek. 1970. The Antilles: Fragments of an Epic Memory. In *What the Twilight Says: Essays*, 65–84. New York: Farrar, Straus, Giroux.

Williams, Eugene. 2017. The Anancy Technique: A Gateway to Postcolonial Performance. *Caribbean Quarterly* 63 (2/3): 215–233.

CHAPTER 2

Guy Régis Jr's Post-earthquake Vigil: Keeping Watch on Catastrophe in *De toute la terre le grand effarement*

Emily Sahakian

Haitian playwright, director, and theater producer Guy Régis Jr (b. 1974) uses theater to foreground the stories and experiences of people who are underrepresented and overlooked, to draw attention to social problems, and to hold his spectators and readers accountable for becoming and behaving more "human."[1] Régis's play about the 2010 earthquake, *De toute la terre le grand effarement* [*And the Whole World Quakes: Chronicle of a Slaughter Foretold*], written immediately after the earthquake and first published in 2011, invites its spectators and readers to keep watch on the catastrophe of the earthquake and its aftermath, and on the humanity of the real people who experienced it. The 2010 earthquake was, for Haitians, a few seconds that upended the world definitively.

E. Sahakian (✉)
Department of Theatre and Film Studies and Department of Romance Languages, University of Georgia, Athens, GA, USA
e-mail: sahakian@uga.edu

© The Author(s), under exclusive license to Springer Nature Switzerland AG 2025
C. Stevens and J. D. Rossini (eds.), *The Coloniality of Catastrophe in Caribbean Theater and Performance*,
https://doi.org/10.1007/978-3-031-85791-1_2

It was, to quote the song that concludes Régis's play, the "event that we'll never, ever, ever, forget—ever. That event of a few seconds that will take years and years to erase. Even centuries. It will take longer than a person's life" (Régis 2022, 60). Moreover, the earthquake was, to quote Régis's subtitle, "foretold" by history: by the "heist" of a tremendous debt paid to France after the Haitian Revolution (Daut 2020), by American occupations, and by neoliberalism (Schuller 2016). And, in its aftermath, it attracted a parade of international aid that both failed the Haitian people and, in many cases, caused further problems.[2] Amidst these catastrophes and failures, theater remains Régis's "dream of the human" (2022, 67). As a white US-based scholar, and as a human, I have reflected deeply on how to write about this play—given that the (ongoing) stakes of this catastrophe were and are life and death, home and homelessness, for so many Haitians, while for me, it is intellectual and emotional wake work from a safe distance. While these questions remain unresolved, my commitments are to the humanity of which Régis writes and to staying watchful and vigilant. My goal was to name with critical precision, through an elucidating interdisciplinary context, what Régis expresses creatively and enacts through invitations to wake and witness in his play. As Régis writes in a postface to the play (which appears in both the French and English editions), "what matters now is for those who know how to NAME to NAME. That way we might come to understand something, little by little" (2022, 63).

In a recent interview, Régis explained how he sees the role of literature and artistic expression in Haiti.

> We think it's necessary, in a country born of a revolt unlike any other, to keep the fires burning. Where those in power are less vigilant, artists and intellectuals must remain so. Our literature is conceived as a kind of collective vigil. We must not forget to stay awake. They can shatter everything, but not our resilience. They can take everything from us, but not our ability to resistance. (Régis cited in Flaugh and Taub Robles 2019, 233)

In this essay, I will read Régis's play as a *veille collective* [collective vigil]. What does that mean? The term has several important connotations. First, it is a call to stay watchful and vigilant, inviting readers and spectators to keep watch on the foreign and local powers exploiting Haitians to hold them accountable. Second, it evokes solidarity in the aftermath of the earthquake: Haitian people kept watch on each other at a time when it was not safe to sleep, whether because of the immediate risk of aftershocks or the longer-lasting vulnerability of being homeless. Furthermore, the concept is situated in the context of death and mourning; *veye* in Kreyòl is both vigil and wake. In this context, the wake, that is, holding vigil beside someone who has died, can more broadly mean honoring each life lost or departing—at a time when death counts went unconfirmed and many victims went unburied. To be in the wake as an aspect of Black being, as Christina Sharpe has influentially theorized, is to "occupy and be occupied by the continuous and changing present of slavery's [and colonialism's] as yet unresolved unfolding" (Sharpe 2016, 13–14). In the Caribbean, a wake, as a funeral tradition, is a time not only for gathering with family and friends, but also for storytelling, which can offer veiled, symbolic subversion of institutions and structures of power, as it did in the time of slavery. Régis's play, as a symbolic wake tale, keeps watch both on the humanity of the Haitian people and on the coloniality of this catastrophe—the vulnerability produced by (neo)colonial powers and the international community's culturally insensitive, sometimes harmful, "humanitarian" response.

To offer a short synopsis of the play, *And the Whole World Quakes* stages a series of poetic exchanges between two nameless women, one older and one younger, who formerly worked in a now-collapsed brothel, living outside and unable to sleep in the aftermath of the earthquake. Their repetitive dialogue evinces a feeling of deep uncertainty and disconnection characteristic of trauma. In the first part, they observe and document the opportunistic international response to the earthquake as they faithfully count shooting stars, representative of Haitian people dying. Next, they discuss how they might begin a new life after the destruction of their brothel, and tentatively connect with one another, putting together the pieces of their own stories, in the absence of a pimp who had dominated them and pitted them against each other. In these tender moments, filled with fear and doubt, the women touch each other and tentatively express their love. Yet, in the consummation of their love, at the play's close, the two women don their respective military uniforms and take turns ritualistically sodomizing each other, evoking an ongoing cycle of colonial exploitation obscuring and coexisting with Haitian solidarity and love. This ending is interrupted by a second ending, a lyrical, sorrowful song, which bears witness to the shock and trauma of the earthquake and introduces hope for a generation to come.

Rather than analyzing a specific staging of the play, which has been produced in multiple contexts, though not yet given a full-scale production,[3] I focus in this essay on the modes of witnessing, engagement, and interpretation the play invites. *And the Whole World Quakes* is a poignant example of what Christian Flaugh has characterized as the author's "human theater," which, according to him, reveals the absence of humanity in our neocolonial world, particularly the Americas, and seeks to restore humanity through a popular, visceral theater that confronts its spectators and readers with "the abject realities" of a marginalized population "that is unheard and dehumanized yet resilient" (Flaugh 2016, 42). It also offers, as Axel Arthéron has argued, a space for remembering the traumatic event and for mourning (2022). By reading the play through the concept of the collective vigil, I bring together these themes of humanity and mourning. In the sections below, I will show how the play honors Haitian humanity and holds neocolonial powers accountable, how it exposes and upends modes of viewing that associate Haiti with catastrophe, sexual violence, and suffering, and how it uses symbolism—under the sign of the Haitian national *Iwa* (spirit) Ezili— to dwell in coexisting meanings, simultaneously unveiling the continuity of coloniality and foregrounding another, Haitian story of humanity and love. As I will argue, the play offers different invitations and messages to differently positioned spectators, calling on us to witness and wake collectively as humans. Under Ezili, the play ultimately explodes the central theme of watchfulness by holding up a revealing, unsettling, fluid mirror to its spectators/readers, inviting us to gaze into and renegotiate our own values, choices, and interpretations.

Eyes on the Coloniality of the Catastrophe

The concept of the vigil—as in watching over and staying alert—is introduced as the play opens, with Young Woman repeatedly asking Older Woman if she is sleeping. Sleeplessness is a practical safety consideration, because of the ongoing aftershocks, and the risk of being trapped under slabs of concrete, and it additionally introduces a tone of disorientation and shock (e.g., not knowing what time it is; wondering if one is going crazy). Speaking about the play's genesis, Régis has described returning home to Haiti just after the earthquake (he was away staging a play in Burkino Faso) and experiencing how he and the people around him were living in a kind of standstill—unable to sleep or stay inside—as the death count mounted.[4] This collective state of being on watch is emphasized by Older Woman, who announces in Kreyòl that no one can sleep ("*Pèsòn pa ka dòmi!*") and insists on the "*veye*" (wake, vigil, keeping watch, and remaining vigilant): "An eye. Always one. One eye to see" (31). Perched on a hill, the women observe below survivors chanting and praying and the arrival of foreign aid workers to the airport and also look tirelessly into the sky to honor the dying.

They assiduously bear witness to the lives lost and attend to those who are dying by counting shooting stars, people, who, as the older insists, "really counted for us": this is their "long-haul game" and "endless ritual" (32). Their counting is an act of love and recognition, an effort to honor the victims, to hold space for those who are transitioning, to mourn those lost, and to undo their erasure. It is hard work, demanding wakefulness and care; as Sharpe writes:

> What does it mean to defend the dead? To tend to the Black dead and dying: to tend to the Black person, to Black people, always living in the push toward our death? It means work. It is work: hard emotional, physical, and intellectual work that demands vigilant attendance to the needs of the dying, to ease their way, and also to the needs of the living. (Sharpe 2016, 10)

As the stars fall rapidly, interrupting their dialogue and disappearing quickly into the sky, the heroine's count moves quickly from one hundred to one hundred thousand (50). The task seems daunting, but Older Woman insists it must be accomplished before they can find calm and finally sleep. They have taken upon themselves the task that official leaders and organizations are failing (or neglecting?). Citing both published and unpublished reports, Mark Schuller explains that the official death toll count was elusive, varying by hundreds of thousands of lives (between 65,000 and 316,000), and observes: "The fact that there could have even been a debate about the death toll highlights that some lives literally don't count: they weren't registered by the state, and therefore their deaths weren't enumerated" (Schuller 2016, 3, 55). Thus, the set design and third "character" stipulated by Régis, a neon sign reading "*Omnia Mors Aequat*" (death makes everyone equal), is satirized (28). The opening scene, with the theme of counting that continues throughout the play, reveals how the Latin phrase must be read under a "both/and" principle, in which it is acknowledged both that everyone dies, and that some deaths (and lives) are institutionally positioned as counting more than others. This is an important, sobering truth that Régis calls on his spectators to witness as humans.

In their commitment to counting, the women bear witness to the loss of life, the humanity of the victims, and the wake work of being Black and Haitian in a world where Black/Haitian lives are precariously positioned. The vigil, as such, becomes an invitation (1) to see humanness, or the meanings of being human, in the wake of the earthquake, and (2) to witness what one might call, following the theme of this volume, "the coloniality of catastrophe," that is, the interweaving of the two, within a long history. The goal of the play, according to Régis's postface, is "to illuminate a disaster already foretold, one that had been in the works far too long" (63). Scholars like Laurent Dubois (2012), Myrtha Gilbert (2010), and Mark Schuller (2016, 19–44) have detailed the non-coincidental histories, economic factors, and foreign occupations/ interventions that have produced Haiti's vulnerability to catastrophe. From this vantage point, Régis's play situates the earthquake within the context of a prior "metaphysical catastrophe," to cite Nelson Maldonado-Torres's third thesis, which produces a "zone of subhumanity" subject to normalized violence and war (Maldonado-Torres 2016, 12–13). Or, as Sylvia Wynter, might say, a long history of coloniality and overdetermining white conceptions of "Man" normalizes and foretells the horror wrought by the earthquake by creating the illusion that Haitians have been "dysselected-by-Evolution" (Wynter 2003, 325) with "Haiti being produced and reproduced as the most impoverished nation in the Americas" (Wynter 2003, 261). In other words, coloniality produces premature Black/Haitian death as normative; the earthquake carries out that norm on a catastrophic level.

The heroines of *And the Whole World Quakes* point to the coloniality of their catastrophe. The women ponder why the international community insists on saving them without understanding or caring for them, and they point out that their suffering is an occasion for those in power to profit. They evoke an "endless puppet show" of "comings and goings of catastrophes and peoples" (36). They satirize the tagline of "international solidarity" and ask: "Why don't they huddle together in their good fortune? Why all of a sudden such interest in us, such a need to wipe their conscience clean? With their summing up, their reporting. Why? Instead of keeping busy with something else" (38). Evoking what journalist Naomi Klein has called disaster capitalism (2009), they sarcastically hope that "our misfortune will feed them well—those opportunists—bring them lots of money" (39).[5] This complaint about opportunism should be contextualized within the unequal spending after the earthquake—for example, two days of per diem for a foreign aid worker ($500 USD) was also the maximum amount a displaced Haitian could receive (to be paid to their landlord) in rent for one year (Schuller 2016, 87). Thus, the vigil also functions as an "accusation," to quote Régis's prefatory remark, against the international community—and particularly the main players, France and the United States—for failing to see and help the Haitian people, and instead, competing over their "savior" status, engaging in a "frivolous quarrel" over the landing strip of the airport, which "register[ed] as a lack of solidarity with the traumatized country it had supposedly come to help" (25). With their eyes, the women protagonists both count the human, Haitian lives being lost, and hold the international aid workers accountable for their interventions in the traumatized country.

Acts of Viewing

Régis's insistence on his heroines' watchfulness additionally serves to interrupt and reverse dominant, colonial modes of viewing Haiti from the outside, which are enmeshed with *the coloniality of catastrophe*, as described above, and to invite instead a different mode of engagement: witnessing as humans. To understand how this works, it is important first to observe how in the aftermath of the earthquake, the mainstream media, particularly in the United States, was saturated with images of Haitians suffering. As opposed to emphasizing Haitian people's collective efforts to help one another, the media produced an image of Haiti as helpless and broken, which both dehumanized Haitians and justified foreign intervention as (continually) necessary. As part of her call for new Haitian narratives, Gina Athena Ulysse has poignantly commented on several examples, including one reporter who saw earthquake survivors roaming the streets (many covered with dust) as indifferent—rather than traumatized or shocked—speculating "perhaps it is because they are so used to hardship that they are nonresponsive," and another who seemed to view a mother as not affected by the loss of her child, asking "Why don't you Haitians cry?" (Ulysse 2015, 30–31). Kaiama L. Glover explains how depictions of Haiti following the earthquake, like the Sally Struthers "for the price of a cup of coffee" commercials, combined categorization and devaluation with humanitarianism, therefore suggesting that:

> disaster is a state of being, as opposed to an event. It is implied that Afro-bodies are at once essentially prone to and built for suffering, a narrative that echoes, of course, slavery-era claims regarding Africans' racial "fitness" for enslavement. (Glover 2017, 242)

Glover argues that these "benign denials [...] at once reflect, sustain, and allay 'First World' anxiety in the face of undesired (but increasingly inevitable) proximity to the 'Third World'" (Glover 2017, 235). These dominant modes of viewing, which preceded and proceed the earthquake, deny Haitian humanity by normalizing the people's suffering, positioning them as essentially helpless, and judging, effacing, and misreading their human responses to trauma.

The protagonists of *And the Whole World Quakes* name and reverse this colonial mode of viewing. They watch the foreigners below and comment on their so-called humanitarianism with irony. "They're moved," declares Young Woman, "and us—we can't hide any more. They cage us, stigmatize us. That's how it is. All our suffering exhibited right in their faces; they stigmatize us. That's all we are in their eyes" (38). Régis's heroines directly point out how the foreign interventions are both dehumanizing and largely one-sided and they look back. "They don't even have time to ask if we see them, if we see them with our own two eyes—us too" (34). Watching researchers "analyzing" their situation, the women look at these "specialists," taking notes and "summing things up" and question whether they (the women) really see them (the foreign researchers). Reversing the status quo, Young Woman concludes, joking, "I see them, but I don't see them" (35). Watching NGOs and foreign government coalitions, they observe how they compete with one another as if the Haitians and their lives did not matter. Rather than prioritizing help, these coalitions "fight for their position" as saviors to the country (34).

Régis's theater-based act of reversing the view here might be understood as speaking on two different levels or to two different audiences. First, and primarily for Haitian spectators, it serves as a manifestation of a Haitian performative impulse. Summarizing his team's research, Schuller reports that many Haitians living in camp communities expressed in their interviews "the importance of aid agencies 'seeing' them" (Schuller 2016, 130, 163). He cites the example of a displaced person's performance of a reversal of information collection, when she grabbed the notebook from an NGO worker collecting information about the camp residents (yet again) and began their script with the roles reversed: "Ma'am, could you give me your name?" (165). Secondly (perhaps more so for white, Western audiences), reversing the view might also serve, as Flaugh has noted, to force the reader and spectator to "see and hear [nontraditional, subaltern characters], to learn of their reality and thereby their humanity" (Flaugh 2016, 63). Such multiple modes of spectatorship and readership might operate separately, or they might interact, as spectators watch each other watching (the protagonists' watching). Dance scholar Susan Manning has theorized "two-way cross-viewing," as occurring when spectators of different races and positions watch each other watching a performance (Manning 2004, xvi). Because of the characters' watchfulness, a three-way cross-viewing occurs here, with spectators from different positions watching other spectators watching the two characters' acts of watching.

In place of the colonial modes of viewing, Régis invites spectators/readers to witness together as self-reflexive, politically positioned humans. Watching the protagonists' acts of watching, the spectator/reader is invited to observe how their own process of watching plays out and they must confront their own positioning to do so. Theater cultivates a "collective vigil" insofar as it facilitates the acknowledgment of differently positioned humans who together bear witness to truths that have been obscured and wake both to those truths and to their own (and shared) humanness. For Haitian, Black, and racialized spectators, this might generate a deeper consciousness of the coloniality of catastrophe and a mutual acknowledgment, through watchfulness of a shared state of being. Sharpe addresses such recognition through shared watching as part of Black being in the wake: she recounts finding a post-earthquake photograph of a young Haitian girl, with the word "ship" taped to her forehead, who looks into the camera. Through her act of looking at the girl's looking, Sharpe recognizes herself and "the common condition of being Black in the wake" (Sharpe 2016, 45). Theater thus invites a collective vigil that holds space for Haitian and Black spectators to engage in wake work together and with the support and solidarity of a wider community bearing witness to their/our humanity. For "First World" and white spectators, the invitation to wake together might interrupt what Glover (2017) calls the "benign denials" of Haitian realities and legitimate complaints. These reader/spectators, in other words, are invited to bear witness to Haitian humanity, to the coloniality of the catastrophe, and to their own fragile and precious humanness (which they share with Haitians), thereby confronting the coexisting truths evoked by the neon *Omnia Mors Aequat* sign. Thus, international and white spectators/readers who choose to witness and engage as humans in the wake—rather than through the mainstream scripts of benign denial, pity, opportunism, and indifference—participate in the collective vigil.

Interpreting Polyamorously Under the Sign of Ezili

As sex workers, as women, and through their same-sex-loving dimensions, the heroines are positioned as the children of Ezili, the lwa (spirit) of love, femininity, (in)fertility, maternity, sexuality, pleasure, fluidity, and creativity, whose structuring presence reminds (culturally literate) spectators and readers to tune in to multiple, coexisting meanings and signs. Ezili is recognized through her three coexisting most common forms: Ezil Dantò, the dark-skinned, hard-working single mother, Ezili Freda, the light-skinned, sensual lover of luxuries, and Lasyrenn, the fluid mermaid, associated with water. While the Ezili is part of a pantheon of lwas of the Vodou religion, providing a link between humans and the divine, Ezili also represents the mother of Haiti and is a useful trope for analyzing Haitian women-centered and queer knowledge. With the Ezili, we interpret the play, as Omise'eke Natasha Tinsley might say, by embracing theoretical, symbolic, and interdisciplinary "polyamory," through which multiple modes of interpretation are married together, each accorded explanatory power, and each considered fairly (Tinsley 2018, 172–177). As I have argued elsewhere, theater by francophone Caribbean women enacts processes of creolization, which remix cultural codes, unsettle expectations, and challenge the status quo: this can be understood as a form of moral repossession via renewal of the syncretism of Caribbean religion and performance (Sahakian 2017, 102–105). Crucially, the coexisting signs and modes of interpretation are not balanced out or resolved but rather should be understood as coexisting in a permanent, unresolved disequilibrium, which must be continually renegotiated and reread by individual spectators and readers. With my understanding of Caribbean theater and performance as creolization, I am riffing here on Tinsley's concept of "theoretical polyamory" to propose a practice of spectating/

reading Régis's play's multivalent symbolism under the structuring presence of Ezili.[6] Ezili is both multidimensional and invites coexisting modes of interpretation. "For men," writes anthropologist Karen McCarthy Brown, Ezil "can function as the target for dreams of conquest. Speaking for women, she reminds all people that these values can be superficial and even dangerous" (McCarthy Brown 1991, 255). Moreover, Ezili's power, and particularly Dantò's, is recognizable in her act of looking back at her viewers: "as you look into Ezili Danto's eyes, she looks also into yours" (White 1999–2000, 68). Reigning over the three-way cross-viewing described above, Ezili's structuring presence demands that spectators/readers commit to shifting, unresolved, disjointed interpretive strategies and modes of witnessing in order to collectively wake to humanity, against reductive, dehumanizing narratives of the earthquake as "natural" and erasures of the coloniality of the catastrophe. And she forces us to submit to unpredictability. Even as the trope of Ezili helps me to deepen my analysis of the play, she continually reminds me of the limitations of my interpretations, and of the need to continually wake, witness, and interpret anew.

Ezili foregrounds the multiplicity and multi-dimensionality of specifically feminine, womanly, and queer experiences, viewpoints, and power; as such she rejects the social scripts of purity and (de)sexualization imposed upon women's—and particularly women of color's—bodies. Colin (Joan) Dayan has compellingly argued that Ezili "dramatizes a historiography of women's experience in Haiti" that rejects the imposition of Western ideas about purity and morality to foreground a deeper understanding of Haitian womanhood, "whether, black, mulatto, or white," within the contexts of slavery and its afterlives, with enduring class and racialized inequities (Dayan 1994, 6). Under Ezili, Régis's characters are positioned as *both* allegorical (generalizable) *and* portraying real, complex, messy womanhood. As he notes in the postface, they "symbolize the great Haitian family—without given names that have been recognized by a government official or inscribed in court documents" (64). With their names emphasizing their relative ages, they also represent two generations of Haitians; their solidarity and love are posed to challenge laws that disenfranchise those younger than 18, who represent more than half of Haiti (64). Even as they are generalizable and symbolic, the women are presented as humans, whose choices reflect their desires for love, intimacy, and livelihood, their fears and losses, and their need for survival.

The stories, memories, and thoughts they share with each other foreground their womanhood, including their bodies and reproductive lives. For example, though she desires to replace the lives lost by making "babies, lots of babies, lots" (47), Young Woman shares that, due to multiple abortions of fetuses fathered by their pimp, she can no longer become pregnant (48). Matter-of-factly, she views her final abortion as a (constrained) human choice, counting *both* childbirth *and* the stopping of menstrual blood and with it, reproductive capacities as the fate of "[e]very woman who exists" (49). This example illustrates how the women interrupt and surpass the limiting views of women in the context of the coloniality of the catastrophe, with Ezili guiding them in expressions of womanhood and humanness within the pain, loss, crimes, and violence of coloniality.

Régis's heroines laugh in the face of paternalistic protection and explode the white patriarchal trope. At first glance (and for some spectators), the choice of Haitian sex worker protagonists might be understood as representing those whom society does not protect—given the Western, patriarchal notion inherited from the time of slavery that white women and virgins are the most morally "pure" and therefore deserving of society's protection. As such the former sex workers stand in for those who are benignly dehumanized: Haiti after the earthquake. Yet, Régis's heroines also interrupt such clichés insofar as they are not seeking protection, and their former profession is evoked only matter-of-factly, never to incite any form of moralizing or pity. It is important here to note that, following the earthquake, gender-based and sexual violence was highly covered in the international media. Glover points to the coloniality of the media's post-quake preoccupation with an "epidemic of rape," which failed to acknowledge sexual violence against women as a global phenomenon, and instead reiterated the portrayal of Haiti (and particularly its women) as in need of rescue. Moreover, it contributed to benign denials by "playing directly [...] on our fears of contagion—of catching whatever it is they've got" (Glover 2017, 244). In contrast, Régis's heroines upend the dehumanizing fetishization of "pure" female victims in need of white male saviors:

> OLDER WOMAN: Maybe we could sell? Like other women—sell, do some business, sell small things. They do that. Everybody sells. To fool their misery, like they say, they sell.
> YOUNG WOMAN: What?

OLDER WOMAN: Things, small things.
YOUNG WOMAN: We don't know how. It won't work. We don't know how. (*Laughs to herself*) We don't know how to sell anything else. (41)

Whereas the common script at the time recounted how women were raped or forced to turn to transactional sex (both were documented lived realities) in the earthquake's aftermath, Régis's heroines have reversed the course. They invite the spectator/reader to call up this sensationalized image of selling one's body for sex, only to interrupt it with the idea of "small things" (a reference to street vending, a common means of income, particularly for women, before the earthquake, which dwindled in the quake's aftermath due to limited availability of merchandise), and then return to the first image as part of a morally neutral repertoire of human survival—via Young Woman's joke. They also make clear that they are not in need of protection, but rather protecting themselves from the "taking it out on women" happening below by remaining perched on the hill under their tree, though the young woman, craving life and contact, questions their isolation (50). It is clear that, with the destruction of their brothel and the death of their pimp, they will not return to sex work, but will actively seek out a new life, as Young Woman envisions, a clean slate: "*Tabula Rasa!*" (47).

The play frames this idea of a clean slate as complex and potentially deceptive in the context of coloniality, reflecting how Ezili's mirrors facilitate destabilizing modes of viewing and polyamorous interpretations that are both profoundly revealing and (sometimes dangerously) disorienting. As the author discusses in the postface, decolonization is a long path that defaults at times to a "return to the colonizer" (65). He hopes that the catastrophe of the earthquake might just be a "launching place for Liberation, for Hope, for another possible Future" (65). The play presents liberation through a polyamorous, metamorphosizing lens. The willed end to their pimp's life, facilitated by the earthquake, is established as a potentially transformative yet disorienting event. Young Woman reveals that their pimp was on top of her when the earthquake hit, and that, instead of pulling him out of the rubble, she "helped him to die" (57), though she also expresses uncertainty as to whether that is true. The death of the pimp, though not foretelling the end to coloniality, "re/forms," as Flaugh might say, "the heteroimperiality imposed on sex/gender expressions of Afro/Caribbean lives" (Flaugh 2024, 139). It frees the women from their societal (working) roles, which positioned them as sexual objects to (often international) male clients, and makes room instead for their own polyamorous desires, which exceed the rules of gender and sex stipulated by colonial patriarchy.

With the lwa of love and creativity, the women reach for a new form of love, a love to replace the existence and community they had at their collapsed brothel, which was (deceptively?) named Bèl Amou (Beautiful Love) in Kreyòl. Love, for Ezili's children and devotees, is not an ideal, but rather a complex human practice that involves conflicting desires, confusions, jealousies, patience, commitments to others, and tending to one's own needs. Relying on one another for companionship and protection in this precarious moment, they approach the possibility of greater physical intimacy through a kind of tentative dance. As they imagine a new life, from the context of their vulnerability, their grief, and what the author calls the great "sense of collapse" surrounding them (28), they tentatively express their desires for one another. Older Woman, the more cautious, confesses to Young Woman that she thrills and moves her, and she asks to touch Young Woman's body (51). Young Woman, who appears aligned with Ezili Freda as the object of desire, is thrilled by the older woman's "soft and gentle looking" and wants to be touched longer and more by her: less inhibited, she has asked for this touch since the opening of the play (29). But Older Woman, who seems aligned with the self-sufficient Ezili Dantò, fears that it is the catastrophe that has brought them together (53). She presents "[b]eautiful human love" as out of reach, something she "would've wanted," an "impossible dream" (53). While the death of the pimp makes room for an expression of polyamorous desires and multiple affective responses, the potentially transformative moment, and with it the possibilities of liberation and of love, is refracted in disorienting ways.

The ending of the play explodes the coexisting modes of viewing established above by presenting the anticipated consummation of the women's love as a "*tragic, surreal ritual*" in colonial drag. Young Woman first (and then Older Woman) puts on a strap-on, which she forces into the other woman's mouth, and then "*forces her down on all fours and savagely plays at sodomizing her*" (59). As the stage directions stipulate, this "*game*" is performed without emotion, in a cycle, in which they continually switch roles against the backdrop of the neon sign proclaiming OMNIA MORS AEQUAT (59). Arthéron has read this final ritual as an act of love that provocatively laughs in the face of death, a profanation in response to collective trauma that plays on the specular dimension of the theater

(2022, 26). We might also understand the ending through Flaugh's argument that the play enacts "dirty love," in which relationships between revolting subjects evoke both love and aversion, simultaneously inviting and disavowing the consumption of the Haitian people (2019, 49–66). Reading polyamorously with Ezili, the final scene can be understood as exploding the tensions between the continuity of coloniality and the liberating hope for radical, decolonial love. Insofar as the ritual repeats emotionless, apparently one-sided sexual acts, it invites readings through the larger pattern of the violent exploitation Haiti has endured—first colonized by France and then occupied by the United States. It is preceded by the donning of military uniforms: first, Young Woman puts on a US military uniform and then she orders Older Woman to take off her dress and put on the United Nations/France uniform. In these uniforms, the women enact—and grotesquely mock—for the audience the competition between the United States and France over the status of white "savior," through which their Haitian bodies (under the uniforms) are violated.

As spectators gaze into this reflection of the continuity of coloniality, the roles, desires, and positionings of the two women become distorted and blurred, which explodes the play's central device of the vigil. Young Woman reveals that she took the uniforms from their pimp (who presumably got them from their clients). Remembering how the uniforms were a status symbol for their pimp that made him look like a hero, she asks, "So what about a heroine? A woman soldier?" (58). As humans, the women (like Haiti's rulers) can put on the uniforms of their colonizers and repeat colonial acts. The heroines are, to quote the postface again, taking their lives "in their own hands after years of abuse" (64). Will they repeat the abuse, or will they break the cycle? These unresolved questions about the future perhaps anticipate Régis's later play *Reconstruction(s)* (2018), a parodic critique of the government in the aftermath of the earthquake. And yet, even beyond this unresolved dichotomy, the strap-on interrupts the sexual exploitation metaphor and unpredictably encodes the queer challenge to heteroimperiality in the costume of coloniality (the uniforms). This blocks readers'/spectators' efforts to classify or categorize the sexual act and calls on them to submit to unpredictability. Once again inviting multiple modes of viewing, this final scene explodes the play's central theme of watchfulness. Made witnesses to a disorienting (long-anticipated) sexual act, spectators and readers are invited to gaze at Ezili, into her waters, which, as Brown notes, "is like gazing at your own reflection. It is seductive because she gives a deeper and truer picture of self than is likely to be found in the mirrors of everyday life. But it is also dangerous to try to get too close or hold on too tightly to the vision" (Brown 1991, 223). What were we, as spectators and readers, anticipating and how do we reconcile this final ritual with our expectations?

As this onstage tragic ritual explodes the central theme of watchfulness, it is interrupted by a song, which shifts the primary mode of communication. In Haitian performance culture, song is associated with Ezili and it is a privileged medium for expressing coexisting truths, affective states, and tones. Régis's beautiful final lament evokes the sounds and sights of the earthquake, the city, the island, with the surf and the sea, an unrealized marriage, funerals, nature, trees, animals, earth, blood, sweat, man, stumbling, and sleep. It expresses unnamable pain and tragedy with poetry and finally concludes with "maybe at the end—hope" as it calls up the image of a sleeping child "becoming forever rewarded" (60). The song seems to tell a bigger story and acknowledge broader truths the women could not say, and it serves to reorient readers and spectators, by focusing us on what is important. As Elizabeth McAlister argues, "Haitian quake survivors used religious music to locate themselves in the midst of the material destruction and psychic disjuncture, to move toward equilibrium. They sang to reconstitute themselves as individuals and as groups" (McAlister 2010, 97). The song moves readers and spectators to a new register beyond both the visual and the protagonists' speech. In the limitation of their speech, the women evoke Ezili Dantò, who is often portrayed as unable to speak, her tongue cut out by Haitian revolutionaries (her children) to keep her from speaking to the enemy, which has made her dependent on others for interpretation of her messages (White 1999–2000, 70). Indeed, Ezili's divine power and truths are often expressed through Kreyòl songs honoring her. Through its sadness, the final song also mirrors how Ezili Freda always leaves a Vodou ritual (the play) in tears. While the heroines had attempted to stop their tears from coming in their earlier dialogue (46), the song allows the tears to flow freely, weeping for the tremendous losses while cradling hope for the next generation and for the future, the reward, forever, for the sleeping child.

In conclusion, by reading *And the Whole World Quakes* as a symbolic wake tale, I have contextualized the theme of watchfulness within the lived realities of the earthquake's aftermath, to show how the play keeps watch on the coloniality of the catastrophe and on the humanity of the Haitian people (the living and the dying). Teasing out how the play speaks simultaneously to differently positioned spectators, inviting them to witness and participate in intersecting modes of watching and waking, I have argued that it cultivates a collective vigil. Lastly, reading polyamorously with Ezili, I have uncovered the play's insistence on coexisting meanings and signs: how the protagonists are both human/woman and symbolic, and how the play ultimately explodes an unresolved cycle of colonial exploitation coexisting with another, Haitian story of humanity and love. Under Ezili, the play invites spectators and readers to gaze into their own values and renegotiate their (constrained) human choices alongside the coloniality of catastrophe and the possibility for an unknown future and a decolonial love that surpasses the limitations and classifications of colonial patriarchy and heteroimperiality. Régis's theater-based collective vigil exposes and interrupts problematic humanitarianism in the wake of catastrophe, asks unresolved questions about the future, forces us to submit to unpredictability, and thereby invites his readers and spectators to dream with him his "dream of the human."

Acknowledgements I thank the editors and Christian Flaugh for helpful comments on an earlier draft of this essay.

Notes

1. For more on Régis, see Flaugh (2016).
2. As has now been widely reported and acknowledged, in the aftermath of the earthquake, UN troops brought cholera to Haiti, which killed 10,000 people, on top of the earthquake's casualties. Furthermore, anthropologist Mark Schuller, drawing from more than 150 interviews, surveys, and research in over 100 camps, documents in detail several other problems, including: focusing on the perceived selfishness of the Haitian people rather than their acts of solidarity; misunderstanding cultural norms; incentivizing the breakdown of communal family units; targeting women for aid in ways that resulted in increased gender-based violence; carelessly appointing camp managers that abused power; making displaced persons wait in long lines for small-scale aid (e.g., four bars of soap) to ensure photo ops; failing to embrace a model of solidarity, as opposed to charity.

3. A preliminary version of the play was first staged at the international theater festival in Avignon in 2011 (https://www.dailymotion.com/video/xjz0xt). In 2012, a version of the play, interspersed with testimonies, was performed as a sonic and visual experience aboard a bus at the author's Festival 4 Chemins in Port-au-Prince: spectators listened to a recording and observed a bus tour of the earthquake's ruins (Arthéron 2022, 12). Judith Miller's English translation was staged as a reading at the Martin E. Segal Theatre in 2020 as part of The ACT (Actions Caribéennes Théâtrales) project, directed by Stéphanie Bérard (https://www.youtube.com/watch?v=uE_RnnaVY0E); director Kaneza Schaal has plans to stage a full-scale production in English. The quotations in this essay are taken from Miller's translation.
4. See, for example, Régis's comments at the staged reading of the translation of his play cited above. His later play, *Reconstruction(s)* (2018), satirizes the government's response to the earthquake, whereas *And The Whole World Quakes* dwells in the disorientation, trauma, and possibility of the catastrophe's wake.
5. The word "capital" is repeated on pp. 34–35.
6. I am also indebted to Tinsley's call to speak of Ezili as a definitive theorizer (2011, 419).

Works Cited

Arthéron, Axel. 2022. *De toute la terre le grand effarement* de Guy Régis Junior ou quand le théâtre devient l'espace du deuil. *Études caribéennes* 52. https://journals.openedition.org/etudescaribeennes/23493.

Brown, Karen McCarthy. 1991. *Mama Lola: A Vodou Priestess in Brooklyn*. Berkeley: University of California Press.

Daut, Marlène. 2020 (updated 2021). When France Extorted Haiti—The Greatest Heist in History. https://theconversation.com/when-france-extorted-haiti-the-greatest-heist-in-history-137949.

Dayan, Joan. 1994. Erzulie: A Women's History of Haiti. *Research in African Literatures* 25 (2): 5–31.

Dubois, Laurent. 2012. *Haiti: The Aftershocks of History*. New York: Metropolitan Books.

Gilbert, Myrtha. 2010. *La Catastrophe n'était pas naturelle*. Cahier No. 1. Port-au-Prince: Imprimateur II.
Flaugh, Christian. 2016. Engaging Reality and Popular Performance in the *Théâtre Humain* of Guy Régis. *The Journal of Haitian Studies* 22 (1): 46–80.
Flaugh, Christian. 2019. Dirty Love: Marie Chauvet, Guy Régis Jr, and Enfleshed Performances of Revolting Subjects. In *Marie Vieux Chauvet's Theatres: Thought, Form, and Performance of Revolt*, ed. Christian Flaugh and Lena Taub Robles. Leiden: Brill. https://doi.org/10.1163/9789004388086_005.
Flaugh, Christian. 2024. Afro/Caribbean Crossings: Gaël Octavia, Guy Régis Jr, and Sex/Gender/Theatre Work with Heteroimperiality. In *The Methuen Drama Handbook of Gender and Theatre*, ed. Sean Metzger and Roberta Mock. London: Methuen.
Flaugh, Christian, and Lena Taub Robles, eds. 2019. After-Words: A Dialogue with Kaiama L. Glover and Guy Régis Jr. In *Marie Vieux Chauvet's Theatres: Thought, Form, and Performance of Revolt*, ed. Christian Flaugh and Lena Taub Robles. Leiden: Brill. https://doi.org/10.1163/9789004388086_016.
Glover, Kaiama L. 2017. 'Flesh Like One's Own': Benign Denials of Legitimate Complaint. *Public Culture* 29 (2): 235–260.
Klein, Naomi. 2009. *The Shock Doctrine: The Rise of Disaster Capitalism*. New York: Picador.
Manning, Susan. 2004. *Modern Dance, Negro Dance: Race in Motion*. Minneapolis: University of Minnesota Press.
McAlister, Elizabeth. 2010. From the Rubble to the Telethon: Music, Religion, and the Haiti Quake. In *Haiti Rising: Haitian History, Culture, and the Earthquake of 2010*, ed. Martin Munro. Kingston: University of West Indies Press.
Régis, Guy. 2011. *De toute la terre le grand effarement*. Paris: les Solitaires intempestifs.
Régis, Guy. 2018. *Reconstruction(s)*. Paris: les Solitaires intempestifs.
Régis, Guy. 2022. *The Whole World Quakes: Chronicle of a Slaughter Foretold*, trans. Judith Miller. In *New Plays from the Caribbean: Haiti, Martinique, Guadeloupe*, ed. Stéphanie Bérard. New York: Martin E. Segal Theatre Center Publications.
Schuller, Mark. 2016. *Humanitarian Aftershocks in Haiti*. New Brunswick: Rutgers University Press.
Sharpe, Christina. 2016. *In the Wake: On Blackness and Being*. Durham: Duke University Press.
Maldonado-Torres, Nelson. 2016. Outline of Ten Theses on Coloniality and Decoloniality. https://fondation-frantzfanon.com/outline-of-ten-theses-on-coloniality-and-decoloniality/.
Sahakian, Emily. 2017. *Staging Creolization: Women's Theater and Performance from the French Caribbean*. Charlottesville: University of Virginia Press.

Tinsley, Omise'eke Natasha. 2011. Songs for Ezili: Vodou Epistemologies of (Trans)gender. *Feminist Studies* 37 (2): 417–436.

Tinsley, Omise'eke Natasha. 2018. *Ezili's Mirrors: Imagining Black Queer Genders*. Durham: Duke University Press.

Ulysse, Gina Athena. 2015. *Why Haiti Needs New Narratives: A Post-Quake Chronicle*. Middletown, CT: Wesleyan University Press.

White, Krista. 1999–2000. Espousing Ezili: Images of a Lwa, Reflections of the Haitian Woman. *Journal of Haitian Studies* 5/6: 62–79.

Wynter, Sylvia. 2003. Unsettling the Coloniality of Being/Power/Truth/Freedom: Toward the Human, After Man, Its Overrepresentation—An Argument. *The New Centennial Review* 3 (3): 257–337.

"We Must Face Haiti": Rawle Gibbons's 1993 Production of *The Black Jacobins*

Raj Chetty

Writing for PBS.org on the first anniversary of the catastrophic 2010 earthquake that ravaged Haiti, Gina Athena Ulysse warned, "Watch. After the anniversary coverage, the cameras will retract and journalists will depart even before filing their bylines. And you won't hear about Haiti again unless or until there's another big disaster" (2015, 62). Ulysse's op-ed points to this volume's central concern: the relation between natural disasters like earthquakes, and the *ideas* and *practices* of a catastrophic Western colonialism whose aftershocks continually produce their own ecological, social, and political devastation, such that natural disasters like earthquakes cause disproportionate destruction in currently colonized and formerly colonized places. Or, as Nelson Maldonado-Torres has put it in his afterword to *Aftershocks of Disaster*, "Europe cannot so easily disentangle itself from the catastrophe that is the long presence of colonialism, naturalized slavery, extractivism, and their aftermath in the

---

R. Chetty (✉)
Department of English, St. John's University, Queens, NY, USA
e-mail: chettyr@stjohns.edu

© The Author(s), under exclusive license to Springer Nature Switzerland AG 2025
C. Stevens and J. D. Rossini (eds.), *The Coloniality of Catastrophe in Caribbean Theater and Performance*,
https://doi.org/10.1007/978-3-031-85791-1_3

Caribbean. This points to the need for an account of Western modernity as catastrophe instead of, as is more common, in terms of crisis" (2019, 333).

While Ulysse's focus in her op-ed above is on the colonially exacerbated material and discursive fallout on the Haitian people from the 2010 earthquake, international attention to Haiti also persistently erupts in moments of political crisis that similarly cannot be disarticulated from what Maldonado-Torres calls "the catastrophe of modernity/coloniality" (2019, 339). So much is clear now in the mainstream news coverage of Haiti as it reels from political instability and violence, the product of internal political failures by state elites, and external/colonial political interference. There is a "chasm between privileged rulers and the poor and marginalized majority," as Robert Fatton recently put it, "and the former's willingness to make all kinds of compromises and deals with imperial powers. This behavior remains an unchanging pattern of Haitian politics" (2024). Coverage of Haiti's current political crisis is but another in a series of aftershocks that can be traced back to the racist, colonial coverage of the Haitian Revolution as it unfolded, a racism precisely pitted against both the self-liberation of the formerly enslaved and the establishment of a Black independent state.[1]

If the "catastrophe of coloniality" has been a persistent feature of global engagement with Haiti, that persistence has been met and exceeded by Haitian people's struggle to preserve, restore, and cement their self-liberation. It should be no surprise, then, that narratives about Haitian revolutionary struggle persistently have inspired readers and audiences. This is exemplified perhaps most powerfully, at least in English, through C. L. R. James's cross-genre work on the Haitian Revolution: from his 1938 history, *The Black Jacobins: Toussaint Louverture and the San Domingo Revolution*, and its 1963 revision; to his 1934 play, *Toussaint Louverture: The Story of the Only Successful Slave Revolt in History*, and its 1967 revision as *The Black Jacobins*.[2] As Rachel Douglas has documented and analyzed quite extensively, James's work on the Haitian Revolution has persisted in two ways: first, in James's own recursive approach to writing or staging it; and second, in what Douglas (2019) dubs the "afterlives" of the history and the play in visual and performing arts (see also, Douglas 2020, 290–94). Douglas writes, "*Black Jacobins* afterlives must be sought not only on the page, but also on the stage in the fifty years since the 1967 premiere [of *The Black Jacobins* play]" (2019, 194). I am most interested in James's Haitian Revolution work "on the stage" and the way the play's revisions and afterlives articulate with and address colonial conjunctures of catastrophe.

To put a finer point on it: in addition to James's commitment to revising his work on the Haitian Revolution, his recourse to the form of theater itself—the ephemerality of each production, its potential for synchronic and diachronic co- and re-creation—enables the sort of conjunctural revisions that distinguish the 1934 *Toussaint Louverture* play from 1967's *The Black Jacobins*, and that in turn undergird the adaptations of *The Black Jacobins* from the 1970s to the present.[3] Crucially, these revisions and adaptations carry a persistent indictment of colonialism and the catastrophes it both produces and exacerbates. In this essay, I focus in particular on one of the afterlives of *The Black Jacobins*: Trinidadian playwright Rawle Gibbons's 1993 stage production in Trinidad. Emerging in the wake of the 1991 coup that deposed Haitian president Jean-Bertrand Aristide, Gibbons's adaptation not only directly engages with the political violence of this particular context—its catastrophe—but does so in a way that invites local Trinidadian engagement with, and broader Caribbean attention to, Haiti's early 1990s crisis. What's more, in his production Gibbons foregrounds contemporary violence against women in 1990s Haiti, in this way deepening the revisions the play had undergone from the 1930s to the 1960s toward incorporating women's participation.[4] By centering violence against women even more than in earlier iterations of the play, Gibbons's adaptation articulates the problem of colonial catastrophe with gender-based violence.

The Evolution of James's Play

Christian Høgsbjerg's archival and editorial work has made it easier to compare James's 1934 *Toussaint Louverture* play on the Haitian Revolution with its 1967 iteration as *The Black Jacobins*.[5] In an interview with Daryl Cumber Dance, James states, "Now that was in 1936. Then came the independence of Ghana and the whole revolutionary movement, India, China, all of them. So that after twenty-odd years I thought that that idea that I was expressing should be differently expressed, and I rewrote the play. [...] Some of the first version went into the second, but the second version meant that writing about struggle for independence in 1956 or 1960 was very different from what it was in 1936" (1992b, 115). This opens deeper possibilities for thinking about the place of theater and public performance in the evolution of James's thinking on that revolution and anticolonial and revolutionary politics more broadly, in addition to the way such evolution has continued beyond James's passing in 1989.[6]

Toussaint Louverture (1934) and *The Black Jacobins* (1967), both featuring three acts in their playscripts, present a chronological depiction of the Haitian Revolution that dramatizes political interactions between major and minor historical actors. Across its 11 scenes, *Toussaint Louverture* offers significant stage time to real and fictional white settler colonists, French colonial officers, and French leaders (most notably, Napoléon Bonaparte), in order to emphasize the profoundly and openly anti-Black racism of Saint Domingue's plantation slavery and to contextualize the Haitian revolutionaries' actions as dialectical responses to oppressive exploitation and violence as well as assertions of a fundamental desire for freedom. The play also retains a focus on Toussaint Louverture as he develops into the leader that Haitian revolutionaries' actions demand, with a final scene featuring Dessalines carrying Toussaint's emancipatory leadership through to Haitian independence in the wake of Toussaint's death in imposed exile.

While retaining this chronological approach, *The Black Jacobins*, with nine scenes, grants far less stage time to white characters and historical figures and correspondingly far more time to Black revolutionaries, and among these latter, more significant stage time to historical figures outside of the well-known male revolutionary leaders (Toussaint, Dessalines, Christophe), including revolutionary Haitian women. These women include Marie-Jeanne, who is a central figure in the play's (and the revolution's) development (Chetty 2019). This revision also features more in the way of total theater—dance, song, gesture, and action, a Vodou ceremony—and less reliance on dialogue to advance the play through the historical progression of the revolution. *The Black Jacobins* is far more invested in the problems of postcolonial Black leadership, as both Toussaint and Dessalines, central heroes of *Toussaint Louverture*, take steps as leaders that forestall the radical transformation the Haitian Revolution promised. *The Black Jacobins* features a new scene in which Toussaint has his nephew, Moïse, executed for insubordination. Clearly depicted as having a radical closeness to and connection with everyday Haitian revolutionaries, Moïse challenges Toussaint's decision to retain working relationships with France and French colonial officers. In Dessalines's case, at the close of the play, he dismisses Toussaint as foolish and declares himself Emperor of Haiti, far from the unifying rhetorical embrace of Toussaint at the close of the earlier play. What's more, Dessalines declares Marie-Jeanne—now his wife—Empress of Haiti, and when she falters, grief-stricken, as news of Toussaint's death arrives, he pulls her into dancing a minuet with him and they both freeze, the play's curtain descending on this final tableau. In other words, one of the central tragedies *The Black Jacobins* underscores is the way independence—in Haiti in 1804, but also in the wave of independent postcolonial states across the mid-twentieth-century—occurs "in a context in which women's freedoms are pushed off-stage even while women are pulled into the limelight" (Chetty 2019, 102).

The Black Jacobins was first staged in post-independence Nigeria in 1967 under the direction of Trinidadian playwright Dexter Lyndersay, who collaborated with James in reimagining and revising the play for the production. Even with James's comment that "writing about struggle for independence in 1956 or 1960 was very different" from the writing in the 1930s, both the 1934 and 1967 versions emerged in a context structured by colonialism. Italy's invasion of Abyssinia/Ethiopia in 1935 became the explicit historical event that prompted its 1936 stage production in London, with Paul Robeson in the title role. To be sure, fascist Italy's invasion was no isolated event; it was the last note in Europe's formal colonial division of the African continent, dating back to the Berlin Conference in 1884. Thus, if drawing attention to Ethiopia's struggle against Italian invasion was a direct motivation for the 1936 production, the play also cast a broader net in its indictment of European colonialism of the African continent, the Caribbean, and elsewhere.

The 1967 production of *The Black Jacobins* shifted its attention to the persistence of colonial structures—what numerous scholars, following Aníbal Quijano (2000), have termed "coloniality"—even in the wake of anticolonial struggles that resulted in formal independence across Africa, the Caribbean, and Asia. As I have pointed out elsewhere, James's revision of the play to become *The Black Jacobins* took place "in the context of James's own political fallout with Trinidadian Prime Minister Eric Williams and in the broader context of the short-lived West Indian Federation" (Chetty 2014, 80). Though James had returned to Trinidad after more than 25 years away to participate in the newly established independent West Indian Federation, eventually he would find himself placed under house arrest in 1965 by Williams, Trinidad's first Prime Minister, and James's one-time student, accused of political subversion after James broke with Williams's People's National Movement party and formed another in opposition to it.

This 1960s Trinidadian political backdrop, and its particular relevance for James personally, is one half of the specific conjuncture of coloniality that undergirds the 1967 staging of *The Black Jacobins*. It seems no stretch to imagine that Lyndersay, a Trinidadian playwright and director living and working in Nigeria, would have been keenly attuned to the relevance of the play both for Trinidad in its broader post/colonial Caribbean and for Nigeria in its broader post/colonial African context. In fact, the most immediate context for the premiere of *The Black Jacobins* is the Nigerian-Biafran War, as Douglas has teased out through analysis of James and Lyndersay's correspondence: "Written during the escalation and at the height of this civil war, the director-playwright correspondence reveals these tumultuous Nigerian events backstage" (Douglas 2019, 151). As various commentators have pointed out, the Nigerian-Biafran War cannot be understood without reference to the lasting effects of British colonialism and a lingering British colonial influence because of, among other reasons, continued colonial interest in oil.[7]

I have dwelt on these contexts to highlight how the stage premieres of James's two plays on the Haitian Revolution—in 1936 and 1967— directly articulated with what could be called political crises: the Italian invasion of Ethiopia in the former case, the Nigerian-Biafran War in the latter. However, following Maldonado-Torres's etymological distinctions between crisis, disaster, and catastrophe, it seems more appropriate to foreground the catastrophic nature of these political moments, precisely because they are a consequence of "a normalization of catastrophe, evident in the form of continued dehumanization, expropriation, slavery (and its aftermaths), and genocide, otherwise known as coloniality" (2019, 337).

Haiti, 1993, and *The Black Jacobins* in Trinidad

After its premiere in 1967 at the University of Ibadan, *The Black Jacobins* has been staged in the 1970s, 1980s, 1990s, and 2000s, in Britain, the United States, Jamaica, Trinidad, and Barbados.[8] These subsequent stage productions have carried forward the conjunctural shifts that animated the revisions from 1936 to the 1967 versions of the play, as the latter has had to be revised to confront new global historical conjunctures and local contexts. The play was directed most famously in 1986 by Yvonne

Brewster, as the opening production of Talawa Theatre Company, which has since become one of the United Kingdom's leading Black theater companies. In the remainder of this essay, however, I focus on Rawle Gibbons's 1993 production in Trinidad because of the way this adaptation carries the play into the persistent coloniality in Haiti's (and Trinidad's) contemporary circumstances and draws attention specifically to the plight of poor Black women in 1990s Haiti.

Founder of the Centre for Creative and Festival Arts (CCFA) at the University of the West Indies (UWI), St. Augustine, Gibbons has directed various of these post-1967 stagings of *The Black Jacobins*, in Jamaica and Trinidad, including one version in 1979, the first in James's native Trinidad, which James himself was able to attend. Louis Regis has analyzed Gibbons's 1979 thesis, "Traditional Enactments of Trinidad: Towards a Third Theatre," to show how his approach to theater, rooted in African and South Asian performance traditions that have creolized in the Caribbean, emerges from an understanding of the "fluid" interaction between actors and audience. What this fluidity has meant for Gibbons, Regis argues, is a "new design of the theatre space, which is structured on the design principle of sacred spaces like *orisa yard* and also on the secular yard, the living space of the urban underclass. Within those yards were enacted the hundreds of little dramas in which the community participated as audience knowing that their very presence was necessary for the performance" (2017, 184).

This sense of community participation was central to Gibbons's 1993 staging and adaptation of *The Black Jacobins*. Instead of staging the play at UWI, St. Augustine, or in Port of Spain, Gibbons elected to stage the play in the Scherzando Cultural Centre (a panyard) in Curepe. This meant that some of the audience for the play included members of this community outside of the centers of Trinidadian intellectual and bourgeois life. The play program notes that the "Scherzando Steel Orchestra evolved from the liberation movement of the late sixties. In 1969, a group of youths, mostly unemployed, came together to harmonize in steelband and other forms of indigenous music." The group reached the finals of Trinidad's National Panorama Steelband Competition in 1974, becoming the first unsponsored group to do so. Subsequent community and cooperative-based fundraising efforts not only resulted in a "proliferation of unsponsored steelbands," but also allowed the group, known since 1987 as Curepe Scherzando Steelband Co-operative Society Limited, to construct a multi-purpose hall in 1991, the purpose of which is "to encourage self-sufficiency among their members by offering trade skills in welding and auto mechanic and to uplift the community through culture by offering their compound to be used for sporting and cultural events."[9]

Beyond connecting with and involving the community-focused cooperative nature of the Scherzando Cultural Centre, staging the play in Curepe meant asking audience members from the UWI community in St. Augustine to travel to an area "not without its undesirable qualities" (Ramcharitar 1993, 5). Gibbons himself acknowledged, perhaps tongue-in-cheek, the need to "make sure and say that there will be adequate security at the venue," having chosen a venue "in what might be called a slightly seedy area, a burnt wreck of a bus, the detritic paraphernalia lying about the yard itself, and the panmen, (who will be part of the performance)," because with all of this, "the aspect of the immediacy crystallised." Gibbons continued, "That's part of the whole thing, to get people to come to a place where they are not comfortable. People are not comfortable with confronting the Haiti situation. We were asked to stage it in Port of Spain, but we're not going to do that. We want people to come here and meet this thing" (quoted in Ramcharitar 1993, 5).

"The Haiti situation" that provided the immediate context for Gibbons's adaptation was one in which Jean-Bertrand Aristide, elected president of Haiti in 1991, had been deposed after only nine months in office by a military coup d'état led by Raoul Cédras, to international outrage. To be sure, this moment was no mere political crisis, but a catastrophe born of internal political conflicts and long-term external colonial practices. This is one through line in Michel-Rolph Trouillot's classic work, *Haiti: State Against Nation, The Origins and Legacy of Duvalierism* (1990), even though colonialism is not Trouillot's explicit guiding framework. What the book does, quite presciently, is predict implicitly the 1991 "crisis" by analyzing the structural opposition of the Haitian state against Haitian people, which is rooted in colonialism:

> The peripheral capitalist state is often *a colonial legacy*, the result of a political "independence" built upon the remains of a power structure imposed from outside. The ultimate moral and political justification of decolonization notwithstanding, the replacement of a European-led apparatus with a "native" bureaucracy creates as many problems as it solves. The "national" state so created never inherited a blank slate because *the preceding colonial entity*, as well as the conditions of its demise, limited both the new rulers' possibilities and those of their successors. Not surprisingly, the inherent

disjuncture between state and nation, conveniently concealed by the recent notion of the "nation-state," tends to increase in peripheral countries. (Trouillot 1990, 23; italics added)

Trouillot emphasizes a longer and explicitly colonial foundation for the failures of the Haitian state in his 1990s conjuncture, one that resonates for Haiti today, more than thirty years later. In his decolonial reading of the lead-up to the Haitian Revolution, Jean Casimir makes this connection explicit: post-independence Haitian leaders "remained fixated on the maintenance and ultimate reconstruction of the colonial social relations that had created them and continued to shape the image they had of themselves. This made it unthinkable, undesirable, and unacceptable for them to imagine any kind of future for popular sovereignty" (Casimir 2020, 22).

To ignore this colonial foundation and its afterlife and lay Haitian state failures exclusively at the feet of Haitian politicians or everyday Haitian people—or to ignore Haitian people altogether—is to reproduce the violence of that colonial thinking. Such political analysis also fails to understand that one of the real threats to colonial power—as it had been in 1791—was the mass mobilization and self-activity of Haitian masses. Trouillot would highlight this point four years after the publication of *Haiti: State Against Nation*, as negotiations for Aristide's return were on-going: "[Haitians'] first—and only unquestionable—gesture as a people was in 1791–1804, when they stood en masse against slavery and French colonialism. Their second national gesture was in 1990, when a 67% majority elected Father Aristide to the presidency in the country's first free elections" (Trouillot 1994, 46). Trouillot's yoking of these two moments of widespread Haitian participation in their own governance is an example of the "countercatastrophic explorations of time and the formations of space, within, against, and outside the modern/colonial world" that Maldonado-Torres argues for (2019, 340). At the close of that 1994 essay, Trouillot makes even more explicit the reason for Aristide's emergence as the popular leader that he was: "Aristide himself was possible in part because of deep political changes in the countryside, rooted in the rural churches and the emerging peasant movement" (Trouillot 1994, 51). Here, there is a clear echo of James's reading of Toussaint's emergence: "Yet Toussaint did not make the revolution. It was the revolution that made Toussaint. And even that is not the whole truth"

(James [1938] 1963, x). In both cases, colonial powers and neocolonial elite actors thought that by merely removing the leader they could remove the threat to their dominance. In both cases, they underestimated Haitians' political will to freedom and the investment Black people more broadly had in a free Haiti that offered hope for their own freedoms.[10]

Gibbons's 1993 production of *The Black Jacobins* emblematizes this Black Internationalist ethos: the play's program included a letter from President Aristide in support of the play and of intra-Caribbean unity. The play's very production was part of a broader organized effort in Trinidad to draw attention to "the Haiti situation" of the time, an effort formally organized by the Haiti Action Support Team (HASTE). Also outlined in the play's program, HASTE's specific aims were to counter what it saw as Caribbean and Trinidad and Tobago societies' lack of attention to Haiti's issues and their "passive" acceptance "of media analysis and coverage emanating largely outside of the region, accepting uncritically the bad press on the Haitian people and the negative international attitudes to ever resolving their problems." Instead of dealing "with the situation as if it is the US's or someone else's problem," HASTE states in the program that its "programme of events is [...] geared towards finding commonalities, historical, social, cultural and economic and encouraging discussion on what our responsibilities to Haiti are." The statement asserts that "Haiti is predominantly a Caribbean responsibility. We must take responsibility for events in the region as we must begin to take responsibility for ourselves in the region."[11] The power of this statement lies both in its argument against a long history of US imperial interference, including then-President Bill Clinton's intervention to restore Aristide to power, and its argument against Caribbean political disavowal of responsibility.

Gibbons's adaptation of *The Black Jacobins* articulates between Haiti's contemporary issues in the early 1990s and the revolutionary period two hundred years prior by staging a historical play within a contemporary play. This carries forward James's purpose in turning to the Haitian Revolution as a story of anticolonial Black struggle with persistent but evolving relevance for its 1930s and 1960s conjunctures. The contemporary framing that Gibbons has created for this 1993 adaptation features no marked beginning: actors playing modern-day Haitians mill about the staging area, interacting with each other, and offering wares to the audience as though in a Haitian village or market area. Gibbons's production brief notes that a shift to a more demarcated performance occurs when these "Haitian" vendors notice that the audience might be able to influence external exposure and attention to Haiti: "Seeing a number of foreigners (the audience) present in Port-au-Prince a group of Haitian peasants demonstrate peacefully for the restoration of democracy in their country," holding up hand-made signs written in Kreyòl calling for democracy, Aristide's return, and help from other Caribbean nations. The precarious situation in Haiti for these Black "peasants" comes to life as their demonstrations are, the brief continues, "attacked by an army patrol unit who violently break up the demonstrations," a representation of the internal military rule dominating Haiti's politics and terrorizing Haitian people, evoking both the earlier Tonton Macoute, the Duvaliers' paramilitary forces, and the contemporary Front pour l'Avancement et le Progrès Haïtien (FRAPH), a violent, right-wing paramilitary force specifically opposed to Aristide. However, the scattered Haitians "regroup and proceed, surreptitiously, to rally the spirit of resistance and tell their tale from the beginning—The Black Jacobins." Thus begins the play-within-a-play, a staging with the express purpose of politically engaging the Trinidadian audience into support for Haitians and Haitian democracy.[12]

The paramilitary forces, played by the yard's panmen, make the ever-present threat of their violence felt not only by their periodic interruption of the play-within-a-play to disrupt the attempt to "rally the spirit of resistance," but also by their interrogation of the audience as to who supports Aristide. This interrogation occurs at the play's "close," when the already broken wall between the players and the audience is completely removed. Including two of the three acts from *The Black Jacobins*, this adaptation closes with Toussaint signing Moïse's execution order at the behest of Dessalines (Act 2, Scene 4 in the 1967 script) before gunfire erupts off-stage, forcing the end of the historical play by bringing contemporary violence back to the stage to scatter the players and signal the return of the police force. The police enter an empty stage, turn to the audience, and ask, "Where are all the Aristide supporters?" Some shouts of "Here" greet these enforcers as they move out into the audience. From off-stage, the actors playing Haitian peasants return and interact with the audience, talking about Haiti individually with audience members, some announcing a call for democracy. Then an announcement goes out— "Supporters of Aristide, come with us"—and the play spills out into the street, with dance, music, drum, and chanting: "We want democracy in Haiti."[13] Because Gibbons's adaptation has ended with the second act, what is left out is the move toward Haitian independence, which takes place in the final scene of the third act of the playscript for *The Black*

Jacobins (and of *Toussaint Louverture*, for that matter). Here, the suggestion is clear: because of both internal military control and the threat/promise of external military occupation/aid, Haitian independence and democracy cannot be staged in 1993. What is performed instead is a call to rally behind both the return of Haitian democracy, embodied in Aristide's return, and its independence, drawing a clear link between the revolutionary struggle that resulted in Haiti's creation in 1804 and the struggle over Haitian sovereignty in 1993.

Gibbons's adaptation also carries forward and updates the muted sense of violence against women as originally scripted in *The Black Jacobins*. In this 1993 production, the persistence of colonial violence turns around the question of Haitian women. The most poignant scene features a Black woman who has been the victim of what the audience must understand as rape at the hands of the paramilitary forces.[14] In an earlier part of the scene, Act 2, Scene 2 of *The Black Jacobins*, Toussaint has just told the French Colonel Vincent that he has placed Governor Hédouville under house arrest when a laugh and other noises come from off-stage. The actors quickly disguise all indications that a play is being performed, pretending to be simply hanging around as the modern-day police forces enter the staging area. A woman is hauled off, and all are visibly terrified. When the police have left, the play resumes exactly where it had left off, at the point in the playscript in which Toussaint delivers a bold speech to Colonel Vincent announcing Saint Domingue's self-governing role as a protectorate of France, a sort of quasi-independence that is a direct challenge to French colonial rule under a newly reigning Napoléon Bonaparte. In Gibbons's adaptation, the actor playing Toussaint—still on stage—puts his costume back on, while the words attributed to him in the *The Black Jacobins* typescript are uttered by a series of men and women on stage, each one taking a phrase or sentence from the speech. Even when, now fully clothed in character as Toussaint, the actor playing him takes up the speech, at his every reference to the enslavement of Black people he is joined by the chorus of characters on stage. With this directorial adaptation, Gibbons fulfills James's aim via *The Black Jacobins*: to foreground the breadth and depth of the Haitian people's direct participation in their Revolution, and revolutionary leaders' reliance on them.[15]

Quite brilliantly, Gibbons extends this communal, unified voice diachronically from the time of the Revolution to his 1993 present. The collective voice reaches its apogee when the play is again interrupted, this time not by the paramilitary force but by the return of the Black woman who had been carted away earlier in the scene. The play's abrupt interruption this time has a decidedly different feel than the interruptions caused by the police harassment. Here, the performance stops of the actors' own accord, as they rush stage right to reintegrate the violated woman into their community. They move her to the center of the stage, gently sit her on a stool, and the actor playing Toussaint cradles her as the rest of the people on stage form a protective embrace around her. Her face is powerfully impassive, past feeling.

One by one, the actors peel off from the communal embrace to issue direct, pointed challenges to the audience, first in the form of personal testimonials. The first testimonial, uttered by the woman playing Madame Toussaint, explicitly addresses the sexual violence perpetrated against the woman on stage: "This [pointing vigorously at her] is the kind of degradation we go through every day. But who do we complain to? The authorities?" The remaining testimonials deal with other forms of violence, against women and men, culminating in the direct address to the audience, stated by the actor playing Toussaint: "What are YOU going to do about Haiti?"[16] The applause at the close of this call reflects the way this scene functions as a cathartic high point for the audience. Even though the performance of the historical play within the contemporary play resumes, finishing the scene that had begun, now interrupted twice, and ending with the final scene of the second act, there is no point of the play that reaches the emotional high of this scene. This, I argue, is not due to the audience mistaking the scene as the end of the play, but to the emotional investment the company creates in the scene.

Even though it is not the closing image, the communal embrace of the violated Black woman is the emotional equivalent of the closing tableau at the end of *The Black Jacobins* 1967 playscript. In that version, the suggestion of future violence against women in a newly independent Haitian state—in Emperor Dessalines's "almost forceful" pulling of Marie-Jeanne's body, his own wife's body, toward him to dance with him—finds its twentieth-century fulfillment in the sexual and physical violation of the Black Haitian peasant woman's body at the hands of a militarized state.[17] Gibbons's adaptation sounds like a note of hope, both in the possibility for healing through communal reintegration against police brutality and sexual violence and in the call for greater Caribbean engagement with Haiti. Because the play eschews idealizing Haiti as "independent" in 1993 by closing the action prior to the act of independence, it decisively avoids the polarizing thinking that describes Haiti as both "the most or only successful" and "the greatest failure." Instead, Haiti's success and failure are bound up in intra-Caribbean politics. As Gibbons put it in a 2011 interview, "My own belief is as a region we don't move forward until we deal with Haiti. We must face, must come to terms with Haiti. This is how you become a region."[18]

The success of the play versions of *The Black Jacobins* turns precisely on the ability to make the Haitian Revolution intersect with current efforts to imagine alternative global political realities to the catastrophe of coloniality—in Nigeria in 1967, in Haiti in 1993—and demand that audience members engage with the task of helping Haiti rebuild itself. What's more, *The Black Jacobins* as scripted and staged for a Nigerian audience in 1967 by Lyndersay, and as adapted for a Trinidadian one in 1993 by Gibbons, offers a version of anticolonial struggle that foregrounds Black women's struggles as fundamental to imagining and building decolonized futures.

Like the play productions in 1936 and 1967, Gibbons's 1993 adaptation of *The Black Jacobins* derives its power from the usefulness of the dramatic story of the Haitian Revolution for broader anticolonial struggle. However, by distinction from those earlier productions, Gibbons's also centers contemporary Haiti and the struggles it was facing in that early 1990s conjuncture, even as it demands attention and action from a Trinidadian and broader Caribbean public. Haiti finds itself today in what seems to be both a new and familiar internal political crisis, with an external Kenyan police force whose presence, orchestrated by the United States, Canada, and other powers of the Global North, is part of a much longer political colonial catastrophe. It is a testament to James's work that *The Black Jacobins* play continues to be relevant, thirty years after Gibbons's production in Trinidad, sixty years after its premiere in Nigeria, and ninety years after James's *Toussaint Louverture* graced London stages. It is also an indictment of regional and global failures to face Haiti.

Notes

1. For a brief but powerful account of this, see Pierre (2023).
2. Most recently, the playscript of *Toussaint Louverture* has been adapted into a graphic novel by Nic Watts and Sakina Karimjee.
3. In the remainder of this essay, I refer to the 1967 version of the play and adaptations or productions of the same as *The Black Jacobins*.

4. See Chetty (2019).
5. The 1934 play was only relatively recently published; see James (2013). The 1967 play typescript was published in 1992 in *The C. L. R. James Reader*; see James (1992a).
6. For illuminating examples, see Shakes (2013) and Douglas (2019).
7. For a brief and useful overview of the colonial context for the Nigerian-Biafran war, see Otiono (2021). For an in-depth discussion of regional tensions that emerged under British colonialism in the two decades before the Nigerian-Biafran War, see Anthony (2018). Finally, for a discussion of British oil interests during the war, see Uche (2008).
8. In addition to the productions discussed below, post-1967 productions include a BBC play on the "Monday Play" program, broadcast on December 13, 1971; a 1975 production in Jamaica, directed by Rawle Gibbons; a 1979 production in Trinidad—at James's alma mater, Queen's Royal college—by the Yard Theatre; a 1982 production of the Jamaican School of Drama's Graduate Theatre Company, directed by Eugene Williams; and a 2004 production in Barbados at the University of the West Indies, Cave Hill, directed by Harclyde Walcott, on the occasion of the 200th anniversary of Haitian independence. See Douglas (2019, 193–197).
9. Program/brochure for C. L. R. James's "The Black Jacobins" at the Curepe Scherzando Steelband Co-operative Society Limited Hall, a student production presented by Creative Arts Centre, Faculty of Humanities and Education, The University of the West Indies, St. Augustine Campus, 1993. Caribbean Performing Arts: Programmes and Ephemera, SC112. Content holder, The Alma Jordan Main Library, The University of the West Indies, St. Augustine Campus. Many thanks to Danielle Lyndersay, Rawle Gibbons, and Sheldon J. Placide for providing direct access to the files surrounding this production of the play.
10. For one recent example, focused on Black Americans' engagement with the Haitian Revolution, see Alexander (2023).
11. Program/brochure for C. L. R. James's "The Black Jacobins" at the Curepe Scherzando Steelband Co-operative Society Limited Hall.

12. Rawle Gibbons, "Brief: The Black Jacobins – C. L. R. James," for C. L. R. James's "The Black Jacobins" at the Curepe Scherzando Steelband Co-operative Society Limited Hall.
13. DVD recording of C. L. R. James's "The Black Jacobins" at the Curepe Scherzando Steelband Co-operative Society Limited Hall.
14. For a report on rape and sexual violence at the time, see, Human Rights Watch (1994). For Haitian women's testimonies on rape and sexual violence, including during this period, see Bell (2002).
15. For a discussion of how the play stages this level of participation by the Haitian people, including their function as an ever-present witness to both the public and the more intimate moments of *The Black Jacobins*, see the performance review by Smith (1993, 26).
16. DVD recording of C. L. R. James's "The Black Jacobins" at the Curepe Scherzando Steelband Co-operative Society Limited Hall.
17. For a discussion of the Duvalierist regime's use of "Marie-Jeannes" as "a reappropriated historical gender symbol represented by a rebellious slave," see Charles (1995, 140).
18. Rawle Gibbons, in discussion with the author, April 4, 2011.

Works Cited

Alexander, Leslie. 2023. *Fear of a Black Republic: Haiti and the Birth of Black Internationalism in the United States*. Champaign: University of Illinois Press.

Anthony, Douglas. 2018. Decolonization, Race, and Region in Nigeria: Northernization Revisited. *The International Journal of African Historical Studies* 51 (1): 37–62. https://www.jstor.org/stable/45176415.

Bell, Beverly. 2002. *Walking on Fire: Haitian Women's Stories of Survival and Resistance*. Ithaca: Cornell University Press.

Casimir, Jean. 2020. *The Haitians: A Decolonial History*. Translated by Laurent Dubois. Durham: Duke University Press.

Charles, Carolle. 1995. Gender and Politics in Contemporary Haiti: The Duvalierist State, Transnationalism, and the Emergence of a New Feminism (1980–1990). *Feminist Studies* 21 (1): 135–164. https://doi.org/10.2307/3178323.

Chetty, Raj. 2014. The Tragicomedy of Anticolonial Overcoming: *Toussaint Louverture* and *The Black Jacobins* on Stage. *Callaloo* 37 (1): 69–88. https://doi.org/10.1353/cal.2014.0023.

Chetty, Raj. 2019. Can a Mulatta be a Black Jacobin?: C. L. R. James, Feminism, and the Place of Collaboration. *Small Axe* 23 (3 (60)): 87–103. https://doi.org/10.1215/07990537-7912286.

Douglas, Rachel. 2019. *Making the Black Jacobins: C. L. R. James and the Making of History*. Durham: Duke University Press.

Douglas, Rachel. 2020. Unsilencing the Haitian Revolution: C. L. R. James and *The Black Jacobins*. *Atlantic Studies* 19 (2): 281–304. https://doi.org/10.1080/14788810.2020.1839283.

Fatton, Jr., Robert. 2024. Reflections on the Haitian Crisis. By Kevin Edmonds. In the Diaspora. *Stabroek News* (Georgetown, Guyana), April 15. https://www.stabroeknews.com/2024/04/15/features/in-the-diaspora/reflections-on-the-haitian-crisis-robert-fatton-jr/.

Human Rights Watch. 1994. Rape in Haiti: A Weapon of Terror, refworld, UNHCR, July 1. https://www.refworld.org/reference/countryrep/hrw/1994/en/21708.

James, C. L. R. (1934) 2013. *Toussaint Louverture: The Story of the Only Successful Slave Revolt in History: A Play in Three Acts*. Edited by Christian Høgsbjerg. Durham: Duke University Press.

James, C. L. R. (1938) 1963. *The Black Jacobins: Toussaint L'ouverture and the San Domingo Revolution*. Second ed., Revised ed. New York: Vintage Books.

James, C. L. R. (1967) 1992a. *The Black Jacobins*. In *The C.L.R. James Reader*, ed. Anna Grimshaw. Blackwell.

James, C. L. R. 1992b. Conversation with C. L. R. James. By Daryl Cumber Dance. In *New World Adams: Conversations with West Indian Writers*, ed. Daryl Cumber Dance, 109–119. Leeds: Peepal Tree.

Maldonado-Torres, Nelson. 2019. Afterword: Critique of Decoloniality in the Face of Crisis, Disaster, and Catastrophe. In *Aftershocks of Disaster: Puerto Rico before and after the Storm*, ed. Yarimar Bonilla and Marisol LeBron. Chicago: Haymarket Books.

Otiono, Kikachukwu. 2021. Blood in Biafra: Re-evaluating Politics and Ethnocultural Conflict in the Nigerian-Biafran War. *History Compass* 19 (7). https://doi.org/10.1111/hic3.12663.

Pierre, Jemima. 2023. Haiti as Empire's Laboratory. *NACLA Report on the Americas* 55: 244–250. https://doi.org/10.1080/10714839.2023.2247749.

Quijano, Anibal. 2000. Coloniality of Power, Eurocentrism, and Latin America. *Nepantla* 1 (3): 533–580.

Ramcharitar, Raymond. 1993. Haiti Revisited via CLR James' 'Black Jacobins.' *Sunday Guardian Magazine* (Port of Spain, Trinidad), April 11: 5.

Regis, Louis. 2017. Rawle Gibbons and the Theory and Practice of the Third Theatre. *Caribbean Quarterly* 63 (2/3): 183–202. https://doi.org/10.1080/00086495.2017.1352269.

Shakes, Nicosia. 2013. History and Drama in C.L.R. James' *Toussaint Louverture: The Story of the Only Successful Slave Revolt in History*. *The CLR James Journal* 19 (1/2): 38–60. https://www.jstor.org/stable/26752032.

Smith, Faith L. 1993. Reading, Rites and Revolution: A Personal Response to *The Black Jacobins*. *Trinidad and Tobago Review* (June): 26–27.

Trouillot, Michel-Rolph. 1990. *Haiti: State against Nation, the Origins and Legacy of Duvalierism*. Monthly Review Press.

Trouillot, Michel-Rolph. 1994. Haiti's Nightmare and the Lessons of History. *NACLA Report on the Americas* 27 (4): 46–51. https://doi.org/10.1080/10714839.1994.11724636.

Uche, Chibuike. 2008. Oil, British Interests, and the Nigerian Civil War. *The Journal of African History* 49 (1): 111–135. https://doi.org/10.1017/S0021853708003393.

Ulysse, Gina Athena. 2015. The Haiti Story You Won't Read. In *Why Haiti Needs New Narratives: A Post-Quake Chronicle*. Middletown, CT: Wesleyan University Press.

Watts, Nic, and Sakina Karimjee. 2023. Adaptation of *Toussaint Louverture: The Story of the Only Successful Slave Revolt in History*, by C. L. R. James. Verso.

Staging the Païdeuma: Nature and Insurrection in Aimé Césaire's *Une tempête*

Eren Jaye

Introduction

Written during the period of political decolonization of the French colonial territories, Aimé Césaire's reconfiguration of William Shakespeare's *The Tempest* is his fourth and final play. Césaire chose the title *Une tempête*, "a tempest," rather than the French equivalent, *la tempête*, to align his reimagining with a multitude of territorial and social revolutionary liberation movements active during the sixties. His dramatic tempest is one among a myriad of others: "[…] une adaptation d'après Shakespeare, qui s'appelle non pas *LA tempête*, mais *UNE tempête*. Parce qu'il y a beaucoup de tempêtes, n'est-ce pas—et la mienne n'est qu'une parmi d'autres…" [(…) an adaptation of Shakespeare, not titled

---

E. Jaye (✉)
Department of French, University of Virginia, Charlottesville, VA, USA
e-mail: eren.jaye@virginia.edu

© The Author(s), under exclusive license to Springer Nature Switzerland AG 2025
C. Stevens and J. D. Rossini (eds.), *The Coloniality of Catastrophe in Caribbean Theater and Performance*,
https://doi.org/10.1007/978-3-031-85791-1_4

THE Tempest but *A Tempest*. Because there are many tempests, aren't there—and mine is but one of many][1] (Beloux and Césaire 1969).

Césaire's reconfiguration was first produced during the summer of 1969 for an international theatre festival taking place in Hammamet, Tunisia, a neighboring country to Algeria and the native land of the play's unseen character, Sycorax, Caliban's mother and a witch who was exiled from her native Algiers while pregnant with her son. In the Shakespearean text, it is explained that Sycorax was exiled due to her practice of magic too terrible to repeat aloud (I, 2) and so strong she could control the moons and the tides (V, 1). Her pregnancy with Caliban was the only reason she was not put to death in Algiers and, instead, banished to the mysterious, unnamed island (I, 2). In this way, and in Aimé Césaire's reimagining, the mother/son bind of Sycorax and Caliban, forced into exile while the two shared a body, presents as a sort of shadow doubling of Shakespeare's father/daughter bind of Prospero and Miranda, also forced into exile before the play's action begins. Prospero's fate further parallels that of Sycorax, as he was also banished from his home country, sent to sea on a raft with his child, rather than put to death, for immersion into studies of the occult that led to the neglect of his governance duties in Milan. Furthermore, the recurrent symbolic theme of political exile takes on a live form with the premiere of Césaire's *Une tempête* in Tunisia, *mis en scène* less than a decade after the Algerian War for Independence resulted in liberation after 132 years of French colonization. During Algeria's anti-colonial struggle, Tunisia offered refuge to many of the Revolution's leaders in exile, including Aimé Césaire's own student and mentee, Frantz Fanon.

In this essay, I offer an ecopoetic reading of *Une tempête* by tracing the origins of Aimé Césaire's early thought originating from the literary journal *Tropiques* (1941–1945). Within the journal's internal textual dialogue between Aimé Césaire and his wife, Suzanne Césaire, is an ecologic-ethnographic archetypal interpretation of civilization developed first by Léo Frobenius named the *païdeuma*, taken up by Aimé and Suzanne in their own discourse on the relationship between nature, culture, and civilization in Martinique. In the textual creation of Aimé Césaire's *Une tempête*, the *païdeuma* is given a conceptual form that is eventually embodied in live productions of the play. This essay also explores the unique vision behind the 2022 production of *Une tempête* at the American Shakespeare Center in Staunton, Virginia as a continuation of the intertextuality between Aimé Césaire, Suzanne Césaire, and William Shakespeare that ultimately inverts the celebrated ending of the original *The Tempest*,[2] thereby subverting the perhaps extractive dynamic of conventional spectatorship by inviting the audience into the fabric of the ritualized theatre sphere as a site for psychosomatic, spiritual transformation.

Staging the *Païdeuma*

The fecund origins of Césaire's theatrical and theoretical thought can be traced back to the literary journal *Tropiques* (1941–1945), co-founded with Suzanne Césaire and René Ménil. Therewithin, one finds that the dialogue within *Tropiques*'s four-year publication run rests largely on a Martinican political and social identity conceived in relation to the natural geography of their island—the Caribbean Sea, the volcanic landscape, the ordered chaos of the tropical forests, and the rhythms of the Antillean seasonal cycles, interwoven with Martinican folklore, and high surrealist poetics. "Fragments d'un poème" [Fragments of a Poem] by Aimé Césaire was the first published text to appear in the review's inaugural issue, printed in 1941 while Martinique was controlled by the Vichy Regime, resulting in a political situation which caused the authors of *Tropiques* to write under constant threat of censure. In this poem, Césaire centers the natural world of Martinique, preparing the ground for a collectively formed textual universe with ecological touchstones that the authors of the journal would continue to adopt for the remainder of the review's print history. In final lines of the poem, Césaire concludes: "L'oreille collée au sol, j'entendis / passer Demain" [With my ear to the earth, I heard / Tomorrow pass] (lines 316–317). These lines elucidate what is fundamental to Césaire's telluric vision of a Martinican cultural future disentangled from French colonial hegemony. By turning towards the natural world of the West Indian island, the writers of *Tropiques* were reaching for a future created anew, beyond the thresholds of colonial cultural forms of expression emanating from the French metropole.

If Aimé Césaire's "Fragments d'un poème" offers an ecologically rooted poetics as a point of departure for the aesthetic vision of *Tropiques*, it is the very next essay in the first issue that develops the eco-theoretical scaffolding for the journal. Suzanne Césaire's essay "Léo Frobenius et le problème des civilisations" [Leo Frobenius and the problem of civilizations] builds upon self-taught German ethnographer Leo Frobenius's concept of the *païdeuma*, a neologism likely formulated by combining two Greek roots: *paideia* and *pneuma*.³ In regard to the first part of the construction, *pais* or *paidos* means son or child, and *paideia* can be interpreted as education or pedagogy. The Greek term *pneuma* is the equivalent of the Latin term *spiritus*, signifying breath or spirit, though they can more specifically be interpreted as a vital essence which flows in the form of "air in movement," such as the verb "respire." Suzanne Césaire's essay opens a textual dialogue with the late Frobenius and interprets what she names as the "païdeuma fondamentale," the "fundamental païdeuma," as a substantial primordial energy, serving as the essence of a culture and animating its participants: "L'homme n'agit pas, il est agi, mû par une force antérieure à l'humanité, assimilable à la forcevitale elle-même." [Man does not act, he is acted upon, moved by a force anterior to humanity, comparable to the vital force itself] (S. Césaire 1941, 27).

Suzanne Césaire's comprehension of the *païdeuma* constitutes more of a reconfiguration of the metaphysical concept in the context of her colonial reality in Martinique than it does a rehashing of Frobenius's ideas for a Martinican readership. As Anny Dominique Curtius suggests, Suzanne Césaire was focused on Frobenius's research intentions of comprehending the essence of human civilization, as well as the "origin of cultures and their complexities [...] that cannot be apprehended through a cognitive and intellectual analysis of the world because of their relatedness to plants, the cosmos, and seasonal cycles" (Curtius 2016, 524). Suzanne Césaire understands the *païdeuma* through the lens of her Martinican community, describing the *païdeuma* as an essential albeit secret force irrigating the depths of all creation that offers a prism through which to recognize civilizations as supernatural entities. In Césaire's worldview, the vital *païdeuma* can be observed as adhering to a binary archetypal manifestation in the forms of "la civilization éthiopienne" [Ethiopian civilization] and "la civilisation hamitique" [Hamitic civilization]. "La civilisation éthiopienne" is related to "la plante, au cycle végétif" [the plant, to the vegetative cycle] and is otherwise termed "l'homme-plante," whereas "la civilisation hamitique" is linked to that of "l'animal, à la conquête du droit de vivre par la lutte" [the animal, to the conquest and to the right to live by fight] and referred to otherwise as "l'homme-animal" (S. Césaire 1941, 30).

Within the cultural framework of the *païdeuma*, "l'homme-plante" does not seek to dominate what is exterior to himself; rather, he follows a chronology of life identical to that of the botanical cycle. "L'homme-plante" is confident in the continuation of the enduring and material poetry of life's biological rhythms, which is to say: "germer, pousser, fleurir, donner des fruits et le cycle recommence. Poésie vécue, sentie profondément" [germinate, grow, blossom, give fruit and begin again. Poetry lived, profoundly felt] (30). Opposed to "l'homme-plante," l'homme-animal" is he who does not have a strong sense of the continuity of humanity in harmony with kingdoms of flora and fauna, but rather is concerned with individual life and kin, ensuring existence by the immediacy of domination, a mindset of the colonizer. Within Suzanne Césaire's framework, all of humanity is animated by a "saisissement," or seizure, by the "force-vitale" of the *païdeuma*. There is no escaping this essential energy. Suzanne Césaire concludes her analysis by relating the harnessing of the *païdeuma* of "l'homme-animal" to the folly of science, imperial conquests of colonial domination, and the terrible technologies of the First and Second World Wars (35).

Despite Frobenius's idealization and construction of an African essentialism, observed in a critical vein by Anny Dominique Curtius, his ideas provided Suzanne Césaire with a conceptual scaffolding with which to develop and navigate Martinican identity at a time of high anti-colonial sentiments and of social momentum moving away from the cultural eclipse by the French hexagon. This orientation by Césaire is aligned with the core mission of *Tropiques*, to redefine what is possible in the world, allowing new ontological realities to extend like wings, crossing the barriers of what was once inconceivable. Using Frobenius's *païdeuma* as a point of departure presenting a unique cultural analysis, Suzanne Césaire employs the framework as a tool to be used in the vision of transforming a collective consciousness. This approach is also aligned with Suzanne and Aimé Césaire's application of Surrealist methodologies as part of an anti-colonial apparatus.

Suzanne Césaire's theorization of the *païdeuma* informs Aimé Césaire's reconfiguration of Shakespeare's *The Tempest*, demonstrating the crucial influence that both Leo Frobenius and Suzanne Césaire continued to have on his mature works—*Une tempête* was published twenty-eight years after Suzanne's 1941 contribution to *Tropiques*. The framework of the "l'homme-plante"/"l'homme-animal" binary proposed by Suzanne Césaire elucidates the dynamic relationship between the island, its inhabitants, and its colonizers in *Une tempête* as tensions of the *païdeuma* are given representational form in the play, incarnating an essential oppositional knot imposed by a colonial society. Prospero and Miranda emerge as Europeans in exile, attempting to build a simulacrum of the civilization they once knew in Milan on the land where they now reside. Prospero executes his mission through total subjugation into slavery of those existing on the isle before he and Miranda, and by harnessing the natural world of the island by way of his magical authority—a manifestation of "l'homme-animal." Opposed to this microcosm are Caliban, Ariel, and their assassinated mother, Sycorax. They are the expression of a culture adhering to the convictions of "l'homme-plante," representing, in Aimé Césaire's imaginary, those who reigned on the island before the arrival of the exiled Europeans.

STAGING THE INSURRECTION

In the text of *Une tempête*, Aimé Césaire invokes from the outset an "atmosphère de psychodrame" [atmosphere of psychodrama], noted at the bottom of the Dramatis Personae page. In the early to mid-decades of the twentieth century, international theatre took an interest in the "corporeal-based psychophysiological transformation" that could take place by incorporating the public into the performance space as a part of the theater-ritual process, a praxis deeply influenced by the theoretical writings of Antonin Artaud, and first gaining modern recognition with Peter Brook and Peter Weiss's 1964 production of *Marat/Sade* (Ruprecht 1996, 60). In addition, the 1947 translation into French from the original German of Friedrich Nietzsche's *L'origine de la tragédie, ou hellénisme et pessimisme* (translated into English in 1910 as *The Birth of Tragedy, or Hellenism and Pessimism*) also had a profound impact on influential playwrights of mid-twentieth century francophone theater. Particularly compelling to Aimé Césaire was Nietzsche's emphasis on the dramatic phenomenon as a cathartic, transformative site that public and actors created mutually, drawn by Nietzsche from his study of classic Greek tragedy, where the audience, raised in concentric arcs encircling the auditorium, would make it possible to ignore the world outside of the theatre site, creating a mirror-like *mise-en-abyme* between actor and spectator, where both could contemplate their own reflection in the other (Nietzsche 1947, 137). In this way, and in a postcolonial context, the dramatic phenomenon as a ritualistic, metamorphic site has the potential to offer individuals amidst a community the opportunity to act "as if entering another body" and "surrendering individuality in a magical-epidemic transformation," while simultaneously dissociating themselves from an alienating, colonial environment, allowing for the emergence of new relational and cognitive frameworks (Bailey 1992, 114).

Aimé Césaire adds a supplementary character to the cast of Shakespeare's original in *Une tempête*. Eshu, described by Césaire as a "dieu-diable nègre" [black devil-god], is a figure originating from West African Yoruba traditions. He is a deity representing communication between visible, mortal realms and invisible, spirit realms, presiding over carrefours of Earth and Gods. He is the manifestation of time before time, present at the beginning of all creation, manifest also in Haitian Vodou as the loa Papa Legba, lording over crossroads and embodiment of the sun's daily death. Eshu is also known as a "trickster," instigating disorder and order, in turn. Though the figure of Eshu is only written into a singular scene of Aimé Césaire's text, his character embodies dual roles in director Dawn Monique Williams's 2022 production staged at the American Shakespeare Center: first, Césaire's original Eshu, and second as the Meneur de Jeu [Master of Ceremonies] present only during the play's prologue.

During the prologue, the cast, along with Eshu, spills onto the stage, each choosing a mask corresponding with a character to be played for the unfolding of the piece. Eshu, as the Master of Ceremonies, confirms the actors' choices as they each decide on a mask in succession, and subsequently casts himself as, of course, Eshu. In Vodou traditions, Papa Legba is the first to be acknowledged during a ritual as he permits communication and passage between realms, and it is only after an offering to him has been made that a ceremony can begin. According to Dawn Monique Williams, this moment of "casting" Eshu as the Master of Ceremonies is this first offering. Eshu himself also puts on a mask as the orchestrator of the piece, serving as the authoritative force which will set the theatre-rite underway, and heightening the ritual incorporation from the play's beginning (D.M. Williams, personal communication). At the end of the prologue and once all of the characters have been chosen by corresponding actors, the Master of Ceremonies/Eshu turns towards the audience and designates the public to play the role of the tempest: "il y en a un que je choisis: c'est toi ! Tu comprends, c'est la Tempête" [there is one that I choose: It is you! Do you understand? It is the Tempest] (Césaire 1969, prologue).

With this gesture, the audience is woven into the fabric of the spectacle as a tempest-chorus before the first Act, bestowing tangible, human form onto the thalassic elements of the seascape surrounding the stage. As the tempestuous fury approaches the island, we, the spectators, are transformed into the atmospheric chaos shrouding the island's coastline, turbulent seas, blusters of wind, and blinding rains of the wild skies in the collective imagination of the piece. Césaire interpolates the public into a psychophysiological dramatic sphere from the play's departing moments as the ecopoetic force of the tempest, the natural disaster itself, diminishing the boundary between actor and audience, stage, and auditorium. In inviting the public into the piece in a scene of high-tensions—"... il me faut une tempête à tout casser..." [...I need a tempest to destroy it all...] (prologue)—Césaire politicizes the audience by transforming them into an ecological feature, implicating the public in the colonial endeavor. Finally, the Shakespearean structure of the original play is also inverted, as it is only during the final moments of *The Tempest* that the public is integrated into the play as the force of forgiveness, liberating Prospero by way of their applause during the piece's famed epilogue: "But release me from my bands / With the help of your hands. [...] / Mercy itself and frees all faults. / As you from crimes would pardoned be / Let your indulgence set me free" (V, 1).

Parallel with the Shakespearean original, Act I, Scene 1 of *Une tempête* depicts chaos among the crewmates of a ship enmeshed in the magically manifested tempest at sea. The storm has been conjured by Ariel, one of the play's two characters enslaved by Prospero, to lure the ship towards the island from Prospero's native Milan, Italy. During Williams's 2022 production, the audience first views Ariel on a balcony facing outwards towards the audience, looking down onto the stage where the crew of the ship damned at sea attempt in vain to navigate the vessel into the eye of the storm. Ariel, depicted as feminine in this production, is also mimetically[4] doubled as the Orisha[5] Oya, the Yoruba spirit of winds in this production of *Une tempête*, a strong directorial decision textually supported by a response made by the sinking ship's second-in-command to Gonzalo, adviser to King Alonso of Naples:

LE MAÎTRE: Le Roi ! Le Roi! Eh bien, il y en a un qui se fout du Roi comme de toi et de moi, il s'appelle le Vent! [...] Pour le moment, c'est lui qui commande et nous sommes ses sujets. (I, 1)
[BOATSWAIN: The King! The King! Very well, there is one who cares nothing for the King, nor for you or me, he is named the Wind! (...) As of now, it is the Wind who reigns, and we are its subjects!]

These lines foreshadow the undoing of the displaced order of Milan through a vexed appeal to the immediacy of the elements as an alternative source of power and legitimacy. Judith Gleason introduces Oya as: "associated with fierce winds portending a change in weather. Her earliest representation was a gyrating cloth cylinder, *Gboya*, brought out by the Nupe people in times of crisis to cleanse the community of negative energies" (Gleason 2000, 265). Oya, just as Eshu, reverberates through African diasporic Latin American and Caribbean creole religions, and is still worshipped on both sides of the Atlantic. Queen of the dead, her spirit offers opportunities for transformation in the presence of destruction. Oya is the preferred wife of Shango—Orisha of war and thunder—, and her intercession presents to the visible world as winds, turbulent storms, running rivers, and the foam of the sea. During the scenes of *Une tempête* where Ariel is depicted as mystically influencing the theatre sphere, her movements take the form of a folkloric ritual dance attributed to Oya, making meteorologic-inspired gestures that mimic the meandering winds of a tempest and dancing to the rhythm of drums that invoke the patter of rain (Corrie Green, personal communication, 2023). Ariel's position as a supernatural orchestrator exerting her influence over the sea, the tempest, the crew, and the audience serves to further synthesize the piece. Though silent during this scene, Ariel's atmospheric dance guides both the ship on stage and the public seated in its peripheries into the play's intrigue, creating a sort of total theatre which troubles the conventional structural boundary between actors and audience.

As the play continues, we are met with the familiar cast of Shakespeare's *The Tempest*. Congruent with the Shakespearean original, Ariel is also forced into slavery after Prospero has assassinated the sorceress Sycorax, freeing the spirit from entrapment in a tree. Though in *The Tempest* Sycorax had enclosed Ariel into the tree with her magic, in Césaire's rewriting, it is left unclear whether assassinated Sycorax entrapped Ariel in a tree or if Sycorax *is* the tree it/herself. Ariel's first lines of the play respond to Prospero concerning this "liberation":

> PROSPERO: Ingrat, qui t'a délivré de Sycorax? Qui fit bâiller le pin où tu étais enfermé et te délivras?
> ARIEL: Parfois je me prends à le regretter... Après tout j'aurais peut-être fini par devenir arbre... Arbre, un des mots qui m'exaltent! J'y ai pensé souvent: Palmier! Fusant très haut une nonchalance où nage une élégance de poulpe. (I, 2)

[PROSPERO: Ungrateful, who delivered you from Sycorax? Who made the pine tree yawn within which you were entrapped and freed you?
ARIEL: At times I find myself regretting this... After all, I could have also ended up as a tree...Tree! A word that exalts me! I think of them often: Palm tree! Rising so high a nonchalance where swims the elegance of an octopus.]

Parallel with the Shakespearean version of this utterance, Prospero reminds Ariel that he has freed the spirit from a "cloven" pine tree by yawning, or gaping, it: "It was mine art / When I arrived and heard thee, that made gape / The pine and let thee out" (I, 2). However, in Césaire's text, Ariel responds by referring not to a pine, but to a palm, a tree whose family species is native to, and ubiquitous across, the Caribbean archipelago. Ariel acknowledges a nostalgia for a variant of life where the spirit may have themself eventually become a tree, an existence aligned with terrestrial, arboresque cycles. Ariel's response to Prospero on the death of Sycorax elucidates their internal harnessing of the *païdeuma*, as well as a troubled sense of alienation from their life before Prospero's arrival on the island. Sycorax, presented here as both a symbolic and literal creative-mother, a tree-of-life from which all springs and returns, remains imprinted in the latent strata of Ariel's subconscious.

In the same scene and shortly after Ariel's proclamation of sorrow over their truncated future as a tree, the audience encounters Caliban, a lyrical demi-man, demi-monster created by Shakespeare, living free on the island before Prospero's arrival.[6] Caliban's name is almost an anagram of *cannibal*, resembling also *Carib*, *Cariba*, and *Cariban*, terms originating from the Arawakan language of the Taino people of Haiti (Chapon 2013, 2; Taylor 1958, 156). These related terms have been historically employed to name those indigenous to the West Indies more broadly and form the etymon for the derivative, *Caribbean* (Taylor 1958, 156). The presence of cannibals native to the Antilles in the European literary mind finds its likely origins from the chronicles of Christopher Columbus, as he described communities of cannibals in his 1493 letter announcing to a European readership his discovery of the "Indian Islands." With this textual gesture, Christopher Columbus launched the myth of the "savage" indigenous populations of the New World into the collective European imagination. William Shakespeare's Caliban enters the literary sphere shortly over a century after Christopher Columbus's letter as the symbol for the colonized monster of the *terra incognita*.

In contrast to Ariel's more docile nature, Caliban's manifestations of his state prior to his enslavement by Prospero foregrounds the irreconcilable dissonance of the colonial relationship, foreshadowing his impulse towards eventual insurrection. Even though Sycorax is no longer breathing in human form, like Ariel, Caliban still finds his mother in the vitality of the island's landscape:

> PROSPERO: Sans moi, que serais-tu?
> CALIBAN: Sans toi? Mais tout simplement le roi! [...] Le roi de mon île que je tiens de Sycorax, ma mère. [...] Morte ou vivante, c'est ma mère et je ne la renierai pas ! D'ailleurs, tu ne la crois morte que parce que tu crois que la terre est chose morte... [...] Morte, alors on la piétine, on la souille, on la foule d'un pied vainqueur! Moi, je la respecte, car je sais qu'elle vit, et que vit Sycorax.
> Sycorax ma mère!
> Serpent! Pluie! Éclairs!
> Et je te retrouve partout:
> Dans l'œil de la mare qui me regarde, sans ciller,
> à travers les scirpes... (I, 2)
> {PROSPERO: Without me, what would you be?
> CALIBAN: Without you? Nothing but the king! [...] The king of my island given to me by Sycorax, my mother. [...] Dead or alive, she is my mother, and I will not deny her! Besides, you believe her dead only because you believe the earth is dead... [...] Dead, then you trample it, you soil it, you tread on it with a victorious foot! Me, I respect it, because I know that the earth lives and that Sycorax lives.
> Sycorax my mother!
> Snake! Rain! Lightning!
> I find you everywhere:
> In the eye of the pond which looks at me, without blinking,
> through the bulrushes...}

Caliban reminds Prospero of a telos that would have been had Prospero never arrived on his island: Caliban would have inherited the island from his mother, Sycorax, who *is* on the island. He also illustrates an essential discord between his relation to the territory and that of Prospero, who engages with the island as a "dead" object to be "trampled" in the service of achieving his *mission civilisatrice*, a manner of being constitutionally oppositional to Caliban who believes the island to be full of life, harbouring a vital essence through which Sycorax continues to live. The grief of Ariel and Caliban over their individual ruptures from the vital maternal source of island-as-Sycorax represents a latent germ of the internal logic of l'homme-plante," despite their enslavement by Prospero.

The form of Act III, Scene 4, echoes back to the play's prologue, opening with Ariel fervently conjuring a band of island creatures, to which each animal responds by ardently affirming their presence. This conjuration soon awakens Caliban, who asserts a resolve to take on the island's "cancer" the "anti-Nature" Prospero (III, 4). In the final scene, the spectators witness Prospero descend into madness rather than relinquish his death grip on his order of civilization and succumb to Caliban. Prospero is last seen shouting out his various "achievements," listing examples of that which he has subjugated by way of his rough magic, concluding with his "civilizing" of the monster, Caliban. Contrary to Ariel and Caliban aligning themselves in symbiotic harmony with the flora and fauna of the island, Prospero positions himself atop of his individual accomplishments, that which he has harnessed and enslaved. He is "l'homme-animal," a mad, necropolitical agent who is dominated by his capacity to "tuer afin de vivre" [to kill in order to live] on a territory he had colonized by refusing his "subjects" free access to their own sacred relationality with the nature of the landscape (Mbembe 2006, 27, 32). The piece closes with "remnants" of Caliban's song in the distance, heard among the rhythmic sound of the surf and the chirping of birds coupled with Prospero's lunar cries (III, 5).

In the Blackfriars Playhouse 2022 production, Dawn Monique Williams chose to stage the ending of Césaire's play with a gesture by Caliban that further undoes Prospero's supremacy in suggesting the total destruction of the island. During the closing scene, Caliban throws matches into a barrel which then begins to produce smoke. He leaves the stage and explosions are heard in the peripheries of the auditorium, implying that Caliban has destroyed his island with both him and Prospero on it. Though this gesture is not written in Aimé Césaire's original text, this directorial decision is textually supported, as suggested by Caliban in a dialogue with Ariel:

> CALIBAN: Mieux vaut la mort que l'humiliation et l'injustice… D'ailleurs, de toute manière, le dernier mot m'appartiendra… A moins qu'il n'appartienne au néant. Le jour où j'aurai le sentiment que tout est perdu, laisse-moi voler quelques barils de ta poudre infernale, et cette île, […] tu la verras sauter dans les airs, avec, j'espère, Prospero et moi dans les débris. J'espère que tu goûteras le feu d'artifice: ce sera signé Caliban. (II, 1)

[CALIBAN: Better death than humiliation and injustice… Nonetheless, the last word will be mine…Unless it belongs to nothingness. The day that I feel that all is lost, let me steal a few barrels of your infernal powder, and this island, […] you will see it leap into the air, with myself and Prospero in the debris. I hope that you will enjoy the fireworks: they will be signed, Caliban.]

In Césaire's rewriting, if Prospero refuses to leave the island, as he prepares to do in Shakespeare's *The Tempest*, Caliban, in his insurrection, is compelled to instigate total destruction rather than inhabit it with, or under the dominion of, Prospero. The threat of looming political violence that will inevitably lead to cataclysmic catastrophe arises from productive hierarchal tensions of the colonizer/colonized dynamic. Caliban's insurrectionist violence towards his own land is an impulse both purifying and curative. He asserts in one of his final lines of his desire to "heal" the island of the "cancer" that is Prospero (III, 4), performing in a theatre context Frantz Fanon's position in *Les Damnés de la terre* (1961) that violence acts as a detoxifying and rehabilitating force for colonized individuals, or as Jean-Paul Sartre remarks in the preface to Fanon's text: "La violence, comme la lance d'Achille, peut cicatriser les blessures qu'elle a faites" [Violence, just as the lance of Achilles, can heal the wounds it has made] (Sartre 1964, 192).

The 2022 production of *Une tempête* at the Blackfriars Playhouse is bookended with catastrophes: the play opens with a ship at sea fated for wreckage in a violent tempest and closes with an island foreordained for devastation. From the ruination of the destroyed island, all the earthly inhabitants that share its geography can perhaps now form a new order of life, outside of Prospero's tyrannical shadow. "What is born in the air [Oya] plants on the earth," and by way of Caliban as a medium, "destruction takes place so order might exist" (Oswaldo Villamil, quoted by Judith Gleason 2000, 275). Just as Oya, who in the presence of death cleanses a community through timely shifts in aerial weather patterns, Caliban's literalization of his threat to destroy the island is itself also a cataclysmic ecological event, making way for the dawn of a new civilization to emerge from the rubble, taking place just outside of the temporal confines of the play's action. In *Une tempête*, resistance against colonization is not a mere human endeavour, as more-than-human meteorologic, geologic, and spiritual forces join Caliban in dismantling Prospero's order of civilization in a shared impulse to restore balance distorted by colonial, human relations.

A final remarkable aspect of the Blackfriars Playhouse concurrent productions of *Une tempête* and *The Tempest* is the addendum of a second epilogue to their representation of Shakespeare's original. *The Tempest* was produced by the American Shakespeare Center amid their Renaissance Season during which all works by Shakespeare produced were directed collectively by the ensemble of the cast rather than by a single director. Together, the cast of the 2022 production of Shakespeare's *The Tempest*, guided by the only two Black actors of the troupe, those who played Ariel and Caliban,[7] decided to add a second epilogue to Shakespeare's original. In the first epilogue where *The Tempest* typically ends, Prospero takes the stage and pronounces a request for forgiveness and deliverance from his past faults, pleading with the audience to set him free by way of their indulgent applause. By contrast, the new, second epilogue consisted of Ariel and Caliban taking the stage following Prospero's final monologue. Alone, together at last, Ariel looks Caliban in the eyes and pronounces the single word, "freedom," offering a clear gesture to the closing scene of Césaire's *Une tempête* and presenting a continuum of the unfolding dialogue now between Aimé Césaire, William Shakespeare, and this unique play's cast. By making Shakespeare speak back to Césaire, the dialogue endures, now in corporealized form outside of the text, taking on a vibrant life of its own as the plays summon each other in tandem production.

Caliban and Ariel, in their persistent resistance in both versions of *The Tempest / Une tempête*, emerge as tragic heroes that have "*taken unto [themselves]* the destiny of a community" by way of an evocation of the forgotten historical figure who, according to Édouard Glissant, undertook and made his own "the cause of [Caribbean] resistance: the maroon" (Glissant 1989, 220). Even though there is one scene with both Ariel and Caliban together in Aimé Césaire's *Une tempête*, the second epilogue added by the American Shakespeare Center's cast to *The Tempest* is the sole instance where the only two previously enslaved characters on the island share the stage together, a moment not written into Shakespeare's original text. The addition of the second epilogue to *The Tempest* denies the reconciliation between Caliban and Prospero typically interpreted by critical consensus and, furthermore, denies Prospero the forgiveness, relinquishing him of all faults, that he notoriously requests in his final monologue. By way of this addendum, the spectators bear witness to, and participate in, what Glissant calls: "l'ardeur individuelle du lyrisme et la pratique collective du politique" [the individual ardor of lyricism

Image 4.1 Corrie Green as Ariel and Tevin Davis as Caliban in Aimé Césaire's *Une tempête* (*Photo Credit* Anna Kariel)

and the collective practice of politics], opening way for "un nouvel ordre de communauté de la planète-Terre" [a new order of community on planet-Earth] (Glissant 1990, 67). A decolonized Caliban and Ariel revitalize the Shakespearean classic by way of a theatric *marronage*, presenting thus not an orientation aimed at returning to an anterior past preceding Prospero's dominance, but, rather, an impulse deconstructing the center of the world, a gesture born from the ashes of a catastrophic colonial endeavor (Image 4.1).

Notes

1. All translations are my own unless otherwise indicated.
2. The American Shakespeare Center in the United States staged a production of *Une tempête* for an anglophone audience directed by Dawn Monique Williams at the Blackfriars Theatre in Staunton, Virginia, running from October 27 to November 19, 2022. This contemporary production of *Une tempête* was staged simultaneously, and thus in dialogue, with the troupe's Renaissance-style production of Shakespeare's *The Tempest*, and though Shakespeare's original had a longer run than Césaire's reimagining of the piece, the two closed on the same date.

3. The ethnopoetic writings of Léo Frobenius had a fundamental influence on the leaders of the négritude movement, including Léopold Sédar Senghor, Aimé Césaire, and Suzanne Césaire.
4. In his article "Thinking with Spirits, or Dwelling and Knowing in the Work of Aimé Césaire," Jason Allen-Paisant elucidates Césaire's conception of ritual possession as mimesis not in a sense of a being emptied of themselves to be fully animated by an-*other* but are, rather, truly doubled; they are both self and supernatural *other*, as one and at once. Allen-Paisant gives the example of possession in Haitian Vaudou: the loa are said to mount the "possessed" individual, a metaphor for horse and rider; they are still two, though acting as one "body" (2022, 578). In the instances in which the cast of *Une tempête* invoke an Orisha, it is my position that the dual casting of characters should be comprehended in this way.
5. The Orisha form the pantheon of divine spirits in the Yoruba religious traditions.
6. Only in Shakespeare's *The Tempest* is Caliban referenced as a hybrid, half-man half-creature. In Césaire's recontextualization of the play, Caliban is never referenced in the body of the text as being anything but human, despite Césaire's designation in his dramatis personæ list that the characters of his version are the same as those of Shakespeare.
7. "Caliban" was played by Tevin Davis and "Ariel" was played by Corrie Green in both 2022 American Shakespeare Center productions of *The Tempest* and *Une tempête*.

Works Cited

Allen-Paisant, Jason. 2022. Thinking with Spirits, or Dwelling and Knowing in the Work of Aimé Césaire. *French Studies* 76 (2): 576–590.

Bailey, Marianne Wichmann. 1992. *The Ritual Theatre of Aimé Césaire: Mythic Structures of the Dramatic Imagination*. Tübingen: Gunter Narr Verlag.

Beloux, François, and Aimé Césaire. 1969. Entretien avec Aimé Césaire. *Le Magazine Littéraire* 34.

Césaire, Aimé. 1969. *Une tempête*. Paris: Éditions du Seuil.

Césaire, Aimé, et al. 1941–1945. *Tropiques* (revue culturelle), 1–12. Reprinted by Jean-Michel Place in 1972.

Césaire, Suzanne. 1941. Léo Frobenius et le problème des civilisations. *Tropiques* 1: 27–36.

Chapon, Cécile. 2013. Caliban cannibale: relectures/réécritures caribéennes de *La tempête* de Shakespeare. *Comparatismes en Sorbonne-4: (Dé)construire le canon*.

Colomb, Christophe. 2002. *La découverte de l'Amérique, 1642–1643*. Translated by Soledad Estorach and Michel Lequenne. Paris: Éditions La Découverte.

Curtius, Anny Dominique. 2016. Cannibalizing *doudouisme*, Conceptualizing the *morne*: Suzanne Césaire's Caribbean Ecopoetics. *The South Atlantic Quarterly* 115 (3): 513–534.

Fanon, Frantz. 1961. *Les Damnés de la terre*. Paris: F. Maspero.

Frobenius, Leo. 1973. *Leo Frobenius 1873–1973: An Anthology*. Edited by Eike Haberland. Translated by Patricia Crampton. Wiesbaden: F. Steiner.

Gleason, Judith. 2000. Oya in the Company of Saints. *Journal of the American Academy of Religion* 16 (2): 265–291.

Glissant, Édouard. 1989. *Caribbean Discourse: Selected Essays*. Translated by J. Micheal Dash. Charlottesville: Caraf Books published by University of Virginia Press.

Glissant, Édouard. 1990. *Poétique de la Relation*. Paris: Gallimard.

Glissant, Édouard. 2009. *Philosophie de la Relation*. Paris: Gallimard.

Mbembe, Achille. 2006. Nécropolitique. *Raisons Politiques* 21 (1): 29–60.

Ménil, René. 1943. Évidences touchant l'esprit et sa vitesse. *Tropiques* 8–9: 27.

Nietzsche, Friedrich. 1947. *L'origine de la tragédie, ou hellénisme et pessimism*, translated by Jean Marnold and Jacques Morland. Paris: Mercure de France.

Ruprecht, Alvina. 1996. Staging Aimé Césaire's *Une tempête*: Anti-Colonial Theatre in the Counter-Culture Continuum. *Essays in Theatre/Études Théâtrales* 15 (1): 59–68.

Sartre, Jean-Paul. 1964. *Situations V: Colonialisme et néo-colonialisme*. Paris: Gallimard.

Shakespeare, William. 2019 [1611]. *The Tempest*. Edited by Peter Hulme and William H. Sherman. New York: Norton Critical Edition.

Taylor, Douglas. 1958. Carib, Caliban, Cannibal. *International Journal of American Linguistics* 24 (2): 156–157.

Une tempête, by Aimé Césaire, directed by Dawn Monique Williams, American Shakespeare Center, Blackfriars Playhouse, October 27–November 19, 2022

CHAPTER 5

The Coloniality of *Naufragio* and Utopia in Teatro Buendía's *Otra tempestad*

Eric Mayer-García

Narratives written during the early colonial period of the Americas have proved to be some of the most lasting tools of colonial worldmaking. Disaster has been intertwined with the Caribbean ever since it was first conceived through the maps and chronicles of Spanish and Portuguese conquest. *Naufragios*, or biographical shipwreck narratives, could be deemed as one particular subgenre of colonial-era writing. Penned by commentators like Álvar Núñez Cabeza de Vaca or Gonzalo Fernández de Oviedo y Valdés, naufragios chronicle the perishing and survival of European explorers after catastrophe leaves them vulnerable and stranded in a strange and wondrous world full of exotic monsters, dangers, and of course, magical and primitive natives who practice cannibalism. William Boelhower identifies two literary tropes with "structuring horizons" originating in colonial mapmaking—utopia and *naufragium*. As he argues,

E. Mayer-García (✉)
Department of Theatre, Drama, and Contemporary Dance, Indiana University, Bloomington, IN, USA
e-mail: emayerg@iu.edu

© The Author(s), under exclusive license to Springer Nature Switzerland AG 2025
C. Stevens and J. D. Rossini (eds.), *The Coloniality of Catastrophe in Caribbean Theater and Performance*,
https://doi.org/10.1007/978-3-031-85791-1_5

"Utopia and naufragium together represent the two extremes of the same geopolitical and geohistorical experience," yet the latter has remained understudied as a cultural site (Boelhower 2019, 199).

Spanish shipwreck narratives are embellished accounts, not without the use of literary conventions and poetic license, that shaped the European imaginary of the Americas. These narratives of catastrophe represent the Caribbean and Indigenous peoples as undeveloped and godless. They tell the story of encounters with racialized and gendered Others that, when overcome, reify Christian providence to dominate. Naufragios and the world picture they rendered helped to formulate a Spanish sense of modernity.[1] Such representational violence has had lasting effects on neocolonial imaginaries of the Americas.[2] In this sense, colonialism is a catastrophe whose aftermath continues to unfold, and naufragios are early modern narratives projecting that catastrophe onto the Other.[3] Much like Diana Taylor's theorization of the conquest scenario (2003, 28–33), naufragio as a genre, absorbed into literary works and cultural expressions, has mediated the exoticization and subordination of Indigenous bodies and cultures, along with the flora, fauna, and landscape of the hemisphere for centuries. William Shakespeare's *The Tempest* (1611) is one of the earliest and most well-known theatrical interpretations of naufragio, arguably taking inspiration from contemporary texts like The Virginia Company's Bermuda pamphlets and Michel de Montaigne's circa 1580 text "Des cannibales" ["Of Cannibals"].[4]

In my analysis of Teatro Buendía's 1997 production of *Otra tempestad* [Another Tempest/An Other Tempest], I query how Caribbean performances and the ways they theorize through practice and embodiment add to our understanding of utopia and its relationship to the shipwreck. The script and video recordings of Buendía's production reconsider colonialism through a transcultural amalgamation of Afro-Cuban myths, orishas, and rituals, and *The Tempest*—itself a hybrid of shipwreck narrative, romantic comedy, myth, allegory, and pastoral (Mengíbar 2016, 179–180; Woodford-Gormley 2021, 26–27).[5] In a frequently quoted passage from the program notes, playwright Carrió positions *Otra tempestad* with respect to Aimé Césaire's *Une tempête* [*A Tempest*] (1969). Carrió asserts that the play goes beyond negating the colonizer's language in search of a third language, another culture produced through syncretism (Carrió 2000, 59). Following Carrió's logic, Jennifer Flaherty argues that *Otra tempestad* resists the colonizer/colonized binary and disorients hierarchies between various cultural sources in the creation of a mestizo text (Flaherty 2020, 102–104, 109). Inspired by these readings, I push this line of thinking in another direction commensurate with the framing of this volume. *Otra tempestad*'s deliberate arrangement and derangement of texts, bodies, music, space, tone, and affects restages colonialism as a shipwreck, as an orchestrated disaster that violently thrusts together and entangles the worlds of the natives and would-be colonizers in a way that opens up alternative possibilities to the historical violence that transpired. Catastrophe's clearing of the ground leaves the *náufragos* or shipwrecked characters at the mercy of Sicorax and her orisha children. Through a ritual process of fifteen movements, this work of image theatre enacts a reversal of the colonial voyage.

The intergenerational and multiracial collective Teatro Buendía created this performance for their Havana public. The performance had a dense aesthetics that challenged audiences to be active interpreters of interwoven narratives and images without an obvious throughline. However, the production was not created for a niche audience. During the 1990s, anti-illusionism, nonrealism, and physical theatre were mainstream trends in Cuba (Manzor 2023, 268). The production was not created as art for art's sake either. *Otra tempestad* worked through the violence of colonialism and its aftermath by deconstructing Shakespearean figures, interrogating the ideologies they carry, and co-opting their narratives to mediate and reconfigure motifs of conquest and domination. This metatheatrical engagement brought about a meditation on the relationship between coloniality and representation. The ideational journey and process were as much affective as intellectual. *Otra tempestad* enunciated and made space for a Caribbean subjectivity beyond colonial paradigms or colonial mimicry. Its reworking of Calibán approached a presence that was non-derivative, opaque, and fugitive—remaining outside the limits of the play of signs and referents in Western epistemology.

In my interpretation of the script and 1997 performance recording, I argue that *Otra tempestad* wields the trope of the shipwreck to process coloniality through active reception and meaning-making with its audiences. First, I touch on Teatro Buendía's approach to the stage, which highlights a discourse between sources from different cultures and emphasizes the importance of the spectator as a participant that co-creates and completes the communicative act. Within this discourse of ideas, Shakespeare's well-known characters are overtaken by an onslaught of intertexts and associations that produce new meanings and reveal hidden ones. I attend to mask work in particular as a metatheatrical and intertextual tool in Buendía's repertoire that reveals meaning by doubling characters and interweaving narratives. To illustrate this, I focus on three different moments from the video recording of the 1997 production—the shipwreck, the creation of Próspero's utopia, and the Macbeths' ritualized orgy and cannibalistic feast following their rise to power. Each of these moments offers key insight into Buendía's processing of colonialism and its aftermath through a ritual unraveling of representational practices and colonial ideology.

Orchestrated by Sicorax and her daughters Elegguá, Oyá, and Oshún, the tempest and resulting shipwreck place power in the hands of the island's inhabitants from the start (Flaherty 2020, 103; Cornejo Griffin 2022, 6). Próspero's power represents a technology foreign to the island and allows him to wield control over it for some time, but as the ritual plays out, the orishas deal with him in much the same way that they deconstruct the other archetypal figures that wash up on their shores. The subsequent movements are dreamlike enchantments of Shakespeare's characters which in turn engender the characters' semiotic deconstruction. Próspero's creation of utopia on the island, presented by Ariel/Elegguá, satirizes governmental authority and uncovers coloniality in the fictional republic's dependence on subjugation. The Macbeths' hyperbolic and sexual bloodthirst culminates in an inverted mass that demystifies the construction of Calibán as primitive and monstrous as a projection of the West's Christian cult of human sacrifice. Recontextualized within this discourse, Calibán, as the ultimate occidentalist Other, undergoes a semiotic process of resignification. As in other postcolonial readings of *The Tempest*, Calibán is transformed into a sign of disruption and defiance. But *Otra tempestad's* interwoven and unraveling discourse of ideas between cultures explicitly focuses on theatre in its postcolonial critique; and Calibán's opaque and non-derivative alterity makes itself known beneath the fragmented mirrors of representation he comes to master.

Disorienting the Coloniality of Aesthetics

Adaptations such as Césaire's or Buendía's can allow for the simultaneous naming and unpacking of the baggage of colonialism that canonical texts like *The Tempest* have carried into postcolonial contexts. Works like *Une tempête* and *Otra tempestad* create meaning through what Édouard

Glissant has theorized as Relation between African diasporic and "Western" sources (1997, 33–35, 92–95). Césaire's adaptation pays homage to Shakespeare's dramaturgy as it subverts the ideological underpinnings of the text's pastoral colonial fantasy, especially seen in the way Césaire's *Une tempête* demystifies power relations between Prospero and Caliban as colonizer/colonized and master/slave dichotomies. For the colonial allegory to work, Césaire makes one significant change to Shakespeare's play: Prospero does not surrender his power and leave the island. He remains, locked in an endless struggle with Caliban at the play's conclusion.

Buendía's play—attributed to both founding director Flora Lauten and her longtime collaborator, renowned playwright and performance scholar Raquel Carrió—is much more of a departure from Shakespeare's *Tempest*. Through a fifteen scene/movement ritual, *Otra tempestad* brings together characters from numerous plays by Shakespeare with various myths of the orishas from the pantheon of the Yoruba, known as Lucumí in Cuba. The production, very much in the style of Artaud's Theater of Cruelty, is a fantastical hallucination. *Otra tempestad* extends the motif of Ariel's spellcasting by displacing nuclei of Shakespeare's dramaturgy and conjuring them as hallucinations, enchantments, and magical world-building among the *náufragos* and native characters. There is exile, a storm, a shipwreck, an encounter in a strange and wondrous place, a wedding, and Próspero's hounds attack Calibán. But these actions are recombined with aspects of Lucumí and Arará myths, many transmitted through songs and drum, and a handful of Shakespeare's plays, including *Othello, Hamlet, The Merchant of Venice, Romeo and Juliet*, and *Macbeth*. Additional texts, including one of José Martí's *Versos sencillos* ("XLII"), create new intertextualities with *Othello* in particular. The performance also integrates archetypal masks—like *los Hijos* [Children], *la Muerte* [Death], and *el Comediante* [The Player]—that are a key aspect of Lauten's method of scenic writing and are used throughout the play to mediate or introduce a new framing for an action or idea. As mentioned above, I will focus on mask work in what follows as an intertextual tool that facilitates the layering of sources and the interweaving of narratives.

Naufragio, Masks, and Hallucinations

Philosopher Aníbal Quijano defines the coloniality of power as European colonialism's structuring of power through the social category of race. He theorizes the ways Eurocentric hierarchies of knowledge and senses of modernity continued to spread the coloniality of power even after colonialism ended (Quijano 2007, 170–172). The polysemous motif of the shipwreck in *Otra tempestad* frames a discourse on colonialism that exposes audiences to practices of representational violence. Audiences complete the performance through their presence and witnessing, which prompts a working through of the coloniality of the literary canon and other imposed knowledge systems. Processing the ways the Caribbean has been constructed in coloniality implies interpreting the interplay of cultural sources that reveal embedded ideologies. This metarepresentational discourse also allows for the enunciation of a Caribbean alterity that persists outside colonial taxonomies and epistemologies.

To understand how the shipwreck motif operates in Lauten's 1997 staging of *Otra tempestad* in Havana, I must begin by describing Eduardo Arrocha's set, which used multiple levels and platforms, ramps, ropes, and ladders to facilitate stage pictures that worked across the proscenium stage horizontally, vertically, diagonally, and laterally (depth-wise). Through these aesthetics, the set resembles a fragmented caravel or schooner. In the performance's recording, various spaces are used to stage scenes sequentially, allowing for smooth transitions. Characters may even cross the space to join a new scene above, below, or in front. Just as often, the various platforms are used simultaneously to create complex and layered images. The juxtaposition may show a memory, a betrayal, or a retaliation in relation to what is taking place across the stage. Not only does the set facilitate this stylized form of storytelling but it also keeps the shipwreck in sight as a scenic metaphor throughout the performance.

Sound and music are also integral to *Otra tempestad*'s worldbuilding, storytelling, and method of interweaving narratives. With their bird calls and other vocal sounds, actors transform simple tableaus and lighting effects into a rain forest. The offstage musicians and singers accompanying the performance in the recording and referred to in the script as *Iyalochas y Tamboreros* [orisha priests and drummers], do similar work in sound to establish time and place, but go much further through their use of piano, percussion, horns, and woodwind instruments to imbue each image with a nuanced mood.[6] The musicians set the rhythm and pacing of the scene/movement and create audible connections between montaged actions or throughlines for transitions. Most importantly, in their singing of songs from the Lucumí or Arará traditions, they introduce key intertexts that add important meaning to the layering and doubling of characters created through the mask work.

Otra tempestad's first scene/movement begins before the storm, which is both Shakespeare and Césaire's point of attack. In Buendía's performance, a series of tableaus introduces a menagerie of Shakespeare's characters, who appear in the streets of "El viejo mundo" in disguise as a group of itinerant players with a nod to early modern metatheatricality (Fernández 2023, 141). Their disguises bring to mind acts of representation, conjure, and transformation, acts tied up in the history of the stage. Concepción Mengíbar traces a genealogy of masking in *Otra tempestad* from *The Tempest* to *Une tempête* to Caribbean carnival and playing Mas (Mengíbar 2016, 178–181). As characters from Shakespeare's plays, these errant figures are semiotically metatheatrical. For example, Shylock and Otelo are evoked as Shakespeare's characters with all their antisemitic, anti-Muslim, and anti-Black baggage. They are not meant to represent a sixteenth-century Jewish money lender or a Moor and military officer. In fact, they are hardly legible as money lender or military officer without a prior knowledge of the plays they come from. They represent two characters who have shaped the construction of racial and religious difference in the Western imagination and become subjects for the critical examination of theatre's role in this violence. As María José Cornejo Griffin argues, *Otra tempestad* enters into a conscious dialectic with Shakespeare's "racecraft," to refer to Ayanna Thompson's term, and proposes a counterpoint to the ideology behind Shakespeare's treatment of racial difference as comical, monstrous, or exotic (Cornejo Griffin 2022, 10–14).

With *Otra tempestad*, Teatro Buendía approaches Shakespeare's work from a perspective that seeks to extend the postcolonial reworking and allegory that Césaire initiated, while interrogating Shakespeare's characters as figures who engender aspects of coloniality as signs, in a poststructuralist sense. The departure from the "Old World" to an island intimated at the end of the first scene/movement, quickly gives way to the shipwreck in the third. In between departure and shipwreck, and, as a means of creating the space of the island where most of the action takes place, we see, in the recording of the 1997 production, Sicorax giving birth to her daughters, Elegguá, Oyá, and Oshún.[7] Bathed in blue and white lighting, Sicorax is associated with Yemayá, the orisha of maternity and the sea (Cornejo Griffin 2022, 6). The choreographed movement and accompanying sound and lighting create a forest environment full of monstrous and wondrous creatures in the spirit of sixteenth-century naufragios. The four characters emerge through choreography and through images created by the performers' bodies and animal-like vocalizations. The unfolding pile of human limbs calls to mind Stephano describing the four-legged monster he sees when Trinculo has taken shelter underneath Caliban in Act II, Scene 2 of Shakespeare's text. Simultaneously, there is a reclaiming of the monstrosity that Sicorax and Calibán represent through the birth of divine daughters that come to drive the performance and its deconstruction of colonial ideology. Gabriela Fernández contends that *Otra tempestad* embraces absolute Otherness—the *otredad* referred to by the title—through the presence and characterization of Sicorax—a witch, a woman, and a character that never appears or speaks directly in Shakespeare's play (Fernández 2023, 138). Cornejo Griffin reads Sicorax as a powerful feminine foil to Próspero (Cornejo Griffin 2022, 6) while Fernández illuminates the many ways that *Otra tempestad* resignifies Eurocentric representations of race and gender, and in doing so, invites us to consider how patriarchy is linked to coloniality (Fernández 2023, 142).

The birthing sequence seems to illustrate Édouard Glissant's notion of errancy by making it difficult to distinguish between the center and the foreign. As opposed to colonial imperialism where the colonizer imposes their culture on those in foreign lands, Glissant defines errancy as immersing oneself in the culture of the Other to understand one's own difference and existence through the languages, lenses, representational practices, and knowledge systems of the Other (Glissant 1997, 18–22). Errancy in *Otra tempestad* is quite complex. The space of the island becomes a contested space, and its inhabitants do occupy the center, while the figures from the "Old World" and their narratives are literally displaced through the shipwreck. But the figures from Shakespeare's oeuvre make up both *náufragos* and natives, colonizer and colonized. The cultural centeredness in the performance text is not attached to any particular form because of its origin, rather it is about a perspective suggested through the interplay of form ensuring that a simple Lucumí/Shakespeare, black/white calculus fails to produce any meaningful analysis.

At the end of the birthing sequence, the four deities move around the stage like insects, serpents, or reptiles. Finally, Oshún enters, swimming across the stage on her belly and dragging a scale model caravel between her ankles. The musicians begin to play a traditional song for Afrekete, the orisha of the sea in Arará culture, while the three sisters manipulate and dance with the scale model of the ship. On the second level, directly behind the sisters, the traveling players use two poles to create the image of a ship's deck and its crew. Hamlet ascends one of the poles calling "Tierra!" [Land!]. We glimpse Sicorax/Yemayá on the third level behind the other scenes creating the tempest. The drummers pick up the tempo, followed by the movements of the actors. As the storm builds, so does the music in volume and tempo, as does the pace of the actors scrambling to fight the wind and waves about the vessel. In the foreground, Oshún, Oyá, and Elegguá take turns whipping around the small ship, holding it with their feet, arms, chest, and head as they dance. Finally, the ship's crew loses the battle and exits to the wings, struggling with the poles all the while. The musicians segue into a traditional Lucumí song for Yemayá, the Lucumí name for the orisha of the sea. Oyá's net, like a huge wave, envelops the small vessel while Oshún slowly manipulates the model, as if on rocky water, to draw it slowly into Oyá and Yemayá's powerful hold.

The staged tempest conjured by Sicorax and the resulting shipwreck represented by Oshún, Oyá, and Elegguá's dance upends the power dynamics of conquest and colonialism. In fact, this reframing underscores naufragio as the inverse of the colonial worldmaking project. As agents of the shipwreck, the orishas evoke occidentalist imagery of sea monsters through their serpentine movement. The interplay of song, dance, voice, and narrative inverts those images of threatening abjection into an empowered alterity. As they toss the ship around like a toy and take pleasure in drowning a sailor, the three orishas make a pact to do the work of persecuting the crew, which entails unsettling each canonical figure along with the worldview they project. The magic these monstrous beings wield harnesses the power of the natural world and its elements—the sea, rain, and wind—elements which physically hold the essence of the orishas. The progression of Afro-Cuban songs marks the rhythm of the tempest and structures its unfolding. As Cornejo Griffin elucidates, the use of Afrekete's song in the sequence answers Kamau Brathwaite's call to create Caribbean literature, not in pentameter but in the cadence of the hurricane (Cornejo Griffin 2022, 7). Songs sonically resituate the "New World" monsters wreaking havoc on the caravel through divine incantation.

Immediately following the shipwreck, the performance takes up the theme of colonization, particularly through the motif of naming. Upon his arrival, Próspero begins to rename and reorder the island. While the scene critically portrays representational violence as the imposition of a foreign order of language, it also introduces the convention of the mask, which comes to take on subversive properties. At first, the mask is a technology belonging to the invading Próspero, but later it is appropriated to facilitate the undoing of his colonial project. He first encounters Elegguá, calling her Ariel. Elegguá/Ariel is as captivated by Próspero's strangeness or newness as Próspero is by her. Próspero impresses Elegguá/Ariel and commands her to be his servant. When Elegguá/Ariel agrees, she ceases to also be Elegguá, and as indicated in the script, is known as just Ariel until later in the performance. Próspero tells Ariel to look under his frock. Ariel emerges with one of the many masks used in the performance. Holding the golden mask, she asks "Oye, ¿y esto qué es?" [Hey, and what's this?] To which Próspero replies, "¡Alquimia, Ariel! ¡Alquimia!... Todos esconden bajo el disfraz alguna pasión o algún crimen" [Alchemy Ariel! Alchemy!... Everyone hides some passion or crime beneath a disguise] (Carrió and Lauten 2010, 137). This moment sets up an association between Próspero's alchemy and the mask, as a theatrical convention used throughout the performance to reveal meaning by doubling characters and interweaving narratives as plays within plays. Critically witnessing Próspero renaming Elegguá does not erase Ariel's association with Elegguá. Rather, it recounts the violence of renaming and the seduction of colonialism, while reinterpreting Ariel's role as a trickster through a major cultural figure of the African Diaspora. The mask work similarly creates associations by layering roles from different cultural sources, and by doing so, it violates binaries between European and African, canon and folklore, center and periphery.

Utopia, Naufragio's Reverse Image

Now under Próspero's influence, Ariel agrees to bewitch the other *náufragos*—Shylock, Otelo, Miranda, Hamlet, and Macbeth. Ariel weaves each of their accompanying narratives into the world of the play as hallucinations and uses their corresponding stories to entrap them. After Ariel carries out Próspero's wishes to drive the other shipwrecked characters mad, Próspero employs Ariel in helping him to create another kind of mirage—a laboratory, a social experiment from where he can create a utopia. The scene alludes to Thomas More's sixteenth-century treatise *Utopia*, about the creation of an ideal republic. As a worldbuilding enterprise imagined in the Americas, More's *Utopia* along with Francis Bacon's *New Atlantis* (1628), set off of the Pacific Coast of Peru, are embroiled in similar kinds of colonial motifs and fervor that underpin Shakespeare's *Tempest* (Mengíbar 2016, 173–174). Some commentators read Próspero's utopian experiment in *Otra tempestad* as a critical commentary on the Enlightenment with the island being his tabula rasa (Flaherty 2020, 106; Fernández 2023, 140). However, we should also consider, as Boelhower contends, the ways in which naufragio is the extreme opposite of utopia in the colonial-era European imaginary. By giving prominence to the trope of utopia within the narrative of naufragio, *Otra tempestad* exposes them as two sides of the same coin. I am not referring to "naufragio" here in the sense explored above as a performative reframing for deconstructing the coloniality of signs but rather to "naufragio" in the larger scope of colonial-era print culture depicting the Americas and their inhabitants through threat and wonder as a means to justify colonialism. In this sense, imaginaries of utopia and naufragio grow out of and into one another as the extreme ends of the same project.

In the recording of the 1997 production, Giselle Navaroli, the performer playing Elegguá/Ariel, announces the founding of a republic. Navaroli gradually raises her voice into a testimonial style, underscored by piano music played slowly in a contemplative mode. Having seen the light, Ariel delivers one of the most rehearsed justifications of colonialism. They testify to how, thanks to their master, the inhabitants of the island have gone from living like beasts to being blessed with the light of knowledge, receiving gifts like astrolabes, sextants, music, and letters. The monologue dramatizes colonialism's hegemonic seduction, with Próspero standing in for a would-be colonizer, when it suddenly takes a sharp turn in mood, approach, and verb tense. Ariel shifts from speaking in the present perfect to the future tense, from being hyperbolically enchanted to being imperative.

As the speech continues, the actress Navaroli performs mask work that satirizes governmental authority and its dependence on subjugation through *choteo*, a grotesque form of Cuban humor that enunciates its desacralization of authority from a subaltern positionality. As the sequence begins, Ariel describes how the republic will be created through several legal proclamations. Navaroli's voice becomes low, raspy, and irreverent in tone—presenting a kind of masculine dictator camp. Navaroli's Ariel plays with gender presentation and performatives throughout the production, and by this point in the performance, the character's fluidity has been well established. The republic plays out across Navaroli's body in a way that is complicated by Ariel's gender mutability. Her body parts become associated with certain aspects of law based on the masks that cover over and touch them. Navaroli places the masks of the sick, who will be cared for, and the mad, who will entertain, over her breasts. The masks of the lovers are attached to the knees so that kneeling—itself an act of subjugation—becomes their punishment of enslavement and death for transgressing marriage vows. In this moment, Ariel proclaims, "El matrimonio… ¡durará toda la vida! Y el adulterio… ¡se pagará con la más vil esclavitud! Y su reincidencia… ¡con la muerte!" [Marriage will last one's entire life! And adultery… will be punished with the most vile slavery! And its recidivism with death!] (Carrió and Lauten 2010, 145). From her knees she pulls up another veil to expose a golden mask. The mask of the child appears over her crotch as if protruding from between her legs, a derisive allusion to childbirth. Rising to her feet, she pronounces, "Nuestros hijos… nacerán sanos, fuertes, libres… ¡Y no abandonarán el país porque vivirán conformes!…" [Our children… will be born healthy, strong, and free… And they will not abandon the country because they will live happily!] (Carrió and Lauten 2010, 145). In resignifying her body as a woman's body that is unduly subject to governmental forms of control and submission, Navaroli, in her performance, draws on female abjection to debase and push back against her spoken parody of governmentality.

Ariel's nonsensical decrees decontextualize the linguistic performatives of governance regardless of political system or philosophy. Still, certain utterances are loaded and carry risky associations when thinking about the political history of Cuba. In that context, the ideas of utopia and republic together arouse several contradictory meanings. Like Cuba, the state Ariel describes is rooted in colonialism. Ariel's utterance of "república" brings to mind Cuba's first and second Republics, whereas the idea of utopia evokes the socialist project of the 1959 Revolution. More's connection between republic and utopia in his sixteenth-century treatise is at odds with Cuba's political history, which places those concepts in opposition to one another. Correlations to colonial, republican, and revolutionary governments are all at play in Ariel's choteo. Their ironic declaration that Utopía's children will not abandon their country most certainly touched on anxieties around the Revolution's "hijos" leaving "el país" during the balsero crisis of the 1990s, which continued to unfold during the production's creation and premiere (González Crespán 2022, 102–104).

At the end of the monologue, Ariel announces the founding of a new island republic called Utopía. In the recording, we see the other characters enter with palm branches and begin slashing and grunting in a rhythmic pattern in sync with the offstage drummers. Próspero declares that work will be the most important thing for Utopía's inhabitants (Carrió and Lauten 2010, 146). Many ideas are summoned in this non-specific, indistinct utopia performed through work. The slashing of branches brings to mind the slashing of sugar cane in Cuba and other parts of the Caribbean, one of the major crops cultivated through the forced labor of Black people in chattel slavery. The repetitive slashes also suggest the slash of the whip doled out to slaves by slave drivers and others. And yet, no characters are being hit with the branches. Their dance feels orderly and voluntary, like an ensemble of dancers or athletes working together to accomplish a great feat. In this sense, their movement recalls historical references to major mobilizations of labor in the Revolution, like the 10,000-ton sugar cane harvest of 1970 or the literacy campaign of the 1960s.

The slippage in references between different historical regimes in this somatic expression of labor, exploitation, and communal ecstasy draws a connecting line between each reference point. At least within the conceit of Ariel's phantasmagoria, utopia is not built upon a tabula rasa. It is built through domination and subordination, no matter how benevolently utopia's architect, Próspero, sees himself. Ariel's choteo gives audiences a glimpse of how the coloniality of this system is inherited, not effaced by consequent utopian projects.

Macbeth's Inversions and Projections of Cannibalism

Throughout the play's movements, Oyá, Oshún, and Elegguá/Ariel work in concert to dispose of Shylock, Otelo, and Próspero. The repeated cycle becomes something like a ritual of deconstruction ending with each of these three characters hanging from the gallows. The orisha characters double and triple as Shakespearean characters and assume roles in corresponding narratives to expose the coloniality of these canonical figures of the stage. The transition following the collapse of Próspero's utopia serves as an example. With Próspero's corpse dangling from a noose, Oyá turns to the audience and delivers a line from Lady Macbeth, "¿Quién iba a decir que el viejo tuviera tanta sangre?" [Who would have thought the old man to have so much blood in him?] (Carrió and Lauten 2010, 152).

Then tripling as one of the witches, she laughs, raises Próspero's relinquished staff, and calls out Macbeth's name as if declaring a prophesy or a curse. Próspero's corpse now stands in for Duncan, the murdered king.

The Macbeths seize power in the immediate aftermath of colonizer Próspero's demise. Rather than creating a new liberatory order on the island, the regime they assume to replace him is brutal and corrupt. In conveying this narrative, the lines and scenes from *Macbeth* are shuffled and given to other characters. Referring to Peter Hulme's comments, Donna Woodford-Gormley explains how translating Shakespeare's familiar words and placing them into the mouths of other characters transforms meaning (Woodford-Gormley 2021, 28–29). Rearranging Shakespeare's text in this way doubles and triples valences and produces an effect similar to that of the performance's mask work. Whereas Próspero and Ariel critically perform commonplace apologist histories of colonialism—claims of "giving" civilization, knowledge, and technology to primitives trapped outside of modernity—the Macbeths outwardly perform the violent underbelly of colonialism that Próspero covers over with his hallucinatory utopia. The tenor of the Macbeths' regime is best conveyed in an orgiastic knife dance. In this moment, the Macbeths each dance with a knife in their mouth, holding the handle with their teeth and pointing the blade outward. With their heads cocked back and their groins grinding together they cross blades, like two birds touching beaks sensually, arousing one another. With his head nodding quickly up and down, Macbeth rubs the edge of the blade against Lady Macbeth/Oyá's nipple. She takes the knife handle from her mouth, panting, and then groans ambiguously in either pain or pleasure. They fall to their knees. Macbeth takes a knife in each hand, and straddling Lady Macbeth/Oyá who lies on her back, he plunges the knives repeatedly into the stage next to her body. The stabbing becomes sexual as the rhythm gives way to a climactic plunge with both daggers above Lady Macbeth/Oyá's head as Macbeth falls on top of her and they cry out together.

The knife dance ritual irreverently and grotesquely mixes ecstasy and doom, sex and violence. Their erotic and impulsive ritual, soaked in turmoil, expresses the Macbeths' ambition, opportunism, and envy through movement. Whereas Próspero's colonial regime sublimated aspirations of dominance and corruption in the guise of civilization and utopia, their choreographed sounds and movements outwardly portray and embody impulses of domination lying in the roots of utopia that are exposed in its very toppling. The imaginative mating ritual wraps human and animal imagery in their birdlike movements and BDSM foreplay. Indeed, the Macbeths' regime signals a renewal of the coloniality of power through continued domination and subordination. And yet, when compared with Próspero, the externalized and irreverent expression of that power through abjectly hybrid embodiment and playful sadomasochism exaggerates its violence, an invitation to a critical reckoning of utopia's violent underbelly that cannot be missed.

Celebrating their rise to power, the Macbeths deride the characters that have been previously disposed of, beginning with the hanging Próspero. Macbeth taunts Otelo for not making it to the end of the play intact, as Otelo has been transformed into one of Próspero's hounds. Meanwhile, Lady Macbeth/Oyá makes fun of Shylock—who has also been transformed into a hound—for not reaching the promised land. The two hounds carry the corpse of Miranda, another casualty, who dies for her love for Calibán. Macbeth insults Miranda too, calling her the queen of the whores. Then he invites the characters to a banquet which becomes an inverted Catholic mass. The sequence decodes the image of the Amerindian cannibal as a projection serving the colonial imaginary circumscribed by utopia and naufragio. Macbeth's banquet allegorizes colonial extraction and consumption, while desacralizing a ritual forced upon Indigenous populations and a religion used to justify the violent conquest.

In a stylized sequence accompanied by Renaissance music, Macbeth mimes cutting Miranda's flesh. Lady Macbeth and the hounds come close, reaching out with their arms fully extended as if bowing in praise. They grab at the imaginary flesh, place it tenderly in their mouths and chew, all in mime. The Macbeths greedily gorge themselves until they vomit. While the ritual transpires, Próspero removes the noose from his neck and silently helps Miranda up and leads her offstage. Just as he reacts to the ghost of Banquo, Macbeth threatens Próspero for shaking his bloody locks over the table. Lady Macbeth who does not see the apparition, tells her husband that the seats are empty. She helps the shocked Macbeth to his feet and readies him for his coronation (Carrió and Lauten 2010, 155–156).

This banquet sequence alludes to Banquo's haunting of Macbeth in the Act III dinner scene as well as the Eucharistic mass and the Last Supper that it commemorates. The pantomimed enactment of cannibalism focuses on demystifying ideologies rather than presenting a gory and violent illusion. The ritualistic nature of the sequence shaped by a shift in pace and stylized movements, inverts the mass, replacing the body of Christ with the corpse of Miranda. Instead of holding up the host before those gathered, Macbeth holds up his dagger. He invites everyone to partake in the great meal of God and to eat "carne de reyes" [the flesh of kings], not the body of Christ; the daughter of a noble, not the son of God. He makes a single incision across Miranda's corpse and the characters help themselves to pieces of her flesh rather than waiting for Macbeth, who assumes the role of the priest, to place a piece in their mouths. The Macbeths' excessive gorging and vomiting contradicts Christian asceticism, fasting, and denial of the flesh.

The inverted mass outwardly enacts the rite of human sacrifice and cannibalism, demystifying the violence sublimated by the Eucharist. It underscores the hypocrisy of projecting the taboo of cannibalism onto Calibán as a monster needing to be tamed or a primitive Other needing to be civilized. The ritual, reflecting the monstrous images of naufragio and the colonial ideology of utopia, does not grant everlasting life, but rather, ritualizes domination and extraction. Much like the apparitions of the dagger, Banquo, and Duncan's blood in Shakespeare's text, Miranda's escape from the Macbeths' banquet table, escorted by Próspero's ghost, foreshadows the Macbeths' demise.

Conclusion: Macbeth's Crown on Calibán's Head

Displaced from their corresponding texts and recombined with elements from Lucumí myths and other sources, Shakespeare's characters dramatize something beyond any single narrative—a naming and purging of the process of colonization and distinct aspects of coloniality mediated through Shakespearean characters and their dramas. Causality in this performance is not about linear plot points, but rather, like the magic and alchemy wielded by Próspero, Ariel, and Sicorax, causality works through a ritual naming and undoing of representational practices—a metatheatrical and reflexive reckoning of how forms of representation impart colonial ideology.

The final movements of the ritual performance put this in sharp relief, implicating theatre in particular as an apparatus of coloniality. Lady Macbeth/Oyá announces Macbeth's coronation. The entire ensemble returns. All wearing masks, they take their places in Macbeth's court. They crown Macbeth with a golden mask with long horns stretching up like an ibex. Then the music shifts as the drummers begin to play an oro seco, an orisha rhythm without song. The characters dance to the quick tempo and syncopated rhythm. They move into a battle formation. Macbeth prepares for war, raising his dagger. Someone cries out that 10,000 soldiers carrying branches are approaching. As the nobles abandon Macbeth and other calamities transpire, the movement and music suddenly come to a stop. The singers break into a song for Ogun, the orisha of metallurgy and war, with a slow tempo and sustained call and response. A soft horn plays in the background as Elegguá, Oshún, and Oyá lift their courtier masks and announce that Lady Macbeth has died. The percussion picks up tempo and the ensemble dances backwards upstage. The masked characters become the Birnam wood closing in on Macbeth and swallow him up.

The ensemble begins a ritual unmasking, removing their masks and passing them back over the heads of the crowded bodies. Dancing overhead, the animated masks initiate a ritual closing and signify the relinquishing of the power of representation. The ensemble breaks away from the tableau one by one and the actors move to different areas of the stage. As they remove the masks, the characters begin choking as if the oxygen had just been sucked out of the air. Once the characters move away from the center platform, we see Macbeth's body suspended and headless in the background. The lights darken. The sounds of the island forest can be heard. The characters turn their backs to the audience, turn their faces down, or hide in the shadows. Each appears to be tortured, as if each were trapped in a different chamber of hell. They call out "Calibán" and "Caníbal." Calibán enters. He is the image of a monster, adorned from head to foot with a bouquet of faces—the same archetypal masks used throughout the performance to transform meaning through the layering of errant texts. The sound of a horn bellowing fills the stage. According to the program for the 1998 performance at London's Globe Theatre, the sound of the horn represents a more modern ship approaching. As Flaherty persuasively argues, this ending implies a recurrence of the first scene, which prompts a contemplation of how the patterns of colonization dramatized by the performance are part of a larger cycle (Flaherty 2020, 109–110). These shadows of colonization and their undoing continually play on a loop. The ship and all it represents and Calibán and all he represents are intertwined. Given the density of meaning in this confluence and that Calibán does not speak any lines in *Otra tempestad*, I suggest that the ship's bellowing horn can be read simultaneously as Calibán's call, his roar. Displaying an amalgam of masks as his exteriority, Calibán's monstrosity cites the horror of European mimesis of Amerindian monsters. At once beautiful and hideous, dominant and defiant, Calibán's opaque alterity makes itself known in the drama of the horn, the layered faces of the masks, and the measured movements of Juan José Rodríguez, the same actor playing Macbeth whose body had appeared decapitated only moments prior. In the final moment, after Shakespeare's ghosts have been reinterpreted, demystified, and transformed, Calibán stands alone, victoriously adorned with masks, symbolically wielding the magic of theatre and the power of representation.

Buendía's performance disorients the moral authority behind Shakespeare's construction of Calibán as an amalgam of colonialist expressions appropriated from shipwreck narratives and other chronicles from the Age of Exploration. Shakespeare's character becomes a vessel that is overwhelmed by a plethora of intertexts, meanings, and associations. In this sense, it could be argued that Calibán becomes an inversion of the telos of naufragio and its justification of Western domination. From another perspective, the interplay and arrangement of cultural sources triangulates an opaque presence that is not derived from or in reaction to the occidentalist renderings of racialized monstrosity even as the performance takes up those images within its layered discourse.

Notes

1. Antonio Benítez Rojo (1997) describes how the idea of modernity is only made possible through the creation of the idea of the Caribbean, a regional construct created through conquest and colonization, making the two ideas, their histories, and affects interdependent.
2. Some examples of the lasting effects of representational violence include Diana Taylor's (2003) discussion of the conquest scenario and its reactivation through cultural memory, Patricia A. Ybarra's (2009) historiography of the performance of conquest across five centuries of history in the Americas, and Analola Santana's (2018) discussion of the codification of Indigenous and African Others as monsters, which are later pathologized as freaks post-Enlightenment. Nevertheless, Taylor, Ybarra, Santana, and José Esteban Muñoz (1999) detail many of the ways that theatre and

performance are powerful tools for naming, reembodying, disidentifying, confronting, reversing, and reflecting on representational violence and its impacts on imaginaries, ideologies, and cultural memory.
3. Fernando Coronil (1996, 55–57) introduces the term Occidentalism, which is derived from Edward W. Said's critique of Orientalism. Occidentalism places focus on the West and its way of constructing Selfhood through various representations of Otherness—in this case Amerindian Otherness. See also Said (2003).
4. See Fulton (1978), Greenblatt and Platt (2014).
5. For research on *Otra tempestad* by one of the authors, see Carrió (1998a and 1998b).
6. The credited musicians on the video recording were Jomary Hechavarría, José del Pilar Suárez, Agustín Gómez, Alfredo Hernández, Leandro More, Juan Larrinaga.
7. Elegguá is usually a male deity but, within hundreds of variations, also has female manifestations.

Works Cited

Benítez Rojo, Antonio. 1997. *The Repeating Island: The Caribbean and the Postmodern Perspective*. Translated by James E. Maraniss. Durham: Duke University Press.

Boelhower, William. 2019. *Atlantic Studies: Prospects and Challenges*. Baton Rouge: Louisiana State University Press.

Carrió, Raquel. 1998. Ironías y paradojas del comediante (Notas sobre el proceso del montaje de *Otra tempestad*). *Conjunto* 109: 10–17.

Carrió, Raquel. 1998. La experimentación en el teatro de la mujer: Dos versiones. *Assaig de Teatre: Revista de l'Associació d'Investigació i Experimentació Teatral* 10–11: 17–27.

Carrió, Raquel. 2000. Notas al programa. In *Otra tempestad*, by Raquel Carrió and Flora Lauten. Havana: Ediciones Alarcos.

Carrió, Raquel and Flora Lauten. 2010. Otra tempestad. In *Antología de teatro latinoamericano, Tomo II*, ed. Lola Proaño Gómez and Gustavo Geirola. Buenos Aires: Instituto Nacional del Teatro.

Cornejo Griffin, María José. 2022. Theatricality and Race in William Shakespeare's *The Tempest* and Raquel Carrió and Flora Lauten's *Otra tempestad*. *English Studies in Latin America* 23: 1–19.

Coronil, Fernando. 1996. Beyond Occidentalism: Toward Nonimperial Geohistorical Categories. *Cultural Anthropology* 11 (1): 51–87.
Fernández, Gabriela. 2023. Reescribir la tradición: *Otra tempestad* revisita a Shakespeare. *Estudios de Teoría Literaria. Revista digital: artes, letras y humanidades* 12 (28): 132–144.
Flaherty, Jennifer. 2020. Calibán Rex?: Cultural syncretism in Teatro Buendía's Otra Tempestad. In *The Routledge Handbook of Shakespeare and Global Appropriation*, ed. Christy Desmet, Sujata Iyengar, and Miriam Jacobson. New York: Routledge.
Fulton, III, Robert C. 1978. The Tempest and the Bermuda Pamphlets: Source and Thematic Intention. *Interpretations* 10 (1): 1–10.
González Crespán, Araceli. 2022. The Cuban Rafter Crisis on Stage: Humanizing the Experience of Refugees in María Irene Fornés' *Manual for a Desperate Crossing*. *American, British, and Canadian Studies* 39 (1): 100–120.
Glissant, Édouard. 1997. *Poetics of Relation*. Translated by Betsy Wing with notes and introduction. Ann Arbor: University of Michigan Press.
Greenblatt, Stephen and Peter G. Platt, eds. 2014. *Shakespeare's Montaigne: The Florio Translation of the Essays, a Selection*. New York Review Books Classics.
Manzor, Lillian. 2023. *Marginality Beyond Return: US Cuban Performances in the 1980s and 1990s*. New York: Routledge.
Mengíbar, Concepción. 2016. The Permeability of Shakespeare's Plays: Tempests in the Caribbean. *Scripta Uniandrade* 14 (2): 170–185.
More, Thomas. 1737. *Utopia: Written in Latin by Sir Thomas More, Chancellor of England. Translated into English, by Gilbert Burnet, late Bishop of Sarum. To this edition is added, a short account of Sir Thomas More's life and his trial*. Dublin: printed by R. Reilly, for G. Risk, G. Ewing, and W. Smith, Booksellers, in Dame-Street. *Eighteenth Century Collections Online*. Accessed 3 June 2024.
Muñoz, José Esteban. 1999. *Disidentifications: Queers of Color and the Performance of Politics*. University of Minnesota Press.
Quijano, Aníbal. 2007. Coloniality and Modernity/Rationality. *Cultural Studies* 21 (2–3): 168–178.
Said, Edward W. 2003. *Orientalism*. New York: Vintage.
Santana, Analola. 2018. *Freak Performances: Dissidence in Latin American Theater*. Ann Arbor: University of Michigan Press.
Taylor, Diana. 2003. *The Archive and the Repertoire: Performing Cultural Memory in the Americas*. Durham: Duke University Press.
Teatro Buendía. 1997. *Otra tempestad*. Video Recording, 106 min. Havana: Teatro Buendía. Digital Video Library, Hemispheric Institute of Performance and Politics, New York University. https://sites.dlib.nyu.edu/hidvl/gqnk991w. Accessed 3 March 2024

Woodford-Gormley, Donna. 2021. *Shakespeare in Cuba: Caliban's Books*. Palgrave Macmillan.
Ybarra, Patricia A. 2009. *Performing Conquest: Five Centuries of Theater, History, and Identity in Tlaxcala, Mexico*. Ann Arbor: University of Michigan Press.

CHAPTER 6

Making Theater in the Face of the Storm: Shakespeare in Paradise, Healing, and Theater

Nicolette Bethel

The Tempest, William Shakespeare's last great play, opens in a storm, with a ship's crew attempting to keep their vessel from running aground. The scene devolves into chaos. Members of the King's party attempt to command the ship's crew and get in the way of the work. This conflict sets a scene that is recognizable to contemporary Caribbean audiences. On the one hand, humans struggle against nature; on the other, the powerless chafe against the powerful. One can read the squabbling between the emissaries of the Duke of Milan and the crew as emblematic of the realities faced throughout the Caribbean region today and throughout history.

Shakespeare in Paradise is an annual theater festival established in Nassau, The Bahamas, in 2009. What began as a 5-day festival over the

N. Bethel (✉)
Department of Psychology, Sociology and Social Work, School of Social Sciences, University of the Bahamas, Nassau, The Bahamas
e-mail: nicolette.bethel@ub.edu.bs

© The Author(s), under exclusive license to Springer Nature Switzerland AG 2025
C. Stevens and J. D. Rossini (eds.), *The Coloniality of Catastrophe in Caribbean Theater and Performance*,
https://doi.org/10.1007/978-3-031-85791-1_6

October holiday weekend has become 3 weeks in September–October. Anchored by Shakespeare's plays, it presents significant works from the African diaspora as well as serving as a showcase for small international productions and an incubator for new Bahamian plays. Its productions interrogate both the canonicity of Shakespeare and the concept of paradise in ways that are designed to tackle the coloniality of catastrophe through theater. This chapter approaches making theater in the face of the storm from two core perspectives: the *context* in which Shakespeare in Paradise occurs, and the *content* presented by Shakespeare in Paradise onstage. The festival is held during hurricane season in a country where catastrophe occurs daily, where coloniality permeates every exchange and interaction. The people behind this project believe powerfully in the healing, human-centered nature of theater, and are dedicated to producing theater in the face of storms.

In considering the coloniality of catastrophe in The Bahamas, I draw on the concept of *coloniality* (Quijano 2000)—the entrenchment of colonial-era world capitalist structures in post-colonial environments, and the impact of continuing white supremacy and Eurocentricity on societies of the Americas. Building on Quijano, in his article on Bahamian citizenship, Stephen Aranha proposes that the manifestation of *coloniality* among post-independence Bahamian elites includes a deep investment in colonial hierarchies that reinforce a sense of *inferiority* within those elites and the people that they represent and/or govern. This he calls "coloni*ority*," which leads these elites to "yearn for the grandeur of the empire while subconsciously suffering from an inferiority complex that they are not—and never will be—equal to the metropolitan elites of old" (Aranha 2015, 19).

As for catastrophe, I am of course acknowledging the big-C catastrophes that accompany the natural disasters that impact the Caribbean. Most salient in the Bahamian context are the hurricanes which affect the archipelago with increasing frequency and force as climate change makes itself evident. But this chapter will examine the ways the festival also engages with the smaller, everyday catastrophes that Caribbean residents face, such as the deadly violence that shapes our identities and the rampant capitalism that dispossesses and displaces our citizens.

Corrosive Capitalism

For Quijano (2000), the economic, social, and political history of the Americas laid the foundation for the development of world capitalism. Gold from the Spanish-settled American mainland transferred wealth from the "new" world to Iberia, while Caribbean plantation economies generated capital to fuel northern Europe's industrial revolutions. Sugar production on the most profitable islands also reorganized labor in ways that were utilized in the development of factories (Mintz 1986; Williams 1944). What benefitted Europe was catastrophic for the Caribbean. Whole islands were cleared of vegetation to build plantations (Ferdinand 2022; Sheller 2003); whole cultures were eradicated, replaced with human chattel (Beckles 2013). The sole purpose of this region was to generate revenue for places far overseas.

That this history established a relationship between Europe and the Caribbean that continues to this day extends the catastrophe. Even now, 500 years later, the islands of the Caribbean are not regarded as generative places in and of themselves. Independence notwithstanding, the Caribbean continues to be mined for raw materials like aragonite, bauxite, or oil, or to be regarded as empty lands inhabited not by human beings but by "native" servants. It is a region of leisure, of abandon, a place where "humans" can go to lose themselves and their cares before returning to the "real" world (see Sheller 2003; Strachan 2002; Nixon 2015 for more). Aaron Kamugisha (2019) argues that, rather than erasing the oppressive machinery of their colonial pasts, Caribbean leaders have established regimes of their own that in many ways mirror colonial subjugation.

In The Bahamas, where the plantation system did not flourish, creole white mercantile oligarchs governed the archipelago. By the 1950s, The Bahamas had turned to tourism undergirded with financial services and gambling. At that point, as Strachan (2002) contends, a new plantation system was established: the mega-resorts that now dominate landscapes and employ the masses. The independent Bahamas remains in thrall to hotel conglomerates, second homeowners, and foreign investors. Economic inequality in The Bahamas is among the highest in the Western hemisphere (World Economics, n.d.).[1] The catastrophe of global capitalism continues in Bahamians' lives. Shakespeare in Paradise's 2009 production of *The Tempest* sought consciously to speak to the impact of global capitalism, reshaping that colonial tale through an anticolonial retelling. For this, it engaged directors Patti-Anne Ali, an Indo-Trinidadian theater professional, and Craig Pinder, a Bahamian working in Britain. Together, they created a world in which Prospero's island was a private cay in The Bahamas.

Their interpretation intentionally subverted mainstream readings. Prospero is a capitalist himself, the unproductive scion of a resort-owning family. Executives of the company are traveling to view another location for the latest hotel when they ran into the tempest of the title. Ariel is a chickcharney, a half-human, half-bird character from Bahamian mythology, working for Prospero as a sort of house slave; Caliban is an African fieldhand.

The Tempest was not a play about which many Bahamians had knowledge. For many audiences and actors, this was their first engagement with Shakespeare outside an academic curriculum. But it struck a nerve. The production was successful, selling more tickets than any of the other productions in that first festival.[2]

Engagement with the catastrophic capitalist exploitation of Caribbean islands was not limited to re-setting and re-imagining existing Shakespeare plays. In 2017, Shakespeare in Paradise premiered the work *Small Axe* (Bethel 2017). In it, an idealistic civil servant clashes with the nation's Prime Minister over the latter's proposal to lease the island of Andros—the largest of all the Bahamian islands—to a multinational corporation for 99 years.

The play's themes are steeped in the capitalist realities of the Bahamian nation, where foreign direct investment (usually in land) is substituted for government-led development. Prime Minister Mallory King is a leader who comprehends perfectly the global structures of capital but opts to twist them to his own ends. Set against his proposal to lease Andros for cotton plantations is civil servant Henry James's desire to move the nation towards the collection of reparations for slavery. This, however, is doomed; in this play, Aranha's idea of *coloniority* looms large. When asked, "But what about the national parks? What about the people?", the Prime Minister responds:

> Who are we? A freckle on the face of the earth. A sprinkle of freckles in the Atlantic Ocean. What do we have? Nothing. [...] Foreign investment? Come on in. Biggest pocket, biggest reward. [...] But [...] The era of the white man is over. There are five next big countries coming to the

forefront and only one of them white. [...] Mallory King is a man who likes to follow the signs and take control of the tides as much as possible. (Bethel 2017, 16–18)

Small Axe premiered in 2017 to audiences who included students attending matinees. These matinees were usually followed by a talkback where the actors took questions from the audience. During one of those occasions, a high-school student shared his despair at the end of the play. Why, he wondered, did the Prime Minister have to get his way? Where was the happy ending?

The answer, of course, is that in The Bahamas, coloniality/coloniority prevails. Bahamian prime ministers have too much power, too little oversight, and they almost always get their way. Indeed, in February 2018, the actual Bahamian Prime Minister announced that his government was granting some 600 acres of crown land in Grand Bahama to Oban Energies for an oil storage facility (Maycock 2018)—a real-life project with much the same sense of futile engagement with global capital as the stage deal. The cavalier manner in which Bahamian prime ministers offer sovereign Bahamian land to foreign investors endures.

Violence and Homicide

In addition to catastrophes wrought by capitalism, Bahamians face the everyday trauma inflicted by a violence that is endemic; the issue of homicide in The Bahamas is a perennial concern (Sutton 2016). Shakespeare in Paradise has addressed this often, most critically in 2016 with two significant works.

The first of these is Winston Saunders *You Can Lead a Horse to Water*. This play explores the psychology of an unnamed young man executed for matricide. Inspired by a true event and fashioned after Greek tragedy, it features a chorus that serves alternately as the Jury in the case and the young man's neighbors. As the story unfolds, we hear Son's account of his deep love for his Mother and his dream to move her out of poverty; we watch what happens when his dreams are betrayed.

Love and violence are intertwined in Son's homelife. The action of the play swings from violence to affection and back again. His mother is the first one to love him, and the first one to beat him. As the Son tells his Lawyer at the play's beginning when he finally begins to speak about his crime:

SON: We were born in a house which was seven by eleven. [...] I was born first, then Old Fool was born, dumb. Before my sisters were born, it was only us three. And I remember how close we were, cozy, comfortable, sleeping in the same bed, and she would wake us early to go to the market with her; before she went to her job. [...] She was all we knew and we were all she had. And she was always kind and loving... then at least, when there was time. Sometimes she used to fly off and beat me too. (Saunders 1983, 2–4)

As the play unfolds, we witness Son trying not only to save himself from this environment but to save his Mother as well. But this is complicated as she moves from lover to lover. Some of these men are abusive to her and the children. Even those who are gentle bring violence to the home; the wife of one comes to fight the Mother. Like the Jury, which is onstage for the entire play, the audience is a witness to—possibly complicit in—the violence. Son grows up troubled, till an arrest for drug possession makes him leave home to get a job elsewhere. He sends weekly remittances to pay for a respectable home for his Mother. But she spends it in other ways. In so doing she destroys his dream, and he kills her for it (Image 6.1).

Image 6.1 Shakespeare in Paradise's 2016 production of *You Can Lead a Horse to Water*, directed by Philip A. Burrows. L-R: Jonico Pratt as Son, Valene Rolle as Mother, and Gabriel Hudson as Old Fool. Photograph by Peter Ramsay

You Can Lead a Horse to Water is about a single man's crime, but the tragedy is collective. The violence that surrounds Son culminates in the final murder. Violence shapes him, linked inextricably with love; love makes him turn that violence outward.[3] He puts a schoolmate in hospital for insulting his Mother, and eventually he kills his Mother—arguably for love. The Jury, intimately involved in virtually every scene, is as much a catalyst for the action as any of the main characters. The ending is inevitable.

Horse suggests that seeds of violence and homicide are woven into the fabric of Bahamian society and culture. That this is part of the catastrophe of coloniality is evident by the fact that the actual murder that inspired the play occurred in the 1960s, before Bahamian independence. In this way, it challenges current concepts that homicidal violence is somehow new to Bahamian life. At the time of its writing (1983), the new nation was still experiencing a coloniority that is expressed in the play by characters such as the Social Worker, the Boss, and the Boss's Wife. In *Horse*, it is possible to see the extension of colonial violence as described by Fanon, where neighbors are "relentless enem[ies]" (Fanon 1963, 307), into the post-colonial reality.

Ian Strachan's *Gun Boys Rhapsody*, written thirty-three years after *You Can Lead a Horse to Water*, demonstrates that although the intervening generation has not shifted the *place* of violence in the lives of ordinary Bahamians, the *nature* of that violence has changed. In *Horse,* the violence is personal, psychological, home-based, cross-gender and cross-generational. But in *Gun Boys*, young men kill one another for very little reason at all. Violence has become endemic, impersonal, everyday, and male.

The play opens with Odarion, a "low level" pusher, addressing the audience: "I about to die. [...] A fella gone turn right t'rough dis corner and shoot me in my back while I try to run [...]" (Strachan 2016, 5). TK, the high school student he has killed, was guilty of taking Marsha, a fellow student who was once Odarion's girlfriend, out on a date. Marsha has left Odarion and is trying to move on; but Odarion still kills TK for "disrespect." This murder sets off a cycle in which each death is more senseless and tragic than the last.

The overall message of the *Gun Boys Rhapsody* is that in the twenty-first century Bahamas, deadly violence is an arbitrary, daily affair. Strachan's account of violence is more immediately social and structural, moving away from Saunders's psychological introspection; in Nassau today, life is disposable, murder is glorified, guns are power, and the next generation emulates the last. This is the everyday catastrophe with which we live.

Gun Boys Rhapsody illustrates starkly how independence has not eradicated the impulses that lead to violence. Decolonization has not cleansed ordinary Bahamians of their need for violent expression. It has not turned them away from fighting themselves to fighting their oppressors (Fanon 1963). Rather, those oppressors are omnipresent. If the violence apparent in *You Can Lead a Horse to Water* may be partly colonial, the violence Strachan presents in *Gun Boys* is certainly the result of the pervasive coloniality in which Bahamian lives wither and die.

Natural Catastrophes: Hurricanes

The very existence of the Shakespeare in Paradise festival is, in its own way, a stand against catastrophe. From its inception, Shakespeare in Paradise has been scheduled around the October 12 holiday. This date carries the weight of both *history*—it is the date on which Columbus recorded his landfall in the "new world"—and *geography*, falling in the belly of the hurricane season.

The organizers of the festival had their reasons for choosing October. Hurricane season and the downturn in tourist arrivals bring good deals on airfares and hotel rooms. The October holiday is observed not only in The Bahamas, but throughout North America as well. Finally, Shakespeare in Paradise occurs at the beginning of the autumn school term, allowing shows to be presented to students.

But the October dates mean also that the festival is troubled regularly by the unpredictability of late-summer weather. It is impossible to know whether temperatures will be hot and humid, pleasant, or blustery. Even more challenging is the actual passage of storms. During the 2010s, matinee performances were frequently affected by hurricane watches[4] that resulted in school closures, although those watches do not normally impact evening performances. In 2016, the festival was interrupted by an actual hurricane.

Hurricane Matthew passed just east of New Providence on October 6, 2016, a Category Four storm with sustained winds of about 110 mph and storm surge of over eight feet. It flooded south-western New Providence and created tidal wave action in nearby Andros (Stewart 2017). The hurricane disrupted the second week of the Shakespeare in Paradise festival. Evening performances were suspended from Wednesday, October

5 until Friday, October 7. Student matinees for *You Can Lead a Horse to Water* were canceled altogether. The losses from that hurricane were significant.

For festival organizers, however, the principle was *the show will go on*. As soon as the all-clear was given, producers were at the theater ascertaining whether performances could be held. Despite some damage to the grounds, both theaters were in good working order, and the festival resumed on the weekend. This decision was not a mere matter of revenue. Shakespeare in Paradise exists in an environment where professional theater does not exist; although performers are offered compensation of various kinds (ticket discounts, gift bags, and stipends when income permits) the festival is put on entirely by volunteers. The festival's organizers believe fundamentally in the ability of theater to heal. Both the communal nature of rehearsals and performances are utilized cathartically. Such was the case following Hurricane Matthew, as performances provided a little respite from the storm's aftermath. It was also the case in the wake of Hurricane Dorian.

In late August 2019, Hurricane Dorian formed in the Atlantic. Initially, it promised to be a relatively minor disturbance. On the evening of August 31, though, it strengthened suddenly from a Category Three hurricane to a severe Category Five. It made landfall on Abaco on Sunday, September 1, 2019. After devastating Abaco, it slowed to a stop over Grand Bahama before moving away to the north on September 3 (Ali et al. 2020).

In New Providence, storm conditions were bearable. Hurricane Matthew had been worse. Nassauvians were more concerned by what was happening in the northern Bahamas. Glued to live feeds on social media, they watched as first Abaco and then Grand Bahama were engulfed in an ocean that had risen at least 20 feet in minutes.

Hurricane Dorian was the first hurricane in living memory that brought significant loss of life.[5] For Shakespeare in Paradise, the storm struck during the fourth week of rehearsal, at a time when plays are getting up on their feet and actors beginning to work off book. In communal terms, this is a time when bonds are being formed within casts, and when discoveries, emotional and otherwise, are being made onstage that have the capacity to provide catharsis and—often—healing. Of particular significance in this regard were the rehearsals for the evening known as *Short Tales*, a collection of new short plays featuring different casts and directors, that since 2018 has opened the festival.

The *Short Tales* experience has changed the working dynamic of rehearsals. An incubator for fresh Bahamian talent, it hones the skills of writers, directors, and actors as people of all ages and levels of experience collaborate to create a single production. The performance takes place in a black box theater. Each play rehearses in 30-minute slots two to three times a week. Several actors perform in multiple plays. On any given night, the *Short Tales* company forms a large, warm, supportive community whose members are mutually invested in the success of the whole.

Given that reality, and understanding the magnitude of the trauma that all Bahamians were experiencing in the wake of Hurricane Dorian, the decision was taken that rehearsals would resume as soon as physically possible. The first post-storm rehearsal was called for Monday, September 2, but several of the company were unable to leave their homes: floodwaters in their areas made the streets impassable. The next day, people turned up. Little work was done that night. Some of the plays were rehearsed, but much of the evening was taken up gathering over coffee, talking out worries about relatives in Abaco and Grand Bahama who had not yet made contact.

One of the actors was intimately involved in the citizen-initiated rescue efforts. In Grand Bahama, many individuals were stranded in attics, awaiting rescue. Many of them used Twitter and WhatsApp to drop location pins, and the actor in question had monitored her social media feeds since the hurricane for these coordinates, passing them on to official rescue crews. Her efforts were responsible for saving countless lives. She came to rehearsal determined to play her part, but when her time came was unable to get through the scene. She spent the rest of the evening sharing her own trauma and despair at not being able to rescue all the people who contacted her. The support of the company offered her respite and strength.

The COVID-19 Pandemic

In 2020, with the nation still reeling from Dorian's widespread devastation, the COVID-19 pandemic arrived with its attendant lockdowns. The first of these was instituted in March 2020. All borders were closed, all businesses beyond essential services shut down, and inter-island travel was prohibited. This state of emergency lasted for 3 months until the first wave of COVID-19 had passed. It was relaxed somewhat during the summer, but as the months went on, democratic processes were effectively suspended. Rather than creating pandemic legislation, the government of the day chose to continually amend the emergency orders. The nation was placed under the rule of a "competent authority"—the Prime Minister.

Under emergency orders, theaters were categorized as "prohibited businesses," and remained closed from March 2020 through September 2021.[6] Although outdoor performances resumed under strict protocols in the summer of 2021, theaters were not permitted to open their doors to the public until after a general election in September brought a change of government and a repeal of emergency orders.

In the summer of 2021, Shakespeare in Paradise mounted a modified in-person festival which ran from September through December 2021.[7] On December 13, the first indoor performance in eighteen months was presented to the public. This was the premiere of a new work: *Competent Authority* (Burrows and Francis 2021), which chronicled the Bahamian response to the pandemic.

Competent Authority was a piece of theatrical collage which drew from news reports, official releases, and social media posts alongside short original pieces to narrate the Bahamian experience of COVID-19 between March 2020 and December 2021. The play's core critique cohered around the erosion of democracy under emergency orders:

> Some of the orders appeared to make no sense. Certain businesses were allowed to open and others had to be closed. The curfew times jumped an hour this way or an hour that way as if the virus knew the best hours to attack. There didn't seem […] to be any rhyme or reason as to why this was. Some people began to speculate that a select few of the businesses allowed to operate might have had ties to members of the government. Some people began to question some of the decisions being made by the so called "Competent Authority," especially since the power of that authority presided in the hands of only one man. (Burrows and Francis 2021, 24)

Although this man—the Prime Minister—was supported by an advisory team which he frequently consulted, the team's expertise was primarily medical in nature. More human considerations took a back seat, and punishments for transgressions of emergency orders were disproportionately severe. In one vignette, a young man is arrested for violating curfew by selling coconuts to feed his family. The play presented part of his personal testimony as told to reporters:

> At around 3:20pm on Friday, May 15th I was arrested [...] in breach of the [...] COVID-19 emergency orders. [...] The entire experience was frightening and made me feel like a criminal. [...]
> It's me, my mother, my father and my sister and my sister has kids. I'm the only person in our house who was working through this COVID thing. [...]
> The police asked me for a valid business license and I told them I was woking on one so not having one they arrested me and took me to Grove Police Station.
> I was arraigned on Monday and pleaded guilty to violating the curfew and operating a non-essential business. I was ordered to pay $700 in fines or spend one month in prison. (Burrows and Francis 2021, 4–5)

The play shared other vignettes, too, illustrating the grief, rage, ennui, and solitude experienced during the lockdown; but at its core remained the enduring absurdity felt by Bahamians in the face of government regulations. Towards the end of the play, actors playing anonymized reporters catalogued this absurdity, in places using text taken from actual news reports.

> REPORTER 62: If you combine the emergency orders and powers, and the amendments to those orders, from May 8th 2020 to September 24th 2021 the total number of documents released to the public comes to 64 [...]
> REPORTER 63: ... Some of the orders appeared to make no sense. [...] Some people began to question some of the decisions being made by the so called "Competent Authority," especially since the power of that authority resided in the hands of only one man.
> REPORTER 64: Prime Minister Dr Hubert Minnis announced that a national curfew will take effect today [...] He said the emergency order, a radical restriction on personal and business freedoms that will upend life in The Bahamas, was needed to prevent the spread of the highly contagious novel coronavirus. [...]
> REPORTER 65: Attorney General Carl Bethel, explaining what compliance with the curfew must entail, said: "Persons should be in their homes, if their homes are affixed to the soil in some matter, they may go in the immediate area in their yard but not if it's an open yard over to someone else's home and not to mingle with any occupant of any other house unless the yard is enclosed." The penalty for breaking the order is a fine not exceeding $10,000 upon summary conviction or imprisonment for not more than 18 months or both.

REPORTER 66: Oxford Languages lists the following definitions:
A ruler with total power over a country
A person who behaves in an autocratic way.
A chief magistrate with absolute power, appointed in an emergency. These definitions are all associated with the word Dictator.
REPORTER 67: Under the Emergency Powers Act (Chapter 34) Emergency Powers (COVID-19) Regulations, 2020
Under Interpretation it reads, "Competent Authority" means the Prime Minister. (Burrows and Francis 2021, 23–24)

In the end, the show resonated with audiences. Whether due to the novelty of returning to live theater or to the experience of seeing the past eighteen months presented to them in under 90 minutes, the audiences for *Competent Authority* grew. It was not an uplifting experience; audiences found it sobering and sad. It was also cathartic. Its impact was difficult to dismiss. At the beginning of the run, the show played to audiences of sixteen. But word spread. Some audience members returned up to four times. By the end, the show was selling out, reaching the mandated capacity available.

Healing the Coloniality of Catastrophe

The founders of Shakespeare in Paradise believe fervently in the healing power of theater. Long before the festival was created, its parent company, Ringplay Productions, took the following quotation from Oskar Eustis as part of its raison d'être: "Theater is the essential art form of democracy, and we know this because they were born in the same city […] in the same decade" (Eustis 2018).

In any postcolonial society, investment in and attention to democracy are healing. This is particularly resonant in the Caribbean setting, given the genocidal and dehumanizing roots of our societies. Theater is a profoundly humanizing art form, one that, if done well, can provoke catharsis and, ultimately, healing on both sides—for performers and audiences alike. The critical element involved is empathy: "truth comes from the collision of different ideas and the emotional muscle of empathy are the necessary tools of democratic citizenship" (Eustis 2018).

More recently, Sheila Cavanagh (2024) has explored the impact of theater, particularly Shakespeare, on communities as diverse as autistic children, military veterans, and prisoners. Drawing on the work of Bessel van der Kolk (2015), she demonstrates how theater can inspire somatic healing—healing of trauma through bodily performance. In either case, whether the healing occurs within the audience or among the actors, it can provide avenues for reparation and growth.

For Shakespeare in Paradise, the initial intention was to employ theater as a means of healing Bahamian society from the wounds inflicted by coloniality. On one level, it was intended to (re)introduce Bahamians to themselves. Part of the impact of coloniality is the production of a kind of amnesia about oneself and one's culture that extends the damage done by colonial subjugation and enslavement. The work produced by Shakespeare in Paradise and Ringplay Productions is conscious of the need to repair that damage. This is done by producing works of Bahamian, Caribbean, and diaspora theater alongside Shakespeare's works to underscore their equivalency, as well as to demystify this icon of the English canon, to prove that the survivors of the colonial enterprise can master Shakespeare, can claim and conquer this paragon of imperial culture, and thereby find confidence in ourselves.

More pragmatically for The Bahamas, whose literary output is most developed in the dramatic arts, the work of Shakespeare in Paradise and Ringplay Productions is also committed to honoring the works of Bahamian playwrights. By reviving, performing, and publishing those plays, new generations of Bahamians are given touchstones of their own as they face potential inundation by global mass culture—again, an act of healing.

Bahamian theater gives voice to the unspoken. In a culture scarred by colonial and postcolonial violence, wounds are usually hidden. They fester, extending that violence to new generations. Shakespeare in Paradise productions seek to name the unnameable: everything from the secret injury of domestic and sexual abuse[8] to the unmentionable love of same-sex couples[9] to the damage done to migrant workers and their children and grandchildren[10] find expression on the Bahamian stage. This has provided a first step towards repairing the damage.

The gathering of audiences in the same space as performers is a counter-catastrophic exercise, even for a short while, in creating community. That audiences are responding to this is evident in the shift in their reactions to difficult moments on stage. Bahamian actors were once taught that if the audience laughed at a tense moment such as an on-stage rape or murder, it did not mean that those laughing were uncaring or unmoved. Rather, it meant that the only acceptable public reaction to strong emotion *was* laughter. This is the legacy of coloniality and colonioirity. Where survival depends on strength, vulnerability may never be revealed to others. Today, however, audiences openly express a range of emotions. They laugh, they weep, they gasp, they remain silent together. The community created by theater in The Bahamas is now recognized as supportive, possibly even safe. Acknowledging the power of live performance, Shakespeare in Paradise does not record its productions for commercial distribution. The producers' philosophy is that performance is most transformative when it is experienced live.

> [...] whether you knew it or not, you were coming to that theater to be part of an audience. You were coming to have the collective experience of laughing together, crying together, holding your breath together to see what's going to happen next. You may have walked into that theater as an individual consumer, but if the theater does its job, you've walked out with a sense of yourself as part of a whole, as part of a community. (Eustis 2018)

What began as an inchoate conviction in 2009 grounded in anthropological studies about drama and ritual (e.g. Turner 1988; Schechner 1985) became a definite practice after encounters with companies that use theater, often Shakespeare, as a means of connection and healing. These encounters included the anti-violence work of Shakespeare practitioners at the University of Colorado, the Hunter Heartbeat method devised for children with autism (Hunter 2015), the rehabilitative effect of Shakespeare in prisons (Rogerson 2004), and post-traumatic healing among veterans and prisoners (Ali et al. 2020, 2022). Shakespeare in Paradise was founded to empower audiences, build Bahamians' confidence in engaging with Shakespeare, celebrate and enhance Bahamian theater, expand the Bahamian economy beyond the sun/sand/sea triumvirate, and train Bahamian actors. Using the empathy that inheres in theater, it seeks to tackle the self-loathing that results from centuries of colonial and post-colonial oppression and to give audiences a new way to see—and honor—themselves.

That this is critical in a region founded on genocide, enslavement, and colonial oppression, a region that was created from the absolute denial of the humanity of its inhabitants, goes without saying. The activities undertaken by Shakespeare in Paradise, therefore, seek to engage both directly and indirectly with the coloniality of catastrophe through theater. In so doing, the festival seeks to redeem, maybe to repair, the damage of the past.

Notes

1. The Bahamas' Gini Coefficient index was 53.3 in 2019—before the double disasters of Hurricane Dorian and COVID-19. (World Economics, n.d.).
2. Later Shakespeare productions explore a range of other issues affecting the Bahamian context, among them the hot-button topic of migrant-Bahamian relations. In 2012, Shakespeare in Paradise chose to produce *A Merchant of Venice*. The Bahamas does not have a significant Jewish population; a play about anti-Semitism was unlikely to resonate with audiences. A play about Haitian immigrants, however, might. So the festival dropped "Venice" from the title of the play and marketed it as *Merchant*, with Shylock as a Haitian numbers-runner. In Shakespeare's original, Shylock is ordered to become a Christian, to pay a fine to the Duke, and to leave half of his estate to his daughter Jessica. But in Shakespeare in Paradise's adaptation, Shylock is deported to Haiti. In this way, *Merchant* spoke directly to Bahamian audiences both of non-Haitian and of Haitian heritage. The play articulated the ever-present dread felt by members of the Haitian community—that children born and raised in The Bahamas might be sent "back" to Haiti for various unspecified infractions of Bahamian laws.
3. This exposure to casual violence is formative. Studies conducted among Bahamian prisoners indicate that one of the most common denominators among those inmates convicted of murder and attempted murder in The Bahamas is violence in the home. See Bethel et al. (2019).
4. Watches indicate that a storm may threaten parts of the Bahamas within 48 hours. Warnings indicate that it is likely that a storm will hit a specific part of The Bahamas within 36 hours. See Bahamas National Emergency Management Agency (NEMA) (n.d.).
5. Officially, the death toll from Hurricane Dorian was 74, with a further 245 people counted as missing (Ali et al. 2020). Many Bahamians are convinced that the death toll was even higher, given that the hurricane washed away whole settlements of stateless people and undocumented migrants (see Bethell-Bennett 2021).

6. Hotels, it must be noted, were never subject to the full slate of emergency orders; restaurants were permitted to open for outdoor, takeaway service, in May 2020; indoor cinemas were permitted to open in February 2021; and under all Orders, the Competent Authority had the power to exempt any business from the stated prohibition.
7. In 2020, Shakespeare in Paradise mounted a virtual festival, airing videos of past productions in partnership with the local cable company.
8. For example: *Small Axe* (Bethel 2017); *All Our Monsters: Witches* (Hanna 2023); *Class of 2020* (Francis 2023); *Sunk in Love* (Burnett 2023).
9. For example: *Music Box* (Alexander 2018); *Eggs for Breakfast* (Rolle 2020).
10. For example: *Woman Take Two* (Turner 1987); *The Children's Teeth* (Bethel 2008); *All Our Monsters* (Hanna 2019).

Works Cited

Alexander, Anjellina. 2018. *Music Box*. In *Short Tales Vol. I*, ed. Nicolette Bethel. Nassau: Shakespeare in Paradise.

Ali, Alisha, Stephan Wolfert, Ingrid Lam ciyu, Patricia Fahmy, Amna Chaudhry, and Jessica Healey. 2022. Treating the Effects of Military Sexual Trauma through a Theater-Based Program for U.S. Veterans. *Women and Therapy* 45 (1): 25–40. https://doi.org/10.1080/02703149.2021.1978050.

Ali, Alisha, Stephan Wolfert, Jocelin E. McGovern, Jennifer Nguyen, and Adam Aharoni. 2020. A Trauma-Informed Analysis of Monologues Constructed by Military Veterans in a Theater-Based Treatment Program. *Qualitative Research in Psychology* 17 (2): 258–273.https://doi.org/10.1080/14780887.2018.1442704

Aranha, Stephen B. 2015. Citizenship as a Fundamental Right: How the Bahamian Constitution Mis-Imagines the Nation. *International Journal of Bahamian Studies* 21: 7–21.

Avila, Lixion A., Stacy R. Stewart, Robbie Berg, and Andrew Hagen. 2020. "Hurricane Dorian (AL052019)." *National Hurricane Center Tropical Cyclone Report*. Miami.

Bahamas National Emergency Management Agency (NEMA). n.d. Government of The Bahamas Webpage. https://www.bahamas.gov.bs/wps/wcm/connect/7c970dd3-9de2-4a57-bb03-5318f499db43/NEMA_Hurricane+or+Tropical+Storm+Watches+and+Warnings.pdf?MOD=AJPERES. Accessed 25 February 2024.

Beckles, Hilary McD. 2013. *Britain's Black Debt: Reparations for Caribbean Slavery and Native Genocide*. University of the West Indies Press.

Bethel, Nicolette. 2008. *The Children's Teeth: A Play in Two Acts*. Nassau: Lulu.

Bethel, Nicolette. 2017. *Small Axe*. Nassau: Lulu.

Bethel, Nicolette, Ebonesse Bain, Ky'Shaun Miller, Rodericka Collie, and Shantique Durham. 2019. Who Commits Murder? In *Our Prisoners: A Collection of Papers Arising from a 2016 Survey of Inmates at The Bahamas Department of Correctional Services Facility at Fox Hill*, ed. William Fielding, Virginia Ballance, Philip Smith, Alexandre Veyrat-Pontet, and Heather Sutton. Washington, DC: Inter-American Development Bank. https://publications.iadb.org/en/our-prisoners-collection-papers-arising-2016-survey-inmates-bahamas-department-correctional.

Bethell-Bennett, Ian A. 2021. Dorian Unmaking Space: Policy, Place and Dislocation. *International Journal of Bahamian Studies* 27: 117–130. https://doi.org/10.15362/ijbs.v27i1.423.

Burnett, Sarah. 2023. Sunk in Love. In *Short Tales Vol. 4*, ed. Nicolette Bethel. Nassau: Shakespeare in Paradise.

Burrows, Philip A., and Patrice A. Francis. 2021. *Competent Authority*. Unpublished playscript.

Cavanagh, Sheila T. 2024. *Multi-sensory Shakespeare and Specialized Communities*. Arden Shakespeare.

Eustis, Oskar. 2018. Theater and Democracy. Filmed April 2018 in Vancouver, BC. TED video, 3:25. https://www.ted.com/talks/oskar_eustis_why_theater_is_essential_to_democracy.

Fanon, Frantz. 1963. *The Wretched of the Earth*. Translated by Constance Farrington: Grove Press.

Ferdinand, Malcom. 2022. *Decolonial Ecology: Thinking from the Caribbean World*. Translated by Anthony Paul Smith. Polity.

Francis, Patrice. 2023. Class of 2020. In *Short Tales Vol. 4*, ed. Nicolette Bethel. Nassau: Shakespeare in Paradise.

Hanna, S. A. 2019. All Our Monsters. In *Short Tales Volume II*, ed. Nicolette Bethel. Nassau: Shakespeare in Paradise.

Hanna, S. A. 2023. All Our Monsters: Witches. In *Short Tales Vol. 4*, ed. Nicolette Bethel. Nassau: Shakespeare in Paradise.

Hunter, Kelly. 2015. *Shakespeare's Heartbeat: Drama Games for Children with Autism*. Routledge.

Kamugisha, Aaron. 2019. *Beyond Coloniality: Citizenship and Freedom in the Caribbean Intellectual Tradition*. Bloomington: Indiana University Press.

Maycock, Denise. 2018. Oban Energies yet to open office in Freeport. *The Tribune*, July 23. http://www.tribune242.com/news/2018/jul/23/oban-energies-yet-to-open-office-in-freeport/. Accessed 7 February 2024.

Mintz, Sidney W. 1986. *Sweetness and Power: The Place of Sugar in Modern History*. Penguin.
Nixon, Angelique V. 2015. *Resisting Paradise: Tourism, Diaspora and Sexuality in Caribbean Culture*. University Press of Mississippi.
Quijano, Aníbal. 2000. Coloniality of Power and Eurocentrism in Latin America. *International Sociology* 15 (2): 215–232. https://doi.org/10.1177/026858 0900015002005.
Rogerson, Hank. 2004. *Shakespeare Behind Bars*. Philomath Films.
Rolle, Valicia. 2020. *Eggs for Breakfast*. In *Short Tales Vol. III*, ed. Nicolette Bethel. Nassau: Shakespeare in Paradise.
Saunders, Winston. 1983. *You Can Lead a Horse to Water*. Unpublished playscript.
Schechner, Richard. 1985. *Between Theater and Anthropology*. University of Pennsylvania Press.
Sheller, Mimi. 2003. *Consuming the Caribbean: From Arawaks to Zombies*. Routledge.
Sheller, Mimi. 2020. *Island Futures: Caribbean Survival in the Anthropocene*. Durham and London: Duke University Press.
Strachan, Ian G. 2002. *Paradise and Plantation: Tourism and Culture in the Anglophone Caribbean*. Charlottesville: University of Virginia Press.
Stewart, Stacy R. 2017. "Hurricane Matthew (AL142016)." *National Hurricane Center Tropical Cyclone Report*. Miami. http://www.nhc.noaa.gov/data/tcr/AL142016_Matthew.pdf.
Strachan, Ian. 2016. *Gun Boys Rhapsody*. Unpublished playscript.
Sutton, Heather. 2016. *Crime and Violence in The Bahamas IDB Series on Crime and Violence in the Caribbean*. Washington, DC: IDB. https://publications.iadb.org/bitstream/handle/11319/7771/Crime-and-Violence-in-The-Bahamas-IDB-Series-on-Crime-and-Violence-in-the-Caribbean.pdf?sequence=4.
Turner, Telcine. 1987. *Woman Take Two: A Play in Three Acts*. Macmillan Caribbean.
Turner, Victor. 1988. *The Anthropology of Performance*. PAJ Publications.
van der Kolk, Bessel. 2015. *The Body Keeps the Score*. Penguin.
Williams, Eric. 1944. *Capitalism and Slavery*, 3rd ed. Chapel Hill: University of North Carolina Press.
World Economics. n.d. https://www.worldeconomics.com. Accessed 19 February 2024.

CHAPTER 7

Drowning in the Wake

Ian A. Bethell Bennett

Beginnings

St Lucian poet and playwright Derek Walcott reminds us that "The Sea is History" (2007) in his poetic work and I respond:

> The wake pulls, grabs, and swamps.
> Its power destabilizes. Coloniality and dehumanization create a wake that drowns the body colonized by enslavement and captured by crowns.

In Bahamian artist Maxwell Taylor's woodcut "The Haitians (The Men)," a man, more a body, lies on the ground in front of a mass of bodies being rounded up.[1] The performance of death and (in)difference is clear and palpable in this etching. Taylor captures the othering of class, race, blackness experienced in The Bahamas by one group of humans to another, all of whom are darker skinned. Their difference lies in the border between

I. A. Bethell Bennett (✉)
School of English Studies, Liberal Arts, The University of the Bahamas, Nassau, The Bahamas
e-mail: ian.bennett@ub.edu.bs

languages and islands, not far apart, both shaped by the colonial condition. Independence did not liberate. Then comes a wave that drowns both states under the coloniality of disaster.

In what follows, I explore the coloniality of catastrophe manifest not only through the ongoing violence of anti-Blackness in The Bahamas but more precisely through its intensification in the form of anti-Haitian discrimination practiced even by black Bahamians. Beginning with a brief overview of the conditions of this othering, I explore the wide-ranging impacts of this intersecting violence through two contemporary Bahamian plays, at times adopting a poetic voice to manifest the affective horror of these practices of dehumanization.

Anti-Blackness and the Violence of Colonialism

The crisis of colonialism in post-Fordist capitalism is that it is hidden under postcolonies and their sovereign rule. In The Bahamas, ownership is built into economic structures of dominance and domination where local industry has been made to fail through the globalization of finance and consumerism. Local agency—the ability of Black bodies to thrive in the postcolony—is circumscribed by the structural violence of coloniality that views all Black bodies as less-than and slowly erodes their ability to breathe. It is drowning in the wake of the wave as much as it is dry land drowning, where structures oppress and undermine. The sea is beautiful as are the islands, yet to those bodies inhabiting their geographies they can be violent and vicious as waves wash over hardly stable homes in the face of colonially imposed power asymmetries and spatial (in)justices (Soja 2009). As tropical space grows higher than in its capitalist worth or its exchange value over its use value, those inhabitants who use it are displaced as more wealthy persons invade from the North.

In the wake of category 5 Hurricane Dorian in 2019, and of course after María and Katrina, too, the catastrophe of colonial lines drawn in the sand or fault lines resembles Taylor's man prostrate on the ground. The etching catches not only the crisis of migration and the need for thinking through its impact and disaster in the Caribbean but also the lack of inquiry into it and the resistance to it. The rendering of human beings as un-human, inhuman, less-than-human animals has become a common thread in the postcolony, which builds on these old colonial lines and the coloniality of power. Imbricated in this is the immobility of subject people. They are enmeshed by laws and legalities, geography, and politics that are colonially drawn. They become dead weights as their bodies are left in shallow graves on Bitter Guana Cay where their memory will never be remembered, or such is the hope of the coloniality of the postcolonial state. Each crisis builds into a wider and broader disaster that forms a catastrophic wave of destruction. Behind this wave, green gentrification and spatial redesign can take over as foreign direct investment displaces the memory of what came before. This is a kind of death that occurs silently under waves of destructive creation.

This acceptance of the death of the "other" comes out of community death, as in forced death, constructed through populism and media-developed nationalism around Benedict Anderson's (1983) concept of nations being imagined into being. The complication in the Caribbean is that the original context has been erased by the imperial decimation of indigenous peoples. The geographies of difference make it easy for spaces of disaster to develop and become catastrophes where migrants are forced to dwell. Johan Galtung (1969) might refer to this as structural violence while Edward Soja could argue that it is a form of spatial (in)justice (2009). In *Legacy of Violence* (2022), Caroline Elkins documents British colonial power and the de-civilization of subject peoples across the globe. Dehumanizing humans or subject people by referring to them as animals or savages and through Orientalist othering is a continuous historical trend evident in the desire to conquer land/space and to dominate/civilize.

As Edward Said points out in *Orientalism* (1978), this process allows the subject people occupying this land to be othered and exoticized. I riff off Said's Orientalist structures, using Galtung's argument that structural violence is invisible because it is indirect, unlike personal/physical violence but negatively impacts the lives of some people (Galtung 1969). Structures are put in place through spatial coloniality, its geography, history, political and economic structures, that render many people invisible to opportunity but vulnerable to exploitation, as we see with the body in Taylor's etching.

The man in Taylor's woodcut is seen as Haitian. When we understand that colonies are spatially determined and historically defined by political processes that live on beyond independence, we see how legacies of violence can continue through Orientalism and the exploitation of Black bodies. To illustrate this, I use Taylor's etching alongside two plays, *Diary of Souls* (2006) by Ian Strachan and *The Children's Teeth* (2008) by Nicolette Bethel to show not only the continuity of othering across time but also its insidious imbrication into the social fabric. Haitians and darker-skinned colonial subjects are treated less favorably. Blackness is seen by the colonized other as bad. We see this "othering" imbricated in structures and attitudes as well as in the ways people are treated and treat one another.

In The Bahamas, there is huge anti-Haitian/anti-Black sentiment because it is culturally acceptable. Like the wave of disaster that drowns, entrenched coloniality is catastrophic because it destroys through separation. Here, Haitians, like other Blacks are relegated to a particularly low part of society. Edwidge Danticat's early short story "Children of the Sea" articulates this clearly: "They treat Haitians like dogs" (1996, 15). Danticat points out the similarities between Bahamians and Haitians while also marking the Bahamians' self-superiority and casual mistreatment of Haitians. Notwithstanding this superiority, the interior schism wrought by colonialism is deep and impactful; as Frantz Fanon notes in the 1950s and 1960s and M. M. Jacqui Alexander argues in the 1990s, it forms a (damaging) legacy of Black male leadership in The Bahamas and Trinidad. Alexander, for example, argues that Black nationalist masculinity aspired toward imperial masculinity:

> Black nationalist masculinity needed to demonstrate that it was now capable of ruling, which is to say, it needed to demonstrate moral rectitude, particularly on questions of paternity. This required distancing itself from irresponsible Black working-class masculinity that spawned the "bastard", the "illegitimate", and that thus had to be criminalized for irresponsible fatherhood by the British. (Alexander 1994, 13)

Alexander further captures Bahamian anti-Haitian sentiment when she writes: "The Bahamian state has invoked an impending population crisis, positioned Haitian communities as 'immigrants', 'refugees' and repositories of crime. It has vindicated its use of military and police force to expel Haitians from the nation's borders by claiming that they are no longer legitimate citizens; they imperil the nation" (Alexander 1994, 15).

The Bahamas has interpreted the old British colonial tropes of an invading disease of Black bodies from Haiti and applied it to the postcolonial nation-state's construction and understanding of the other. The Other is Black, blacker than "normal," not an acceptable Black but rather an uncivilized Black bringing poverty, disease, and sorcery. In The Bahamas, this is seen in the media portrayal of Haitians: Haitians are a threat to the civility and the prosperity of the nation. Haitians can drown in the sea and not so much matter. Haitians, boat people, can be consumed by waves and not count. Waves of anti-Haitian sentiment wash over Bahamian communities flattening and erasing complex histories.[2]

As a child in The Bahamas, I heard about Haitian strongman ruler François Duvalier because there were so many Haitian laborers fleeing Haiti. This was the 1970s. By the 1980s, immigration law was being enforced to ensure no one overstayed their permits. This crackdown was perceived as violent at the time as it disrupted a normal working of cultural norms to enforce the reality that people had to follow a law that was often ignored or flaunted by those in positions of power. There was a steady stream of Haitian laborers coming through to work on farms, that by the 1990s had begun to disappear under the new promise of independence in the form of better jobs without sweating: tourism jobs. As Haiti's instability grew, The Bahamas' shining lights and well-paying jobs attracted more Haitian labor. Initially, farming required more labor than Bahamians were willing to provide, so Haitian migrants provided affordable, reliable sources of labor for these farms on Abaco, New Providence, and Eleuthera.

As a result of legally enshrined discrimination, and its socially promoted aspect, Haitians can live for generations in The Bahamas and continue to experience legal and social stigmatization and exclusion. This has come to bear on children born in The Bahamas of Haitian parents, especially young men who are disenfranchised and become disaffected by their stigmatization. Simultaneously, this disaster of dispossession is most keenly experienced by young Black men, particularly if they are working-class and poor. They become society's pariahs.

In the wake of Hurricane Dorian, we understand that Haitians and Bahaitians were unequally impacted because of their spatial location and years of legally sanctioned disenfranchisement. Slow violence (Nixon 2011), which builds on Galtung's structural violence, is an important framework for understanding this unequal impact. In his study of slow violence Rob Nixon notes, in line with Edward Said, that the power to describe and to "other" in many ways allows for the poor to be abused, but adds that because this violence is slow, it is often unperceived. This incrementally increasing violence and disenfranchisement over time allows crises to turn into disasters.

Theatrical Work Reimag(in)ing the Violence

In this essay, I explore how the plays *Diary of Souls* and *The Children's Teeth* act as alternative responses and analyses of the drowning waves of colonial violence, moving away from the pervasive media-controlled reductive and threatening misrepresentations of blackness and the media's destructive forms of othering that permeate Bahamian culture. Both plays perform aspects of cultural oppression and structural discrimination that lead to slow violence. Bahamians do not see as violence the violence of intentional exploitation exercised upon enslaved African bodies revisited in the twenty-first century, as well as the violence of exclusion. Waves of coloniality and Black hatred continue to wash over postcolonies. Wave one drowns a boat of Haitians being rescued by a Royal Bahamas Defence Force vessel. Wave two is the anti-Blackness made palpable by Hurricane Dorian's wall of water. Meanwhile, on stage, players assume the roles of those disempowered bodies and disavow the silences around death's erasure in the common space. This is poignant because it is unassuming though powerful. And I think:

> In our lives in the postcolony, I note, There are no dead.
> There are only missing.
> So always suspended between unbeing and erasure.
> Haunting those who bore witness
> Never silenced by the erasure of colonially imagined geographies now redesigned
> Gun boys are bodies
> Haitians are said to be gunboys
> The children's teeth, as Bethel notes,
> are on edge.
> Waves destroy, but never kill
> Even though death is always hemmed into the colonial violence
> Its aftermath
> Catastrophic waves
> Poison in the pits of society's abdomen
> Laid by powers now hidden but relentlessly dominating all spatial relation in paradise.

Wave One: *Diary of Souls*

Strachan's *Diary of Souls* is set in the early 1990s on a beach in the Exumas, on Bitter Guana Cay, to be exact. The audience learns quickly that everyone is dead. The characters are trying to figure out how to get home. They recount the passing that has landed them in this shallow, sandy grave, dumped without ceremony. The action moves between the Haitian souls stuck on the beach, buried in shallow graves, and Ishmael, a Royal Bahamas Defence Force officer who "survived" the ordeal and is back in Nassau in therapy sessions with a psychiatrist who negates his reactions to the events. *Diary of Souls* commingles living and dead, and so, lines are blurred. In much of Caribbean culture, the living and dead cohabit in life, though this is not often articulated. The haunting approach Strachan uses is a trope that could hark back to ideas of Haitian Vodou but also speaks to the abiding African presence in many Bahamian cultural practices.

Strachan picks up after a Bahamian Defence Force vessel apprehends a Haitian sloop carrying numerous refugees through Bahamian waters. The sloop is tied to the back of the vessel and is swamped by a wave. The passengers end up drowning and being buried by the officers on Bitter Guana Cay. In the opening scene, Silvi, Pol, and Ti Twan are reliving their ordeal as they have forgotten where they are and how they got there; that they are in fact dead and buried; and that they cannot leave the cay. Ishmael feels tragically responsible for this disaster on the seas, as he facilitates the bodies' burial and abandonment on the cay. He seeks assistance from the doctor, who refuses to acknowledge there can be any such thing as post-traumatic response or haunting and seeks to disabuse Ishmael of his PTSD or cultural trauma. The culture of xenophobia in the denial of spiritual and cultural trauma and the refusal to address PTSD, along with the negation of Black bodies and their lives, is omnipresent in this production. Strachan uses media reports and fictional makeups for what is omitted to bring the action into our beings, as audience members, to grapple with disenfranchisement and violence—epistemic violence built around structural violence and the silence of being Black colonial subjects.

Strachan intentionally employs Kreyòl throughout the text. The names are important and capture aspects of the characters in both Kreyòl and English. At the beginning of the play, Pol and Ti Twan offer what they remember of the event that leads to them being left suspended between worlds. Danticat's words above from "Children of the Sea" are echoed as

Ti Twan notes: "We were on the boat below deck. Packed in tight. No room to move. Like slaves. It was morning. The wind was blowing. The sea was rough. No food, no water" (Strachan 2006, 13). The likening to enslaved bodies is significant as this is reminiscent of all the bodies left at the bottom of the Atlantic on their way from Africa to "New World" enslavement. Ti Twan recounts the entire experience of their boat being sunk:

> The big boat turned to tow us. I heard a loud cracking noise. The walls fell away. The roof caved in. The boat fell to pieces. People falling on top of people. The children were crying. [...] Blackness. Then I remember climbing. [...] No air. And then I was in the sun again. On this beach. And they were leaving us. They were riding off in the boat and leaving us behind. (Strachan 2006, 13–14)

This exchange between Pol and Ti Twan sets the scene for the rest of the play. It is the loss of life through drowning, a centuries-old event where Black bodies are abandoned at sea to save slave traffickers and governors and other important people from capture and possible prosecution. Death, though naturally occurring, has particularities when it comes in the way Ti Twan describes.

The coloniality of the scene described above is that it repeats itself unchecked, unencumbered. Aimé Césaire notes in *A Discourse on Colonialism* that colonialism destroys the humanity of the colonizers as well as the colonized as the former attempt to turn the latter into animals and dehumanize them. Similarly, Frantz Fanon demonstrates that separation is an essential part of the experience, one that supports stark demarcations between settlers and natives as well as the internalized attitudes of the colonizer in the colonized, which results in the tendency to dehumanize fellow Blacks. But we also get a distinct view as Ishmael, a witness participant of catastrophe, experiences the aftereffects of the trauma of the killing of the Haitians on the sloop they swamped. Ishmael tells the doctor: "Miss, dese jus Highshuns we talkin' 'bout. What you getting your garters in a twis' for? Besides, you shouldn't believe errrting you hear. Who say it was only 100 people?" (Strachan 2006, 58). He throws into uncertainty any of the facts presented as well as clearly shows the disregard in which Bahamians hold Haitians. This is structural violence. They are not people; they are only "Highshuns" and as such can be ignored, violently erased, and dehumanized. The media casts them as a threat. Strachan decenters that colonial vision.

These violent deaths are made even more palpable by the disenfranchisement of Haitians in daily life, as we will see in Bethel's play, *The Children's Teeth*. Many Haitians were not deemed to be citizens by the postcolonial interpretation of Bahamian laws based on and copied from their colonial antecedents. Ishmael's above response is to the doctor's question of why the Haitians were not treated differently. In his mind, Ishmael also prompts the doctor to say "Stick to the lies we agreed upon, sir. I implore you" (Strachan 2006, 58). Lies are important in the coloniality of Bahamian life. Most Haitians born in The Bahamas can only access citizenship between the ages of 18 and 19, prior to which they have no access and after which they must complete a full naturalization process. Even then, it takes years for the process to be completed. Theater shows how easily they can be dehumanized by the structural violence of colonial power structures, but how showing their realities can return their humanity to them.

Wave Two: *The Children's Teeth*

Nicolette Bethel's *The Children's Teeth* is violent. The rape that precedes the action of the play is violent. The dehumanizing effect of violence can be seen throughout this play though, as it is staged, the audience is not enjoined to reject it outright. The subtlety of showing insidious, structural, and systemic violence that harks back to the colonial past is easier on the stage and screen than in real life.

In British colonialism, Blacks were relegated to particular places; they were denied space within the confines of civilized, polite society. They were granted space in less desirable land. Abaco and Grand Bahama, irregular communities where impoverished Blacks could reside, were savaged by Dorian's wall of water. Space is colonial; it is literally carved out by violent discovery and imperial mapping. The second-classing of citizenship for particular bodies is another enduring legacy of colonialism. Alexander sees this as a manifestation of how "[n]ot just (any)body can be a citizen" (Alexander 1994). Citizenship, she determines, is reserved for white colonial rapists, or those Black-skinned, white-masked post-colonial leaders who emulate and follow them. Space is mapped out by and for them. *The Children's Teeth* highlights how some of these tensions are entangled with questions of land and (un)belonging.

The Children's Teeth sets its story in the space of a family and touches upon themes of xenophobia, the violence of rape, cultural isolation, sexism, and structural violence in the legacies of colonialism that have remained hidden in the fabric of the postcolonial state. As we see in the play, notwithstanding independence, The Bahamas deploys the above colonial tropes and tools to focus on and disenfranchise Blacks, in this case more specifically Haitians. The family relations in *The Children's Teeth* are as follows: Donnie is the patriarch Neville's adopted daughter born to a Haitian mother begotten through rape, and this is used against her throughout the play. The other family members hate this child because she is Haitian, and they denigrate her accordingly. Neville strives to overcome his sin of rape by taking care of the victim and later by taking in Donnie. Ellie, his wife, looks after Donnie, who, as an adult, has returned to claim her place in the family and the house. Along with Donnie, Ellie raises her own daughter, Stacey, her son Jeff, her cousin, and adopted "brother", Ross, Blanche's great nephew; she also looks after her mother, Blanche, who hates Donnie. When Neville dies, his hard work and drive to succeed are lost in the next generation, who are more concerned with being cash-rich and discriminating against women and Haitians. The ensuing generations have lost the connection to the space and the pride of ownership; it has been replaced by a superficial, irresponsible, materiality embodied in much of Ross's brash attitude and behavior.

Like in *Diary of Souls*, the Bahamas Defence Force is involved. Bethel's play begins with a domestic scenario in a home where the family described above is discussing and disagreeing over the inclusion of a "daughter" as there is no proof the girl belongs to the father. The presumed father was part of a group Defence Force Officer who raped a Haitian woman during an immigration raid targeting a Haitian village in southeastern New Providence, one assumes in the Carmichael Road area (once called Headquarters and the space allotted for Black settlement). The play revisits this ground to show how the dehumanizing event comes to pass. The hatred and violence directed by Bahamians toward Haitians as they are rounded up and detained dehumanizes both the oppressor and the oppressed, as Fanon and Césaire have noted, though in this instance the woman is not deported or repatriated.

The play mixes living with dead as Neville is a ghost, and similarly to Strachan's play the living and the dead interact as if there were no line between the two realities. The matriarch, Blanche, struggles to maintain the home and family and faces division in the home due to Donnie and Ellie's collapsing relationship. They both share ownership of a house they wish to have separately, and each resents the other; both are sufficiently strong and determined, but Ellie expresses her dislikes openly. The anti-Haitian theme is the most palpable, but just as important is how the play exposes how Bahamian women, after their husbands have died, lose homes because they cannot afford to keep them. As the cost of living rises, local jobs do not keep pace, and increasingly scores of Bahamian homes collapse, as do relationships after the male breadwinner dies. Once "good neighborhoods" where Black bodies can live become dilapidated spaces, as the right of dower, lack of wills and forward planning result in cultural catastrophe and displacement. This catastrophic process is slower and more protracted than in Strachan's *Diary of Souls*.

Bahamian space is deeply divided around colonially imagined geographies of color, class, race, sex and superiority/inferiority, Blacks, especially Haitians, are sent to marginal spaces where death can come, disaster zones, but are kept close enough to tend to the beautiful playgrounds of neoliberal wealth and hedge-fund sharks. Bethel alludes to this segregation in the first scene of the play. Neville states, "When I pay down on this property it was still one of the best places black people could live" (Bethel 2008, 11). The full weight of these words, *Black people could live*, is missed. Yet, the play also alludes to the separation of Haitians from Bahamians within Black spaces. Haitians are culturally represented as bad. Donnie is the viper, detested by the others, especially Blanche. She is the result of the rape of the Haitian woman whom Blanche describes to Donnie as a "slack-leg whore" and a "wutless pisstail Haitian bitch" (Bethel 2008, 26).

In Bethel's play, the house comes to represent all the good and the bad of colonial paternalist patriarchal power while the sea in Strachan's work embodies the violence of a void where no one "knows" what really happened. The play not only speaks to the segregation inherent in colonial spaces it also attests to the inequalities of power between men and women and the reinforcement of these dichotomies that Blanche, Ellie's mother, tries to shore up by deploying patriarchal and xenophobic tropes. To be sure, the play does not simply grapple with the "othering" of Haitian Bahamians but with a plethora of social ills and traditions that seek to disempower colonized subjects. Again, Taylor's image of the Black migrant is powerful in communicating this alterity.

Home ownership in The Bahamas is a vexing topic because land was so carefully guarded away from most Black bodies. The Bahamas, especially,

Nassau, prior to independence was segregated along racial lines; today, that has ended, and it is class that functions as the marker of separation, though often silently. While many families in the country are headed by single mothers, and the matrilinearity of culture is obvious, patriarchy maintains a strong grip on society. Blacks pushed to own land in the wake of extremely oppressive direct colonial rule that denied belonging for most Black bodies and restricted landownership to White men or a few wealthy Black/Brown men, and later women, all the while upholding landownership as a qualifier to vote in any elections in the colony. Owning a home was a sign that one had made it. After the initial independence period of the 1960s–70s, as tourism, cultural consumption, xenophobia, and entrenched structural violence pervade the ecoscape, people fell into the regular traps of neoliberal and late-capitalist cultural materialism: selling off land in search of cash riches.

Woven into the landscape of dispossession that has been reconfigured since the 2000s is structural and systemic interpersonal violence. The land stands for nothing more than money and is being sold out from under cash-poor residents by Janus-faced developers who are well aware of the value of the land but lie and cheat to get it cheap. Bethel's play captures the deep fissures involved in land and spatial relations that show up in interpersonal violence and the social dysfunctions bubbling up in the wake of untreated and unchecked deep cultural trauma. We see this in Neville's fight to build a house with his "own hand" (Bethel 2008, 19) shortly after desegregation occurred, when they broke through the wall, he notes. The wall was a literal wall that ran from the north to the south of New Providence separating Black space from White land.

By the time the play is staged in 2008, the social ethos has changed: Ross embodies the shift towards a new materialism that disregards the multiple meanings of land and sees it exclusively for its monetary value. Ross's "fast living" brashness is evident in the way he talks with Ellie, his cousin. Ross has a sweet tongue and tries to convince Ellie to sell the house to "the man," a developer ready to take over and develop the entire area; they can move to a new subdivision. Ironically, the new subdivisions are further away from what had been up until then the commercial hub, less stable, more explosive, and not as well serviced as the area Neville had built in, but they attract residents because they are newer. However, Neville's dream is challenged by the dissolution of the family and Ross's masculine materiality and philandering. He has simply moved beyond the fight to get one piece of land and cuts his ties with everything. "FUCK the house! When yall ga sell this piece of shit anyhow?" (Bethel 2008, 80). Ross embodies all the cultural violence and contradictions of the catastrophic postcolony. His violence seeps into and eventually destroys the entire family, reflecting the intersection of personal loss and spatial loss.

In Act II Scene 4, Neville, now a ghost, recounts to his daughter, Stacey, still alive, the structural and direct violence he inflicted on people as an officer, which also foreshadows the destruction in Scene 5, which is seen in the excerpt below. He shares how they would raid people in the bush, and this is how Donnie comes into being:

> Me and Hillie and Sparks and Handy—all my fellas and me. They send us up in the back of the bush out Carmichael way. Out that way, look like nothing there but bush, but when you follow this track road or that through the bush, you come out into these camp. Like whole city off in the back there, and people pile up one on top the other in lil lean to shack, in clapboard house what somebody cart from one lot to the next. No power. No water. Just couple hole in the ground with shack over them for toilet. We gone into house after house, and the fella-dem chasing down shadow in the bush, and I pulling people out they bed. (Bethel 2008, 76)

These raids to protect the nation enable the direct violence that spills over into cultural violence, where it is justifiable to exploit those who are "illegal," as Stacey notes. They recite Bible passages as if to enact the cultural duplicity and Janus face of civility that has encapsulated the culture, especially since colonialism. Neville states clearly as he leaves: "My house falling down. Build it up" (Bethel 2008, 78). As the father who has eaten sour grapes, he is aware of the damage that is befalling his family.

The play underscores the multiple levels of violence and dispossession embedded in the colonial system within which young Black males are disenfranchised, women are ignored except to have violence visited upon them, and land is sold out from under many who are unaware of the dissolution of and underhanded goings on in their family units. Likewise, the characters in the play grapple with the complete social dissolution of civility and trust. Ross represents a newer generation who will dislocate his entire family for his own benefit. He and Blanche speak similar languages of hate and xenophobia, but also of self-interested focus. As Ross and Donnie have it out, the seeping violence continues to reverberate through the play. In Act II Scene 5, as he accuses her of abandoning him, she tells him:

> I leave you cause Max give me something to live for. Ain't you was boning everything that move? I'n leave to get married. I leave cause Daddy was dying. I'n know why I leave. But when Max turn round and tell me say, Come with me, I just say yes. Wasn't like you was ga miss me. (Bethel 2008, 84)

The structural violence manifests more directly in Ross's final response to Donnie: "HOLD STILL, BITCH, LEMME KILL YOU!!!" (Bethel 2008, 86). But rather than kill Donnie, in his drunken rage Ross accidentally shoots Stacey; as he seeks his own fortune at everyone else's expense, he represents all the bad of the violence and toxic masculinity that has developed in Bahamian culture.

In *The Children's Teeth* and the world outside the fiction of the play, there are no safe spaces; there are no untinged possibilities. Tourism, the once golden chalice, is as bad as enslavement, as Donnie hints at in a monologue later in the play. The culture of consumption and the consumption of culture condoned through coloniality impact the entire household in different ways. Development is Janus-faced, as what feeds the family also catastrophically devours it.

Conclusion: Violence and Loss

We need to remember the biblical reference that so deeply informs the play's title: "The fathers have eaten sour grapes, and the children's teeth are set on edge" (Ezekiel 18:2). Loss is deeper than the ocean. The violence in these plays folds itself into the very creases of the social fabric and washes through and over like waves. The father's deeds are visited on the children. The foreshadowing is intentional. Independence was for some, but not all. This is similarly the case with the deeds of the colonial power being visited on those who issue from it but claim no connection to it nor benefit from it. Bethel's house in *The Children's Teeth* and the waterscape in Strachan's *Diary* provide backdrops for the coloniality of space. Space is deeply colonized and usually by White, paternalist, patriarchal power. I highlight Strachan's and Bethel's work to act as a foil to the media performance of otherness (that perpetuates the colonized view). Their art recaptures the "forgotten" drownings and discriminations on stage that the media presents in de-contextualized spaces where meaning is transformed into threat/danger. Bell hooks reminds us: "We have to constantly critique imperialist white supremacist patriarchal culture because it is normalized by mass media and rendered unproblematic" (hooks 2006, 61). Theater does this. This duality of stage and performance then transcends the physical into what is later Dorian, which becomes a stage for loss and Black suffering. Dorian becomes an almost metaphysical stage where catastrophe becomes linked to invisible Black bodies left nameless. However, because news reporting was "managed," much of the significance of the suffering inflicted by Dorian disappears from view.

As *Diary of Souls* recounts the experience of a "boat load" of Haitian migrants in The Bahamas, Max Taylor's etching evoked at the beginning of this essay shows the dehumanization of the masses, the loads of human animals, always colonized, always Black, always erased by indifference. Indifference is catastrophic as it marshals thousands to death chambers. In *Diary of Souls*, Strachan's fictionalized event occurs in the early 1990s, yet its repercussions and cultural manifestations reverberate across the decades. The verisimilar nature of the event, the play, and its reverberations when performed are culturally significant when the postcolony lives in denial of such tragedies and territorial strips, colonized spaces that can be cleansed of all human animals. In these older communities, as in Bethel's *The Children's Teeth*, the promise of independence dissolves in spatial recolonization and violent waves of irresponsible masculinity, all of which seem to foreground a deficient decolonial process. The flooding of the cultural space with investor greed and national poverty are invisible disasters, though, and so carry on unperceived. When memories are erased, so too is lived history. As James Baldwin states in the documentary film *I Am Not Your Negro*, "History is not the past. It is the present. We carry our history with us. We are our history. If we pretend otherwise, we are literally criminals." These plays document how criminal such rewritings and erasures can be.

So, too, are the tragedies and disasters that occur on the seas ignored. The collective trauma is dismissed, the impact on the social scape denied. The bodies of the characters Sylvie, Pol, and others become conflated with those who died in the sinking vessel in 2017 and with Dorian's wave in 2019. They are Others exiled to a land they never knew, but were made to see as their home, or relegated to watery graves where their names, though possibly registered somewhere in an official book, cannot be found as if they had never existed and so cannot be counted in Dorian's wake. Walcott notes, "The Sea is History" and I hope to have shown that the colonized seascape is life and death as it holds history firmly in its waves and forces violence-like laws on those it deems lesser humans. This decolonial theatre and writing helps avoid disaster.

Notes

1. See Taylor's etching here: https://nagb.org.bs/national-collection/entries/entry/?folder_id=7b9a8590-d836-11eb-9d7f-23d85b50e27a&page_number=1&entry_id=9bf88f80-a6bd-11eb-b481-fffa0e42c804.
2. In prior socio-cultural work, I spoke to several former law enforcement officers and got first-hand accounts of the cruelties inflicted on young Black Bahamian and Haitians in this Bahamian postcolony. The structures may now be hidden to some extent but they remain operative in othering citizens as they did when Blacks were either property or simply had *fewer* rights in law. In some cases, the law did not and does not "protect" them from exploitation (Alexander 1994, Kamuguisha 2007).

Works Cited

Alexander, M. Jacqui. 1994. Not Just (Any)Body Can Be a Citizen: The Politics of Law, Sexuality and Postcoloniality in Trinidad and Tobago and the Bahamas. *Feminist Review* 48 (Autumn): 5–23.

Baldwin, James, writer, and Raoul Peck, director. 2016. *I Am Not Your Negro*. Independent Lens, Magnolia Pictures.

Bethel, Nicolette. 2008. *The Children's Teeth*. Nassau, Bahamas.

Césaire, Aimé. 2000. *A Discourse on Colonialism*. Translated by Joan Pinkham. New York: Monthly Review Press.

Danticat, Edwidge. 1996. *Krik? Krak!* New York: Soho Press.

Elkins, Caroline. 2022. *Legacy of Violence*. New York: Knopf.

Fanon, Frantz. 1961. *The Wretched of the Earth*. Introduced by Jean-Paul Sartre. Translated by Constance Farrington. London: MacGibbon & Kee, Penguin.

Galtung, Johan. 1969. Violence, Peace, and Peace Research. *Journal of Peace Research* 6 (3): 167–191.

hooks, bell. 2006. *Homegrown: Engaged Cultural Criticism*. Boston: South End Press.

Kamuguisha, Aaron. 2007. The Coloniality of Citizenship in the contemporary Anglophone Caribbean. *Race and Class* 4 (2): 20–40.

Nixon, Rob. 2011. *Slow Violence and the Environmentalism of the Poor*. Cambridge: Harvard University Press.

Said, Edward. 1978. *Orientalism*. New York: Vintage.

Soja, Edward. 2009. The City and Spatial Justice. Translated by Sophie Didier, Frédéric Dufaux. *justice spatiale | spatial justice* 1 (September). https://www.jssj.org/wp-content/uploads/2012/12/JSSJ1-1en4.pdf

Strachan, Ian. 2006. *Diary of Souls*. Nassau, Bahamas: Cerasee Books.

Walcott, Derek. 2007. The Sea Is History. In *Selected Poems*. New York: Farrar, Straus and Giroux.

CHAPTER 8

"No More Drumming. Nor Sticks": The Colonial Catastrophe that Conditioned Caribbean Performance

Shrabani Basu

INTRODUCTION

"Salting the earth," a much controversial aspect of warfare, not only alludes to the indemnity of the victors in possible annihilatory actions against the defeated but also hints at systematic destabilization of the defeated against any future dissent. Roman general Scipio Aemilianus's legendary destruction of the city of Carthage at the end of the Third Punic War in c.146 BCE was followed by plowing the soil with salt to make any resurgence impossible and is considered by many as the most distinctive instance of cultural annihilation. Despite the probable figurative usage of salt to render soil infertile, the act of cultural annihilation and overhaul has been a continuing practice in conflicts. Barbara

---

S. Basu (✉)
Department of English, Deshabandhu Mahavidyalaya, Chittaranjan, West Bengal, India
e-mail: shrabani@dbmcrj.ac.in

© The Author(s), under exclusive license to Springer Nature Switzerland AG 2025
C. Stevens and J. D. Rossini (eds.), *The Coloniality of Catastrophe in Caribbean Theater and Performance*,
https://doi.org/10.1007/978-3-031-85791-1_8

Romaine in her "Evolution of a Storyteller: the 'Ḥakawātī' against the Threat of Cultural Annihilation" refers to the Latin phrase *damnation memoriae* as a method for impugning the memory of a defeated individual or statement once fallen from grace (Romaine 2007–2008, 256). This removal of the defeated from "contemporary and historical consciousness" consistently obliterates a cultural position once a more dominant culture succeeds in disenfranchising it (Romaine 2007–2008, 256). Enforced obliviation of cultural memory is actualized in various ways, all conditioned by the context of the power equation. Romaine's argument on cultural annihilation suggests a mass amnesia imposed on a displaced or overpowered populace, misplacing their cultural self as the dominant culture erases and replaces the memories with elements previously alien to it. This "artificial reconstruction of history" (Kundera quoted in Romaine 2007–2008, 257) creates a void in the disenfranchised culture through epistemic catastrophic violence. Erasing cultural and communal memory acts as the first and the most important step of systematic liquidation of a generation or a heritage of inherited mnemonic identity. Romaine quotes Kundera to establish this practice as a recurrent trope of colonialism where a nation is "hoodwinked" (Romaine 2007–2008, 258) into forgetting not only what they are but also what they used to be. The strategies for effecting this erasure are never uniform and may range from brute force to subtle cultural overhaul, where an alternative norm is fixed as a model and all differing practices are gradually weeded out.

It is not unusual to associate "catastrophe" with literature; many texts either literally narrate a catastrophic event or figuratively dub some event or chain of misfortunes "catastrophic" to a certain community. The inherent association of catastrophe with a persistent rhetoric of loss can also be found in most literary case studies. For instance, Thomas J. Lynn holds Chinua Achebe's short story "Civil Peace" as a tale of personal/communal catastrophe experienced by a Nigerian family in the wake of the Nigerian Civil War (1967–1970). According to Lynn, Achebe creates a time of chaos where war provokes the worst efforts of human survival through violence, deceit, and opportunism, thereby conditioning increasingly apparent conflict and aggression (Lynn 2010, 73). On the other hand, Ken Urban, in his "An Ethics of Catastrophe: The Theatre of Sarah Kane" characterizes Kane's *Blasted* as a realistic portrayal of "intense experience" (Urban 2001, 36) stemming from political angst, social dystrophy, and the playwright's externalization of her social maladjustment. Kane's debut play percolated into the British post-Thatcher sentiment when the personal tragedy of a dying journalist became the center of a political skirmish. Urban, refreshingly irreverent toward the system, applauds Kane as one who defines an "ethics of catastrophe" in her gritty portrayal of social "filth" (Urban 2001, 37). For his part, Alan Rosen, in his commentary on Samuel Beckett's play *Catastrophe*, alludes to Donastus's definition of catastrophe as an act of unraveling, where the outcome of the play is either predicted or demonstrated. For Rosen, a catastrophe predicts the outcome, regardless of the attempts at deterrence amidst the moment of disaster and the moment of the consequence. This inevitability, once added to the perspectives expressed by Lynn and Urban, creates a certain sense that catastrophes in cultures are irreversible. Neither Lynn nor Urban directly addresses catastrophe as a cultural effect. Rather, they place before us a possible definition of a catastrophe or a disaster that is in line with the tenets propounded in Mathematics and Environmental Science yet specific to the context of vanishing cultures and the colonialist impact on indigeneity. A catastrophe or a disaster, hence, can be any "intense experience," perceived communally (or personally), effecting a permanent change in the face of cultural resilience, from which the affected community does not bounce back. Catastrophes, therefore, are non-linear and disruptive, but do not last permanently; if they did, they would have been internalized as a regular event, rather than an aberration from normative linearity. This chapter focuses on the way that colonialism, experienced as catastrophe, irretrievably changes indigenous cultures.

One of the many catastrophic consequences of colonialism is its systematic strategy of annihilating indigenous religious and cultural forms, imposing a homogeneous colonial code of conduct. While certain elements of cultural preservation were recorded in South Asian colonies (funds for the rise of vernacular literature, translation projects, government policies for officials to learn local languages, especially in the Bengal Presidency in India), in the Caribbean islands, there were instances of complete cultural overhaul, with enforced whitewashing of moral frameworks with an insistence of Victorian prudery.[1] This chapter tentatively traces the colonial attempt to eliminate elements of Afro-Caribbean performances associated with the anglophone Caribbean theater, and the subsequent resistance reflected in it. I focus on Trinidadian playwright Rawle Gibbons's *I Lawah* (1985), *Shepherd* (1981), and *Ogun Ayan—As in Pan* (2006), which recreate the heritage of the various Caribbean folk forms to narrate a communal history of an intensely creolized society. Each addresses a cultural tradition—Canboulay and calypso, Baptist mourning rituals, Carnival—to reenact moments in the Caribbean collective memory. From the Canboulay Riots of the late nineteenth century to the mid-twentieth century Windrush era, each presents an instance of a colonial ban or a restrictive policy change targeting Afro-Caribbean cultures. The present study concentrates on *I Lawah* and *Shepherd* from the trilogy, with a cursory look at the third play to establish the effect on secular and religious rituals and the identification of a certain class of people with it. While it is not unprecedented to ascribe colonialism within a rhetoric of catastrophe/disaster (as in Danielle Zoe Riviera and Jenna N. Hanachey's works for instance), it is imperative to hold colonialism as a catastrophe that obliterates representative cultural practices, thereby altering particular cultural outputs. Caribbean theater needs to be reevaluated as a legatee of such obliterations as well as a record of resistance and resilience against the attempts at erasure, by examining specifically whether secular performances and religious performances reacted differently in the face of such ordinances.

The *Love Trilogy* and the Death of the Performance

Rawle Gibbons's *I Lawah*, *Shepherd*, and *Ogun Ayan—as in Pan*, collectively published as *Love Trilogy* in 2012, recreate instances of Caribbean cultural performance in moments of possible extinction: the Canboulay riots of the late nineteenth century and a moment in the history of Spiritual Baptists during the first half of the twentieth century when it was prohibited. The plays may be understood by the reader/audience as an interwoven recounting of crises and survival. Hugh Stultz, in his "Introduction" to the volume, dubs them interwoven secular rituals, insistent in narrating the collective Caribbean past, ensuring its perpetuity in the face of annihilation through "the range of historical, social and psycho-emotional dramas […] show[ing] the triumph of the human spirit over adversity, the necessity of hope against the odds" (Gibbons 2012, xiii). Each of these practices serves as an organic vein connecting the once robust past to the still pulsating survivor(s) of the present catastrophe. This viscerality of the moment, albeit gory, promises a renewal, opening "doorways to our hopes" (Gibbons 2012, xiii).

For Gibbons, performances are essentially acts of dissension, constantly running the risk of stagnation. Hence, while any effort to neutralize performance may irretrievably amputate crucial moments of cultural history, it may also bolster practices by posing the challenge to reinvent themselves. This essentially defines Gibbons's academic centeredness with the idea of "third theatre." Following the analysis of Gibbons's plays by Louis Regis, the "third theatre" appears to be an inherently hybrid performance that supposedly brings forward "the erstwhile marginal or invisible folk to centre stage and invest[s] them with the complex human emotions and passions denied the descendants of the enslaved or the indentured" (Regis 2017, 183). However, Regis also admits that though the plays of the "third theatre" commendably attempt indigenization of theatrical traditions and contribute to the nationalization project, the polarized inheritance of the first (European theatrical tradition) and the second (the ritualistic folk theatre of the Asian, African, and Amerindian traditions) theater is still not resolved in the "third theatre" (Basu 2022, 120). The third theatre, therefore, remains a space of crises, perpetually accommodating the complexities of the multifaceted Caribbean society. These crises pose contemporary theatrical performance as an inheritance of communal experiences that have fashioned theater over the ages, showcasing the disruptions, attempts of renewal, as well as resistances against them. This foregrounding of catastrophe or disaster, as an action of unwelcome renewal, aligns with Danielle Zoé Rivera's thesis that disaster operates not as isolated instances of crisis and damage, but "as compounding and interconnected with societal histories" (Rivera 2020, 126). This argument, though meant as a warning map for climate change, projects disasters as inevitabilities rising from a certain turn in societal histories. Although this position may be criticized as victim-blaming, when more sensitively analyzed, it puts the onus of most societal disasters on oppressive power-play:

> Disaster capitalism unwittingly obscures the history of these practices by focusing almost exclusively on what has happened since the "disaster" (in this case the powerful Hurricanes Irma and Maria), while obviating continuities inherited from the past. (Woods quoted in Rivera 2020, 129)

For Rivera, hence, disasters and crises are both the outcome and the tool for racial violence and colonial oppression. This, for Rivera, distinguishes between colonialism and coloniality, as the latter encompasses similar long-standing effects of political and administrative colonialism, including "the long-standing patterns of power that emerged as a result of colonialism, but that define culture, labor, intersubjective relations, and knowledge production well beyond the strict limits of colonial administrations" (Maldonado-Torres quoted in Rivera 2020, 127). Citing the case study of disaster in Puerto Rico in particular and the Caribbean in general, Rivera proposes a characterization of disaster as the principal effect of the maintenance of something she calls "coloniality of being" (2020, 127). In Riviera's postulation, this reaches its peak (let's call it "catastrophe") when the old dies before the new has a chance to be born, creating a cultural void. This void is what coloniality seeks to create, as it fills it with youth in its own image. This obviation of the past, and a focus on a desperate need for the new, without analyzing the nature of this new or the responsibility of an encroaching power in creating the disaster, magnifies the crisis. At the center of this systematic erasure, is the fundamental manifestation of colonial policy—extractivism, where the exploitation and extraction of natural, material, environmental, and cultural materials from the colonized people gut them of any sense of "self" or "identity." Authors like Naomi Klein present another rhetoric of colonial catastrophe, more pertinent in the postcolonial context, where much of the disasters are strategically engineered to create "interregnums" where normal administrative actions will be suspended, thereby making brutish interventions to change cultural and religious changes easier and unnoticed. These interventions manifest in late-nineteenth century Trinidadian culture through the legal prohibition of flambeaux (1881), the flaming torches at the heart of the Canboulay, reducing a powerful social gathering into a nice, pretty, folksy spectacle. These may also be tacit efforts to strip Carnival and Canboulay of its dissenting social history and narrative of resistance, where the very idea of "people's Carnival"[2] gave way to a sterilization of Trinidadian cultural identity that stripped it of its very character.

"FIRE IS WE. CANBOULAY"

Gibbons's *I Lawah* stages the journey of Lawah, Sophie, and Therese, three disenfranchised characters who, in the context of the 1881 Canboulay riots, generate or succumb to affirmations of their identity in the face of destruction and chaos. In spite of its titular focus on Lawah, a celebrated stickfighter and jamette, Sophie Bella, Lawah's companion and common-law wife, offers a more compelling point of focus as she wades through continual abuse not only from Lawah but from her employer

Monsieur Le Blanc. Sophie Bella's return to Canboulay dancing is a self-assertion away from the suffocation of domestic service, in the face of the riots, dramatizing the phoenix-like emergence of performance from the ashes of oppressive colonial injunctions. Therese, the daughter of the Le Blanc family, is forced to marry the despised Alexander De Gannes, a last gasp effort by the last of the French aristocratic planter class to forestall encroaching British colonialism.

The history of the practice of Canboulay and the ongoing cultural power and tensions manifest in its practice provide a rich context for these actions. Around 1797, when the British imperialist endeavors wrested control of Trinidad away from the Spanish crown, the white upper-class plantation owners were mostly first- and second-generation French creoles, who had settled in the Caribbean answering the call of Charles III of Spain. On two occasions in the eighteenth century, Charles III issued edicts to encourage Catholic settlement in Trinidad, which had been neglected by the Spanish crown and sparsely populated. The Spanish strategy for repopulating the Caribbean offered incentives to Catholic planters willing to pledge loyalty to the Spanish crown to emigrate, which also had the effect of limiting the entry of the British and Dutch navies. The resulting French cultural supremacy affected the religious, linguistic, and cultural practices of the island. French patois found space in common parlance, and the Catholic Carnival became adapted as the chief form of entertainment (Elder 1988, 38–39). Canboulay (a patois adaptation of *cannes brûlées* or cane burning) entered the foray predominantly post-emancipation, with the newly freed slaves burning sugarcane stalks to celebrate their freedom from chains.

> As a 'reenactment of the drama of bondage'[…], Canboulay remembered the brutalities of the colonial experience […] even more significant as a subversive practice because it demonstrates that a masquerade designed to degrade its subject can be taken over, invested with new meanings, and deployed as an empowering strategy. (Gilbert and Tompkins 1996, 79)

Like many other resistant forms of performance, the first explicit historical references emerge not at its inception but at the moment of legislative control and censorship as colonial powers attempted to ban it from the streets of Port of Spain, San Fernando, and Princes Town around 1881. The most glaring of these attempts to neutralize the most authentic cultural display of Afro-Caribbean slave community was Captain Baker's police attack on revelers in Port of Spain. The resulting series of violent altercations between the performers and the police force claimed lives as well as stood witness to mass protest from the largely working-class populace of the island. Consequentially, Canboulay, jamette, and chantwell—popular, yet underappreciated forms of pageantry—became marked as distinctive Black resistance performances, ritualistic dissension, popular street theater, and symbols of survival.[3] This resistance also generated a temporary alliance between the working-class stickfighters and the French Creole planters who saw the British repression as a typical instance of colonial cultural encroachment. This alliance resulted in the British Governor of the island formally reprimanding Baker and forbidding his police force from leaving the barracks for a few days. Moving beyond this explicit violent repression, Canboulay and Carnival also survived (albeit with changes) attempts of "moral white-washing," where the inherent "nonmoralistic exhibitionism" (Elder 1988, 39) was criticized by the prudish middle- and upper-class population who considered such anarchical corporeal display against the increasingly Victorian code of taste. The British effort to induce a transformation on the perceived violence and obscenity of the Canboulay persisted in the twentieth century, with Carnival sponsors attempting to sanitize the skimpy mas.[4]

The onslaught on the predominant culture does generate camaraderie and collective remonstration against the chaos. Gibbons uses this context to explore alternative possibilities, placing Sophie and Therese in a spatial juxtaposition, where each imagines emancipation in the space of the other. Therese views the Canboulay as a fascinating tool of emancipation, distinct from her stifling upper-class reality. On the other hand, Sophie wishes for an escape from the viscerality of the Yard and yearns for a certain respectability, which she imagines her service in the Le Blanc household will provide. The apparent blue-blooded docility of the Le Blanc household stands in juxtaposition with the energy of the Yard.

Whereas the spatial politics of the Canboulay is more subtle, the sound associated with the performance is less nuanced to read. Canboulay cries typically resonate with the deprivations of the working class, systematically tormented by racial and economic sidelining. As the increasingly aggressive jamette/boismen walk down the streets of Port of Spain in Gibbons's work, their voices become indistinguishable and increasingly belligerent as they become aware of Captain Baker's repressive intent. The Canboulay readies itself for confrontation, as erstwhile enemies strike a truce to confront the common foe, reinforcing the possible alliances emerging from a common enemy:

> LAWAH: [...] Word is police out to mash up we Canboulay. I say we join forces and meet them as one! [...] Helles Enfants say we meet them head on. [...] One fight! One signal! Helles Enfants will sound the war horn. Signal for all the yards! (Gibbons 2012, 42)

Lawah's call for solidarity is also reflective of an attempt to reclaim and shift the balance of power. In a symbolic act of resistance to the state-engineered cultural catastrophe, the Canboulay stick (bois) assumes the symbolic stature of a partisan's baton, appropriating the authority of the disaster of colonization in an attempt to neutralize it. Lawah's stick and his companion Zanana's hat are an attempt at colonial mimicry to reclaim power away from Baker's violence. But these machinations are unsuccessful despite various attempts to reimagine the terms of performance.

In addition to these shifting forms of resistance, there is also an explicit argument for direct confrontation and principled insistence on tradition, crucially voiced by one of the women jamettes:

> NEN: [...] No Canboulay? No Canboulay. The White Inspector say no drums, no fire, no bois. [...] Well, is Dimanche Gras and if jamet feteing inside like decent people, I have all the things whitepeople does use. The best of rum, I have paint, even grease, and for decoration? Gle gle, mirrors and swansdown, look mas for so, wire, stocking, papier mache, (Pause) only the bois you don't bound for, the bois and the fire. [...] So dearies, dance like your betters. [...] Dance their music better than self. (Gibbons 2012, 75–76)

Nen's call for dissent can be interpreted not only as a conflict on racial grounds but also for a class-based confrontation. Moreover, Nen's words reinstate the ontology of Canboulay as a celebration of emancipation from the colonizer's bondage appropriating the music (substituting the accompaniments for western music with local made instruments) and performance of them into energetic reveling. Despite this feverish call for rebellion, Gibbons pits the blustering of the boismen against the cold finality of the militia police, in a style strangely reminiscent of disaster films with the approaching giant waves or slow-moving lava juxtaposed with the grit of the fleeing survivors. However, in a curious moment of anticlimax, Captain Baker disarms Lawah and symbolically removes his bois:

> BAKER: No more drumming. Nor sticks. (Retrieves Lawah's) From now, this moment, the brandishing of torches through the streets is strictly forbidden. No torches, understand? What's more, the same holds for your infernal masking. I want none of it. (Removes hat from Zanana.) Your carnival is over. (Gibbons 2012, 72)

Baker's action in retrieving Lawah's bois and Zanana's hat, which he was using to impersonate Baker himself, suggests a ritualistic destruction—the catastrophe seemingly is complete, and the affected population, overpowered. In practice, while not fully banned, the gradual gentrification of the Canboulay performances, as the jamette performers adapt to accommodate the injunctions imposed by the colonial authorities, is perhaps the casualty that no disaster can ever avoid.

But Gibbons refuses this slow evolution, highlighting the transformative power in the moment of conflict. In a moment of near annihilation, hope surfaces amongst the underdogs, in the form of the female jamettes, who plan to take over the acts of dissension. As Nen and the other women start their own flambeaux (procession with flaming torches), Sophie and Therese join the offense. In a symbolic categorization of destructive force, Lawah is relegated to play Alexander de Gannes, Therese's suitor. Elsewhere Therese seemingly sacrifices herself in the fires of the Canboulay, iconically draping a jamette-style costume of fire around her instead of the docile and respectable dress for her engagement with de Gannes.

> MADAME: What is it? What's that burning?
> SOPHIE: Dancing, dancing.
> [...]
> SOPHIE: Free. I will be free. (Gibbons 2012, 80, 81)

Through Therese's self-immolating bid for liberty, Sophie finds her deliverance, as she walks out on the Le Blancs and prepares for her performance. With the fire of dissonance joining her with the now martyred Therese, Sophie returns to her vocation, taking up the bois and standing her ground against the colonial onslaught:

> SOPHIE: Fire. Shantwelle? [...]
> Your tongue is mine. Fire. (Whirls among them)

[…] Fire on my wrist. Take it.
[…] Fire in my arms. Hold me.
[…] Fire, fire in me skin. Touch me.
[…] Foot is fire tonight. We walking, one foot for who we is, one for who we go be. We walking and who stopping we?
[…] Fire is we. Canboulay! (Gibbons 2012, 86–87)

With this unexpected opposition from the women leading the Canboulay, Baker and Todd are taken aback as they are swept away against the onslaught of the frenzied fire that Canboulay literally induces.[5]

Interestingly, Gibbons starts his 2006 play *Ogun Ayan—As in Pan* in the deep Orisha tradition of the Yoruba culture with references to Shango cultism, as the play's spatio-temporal context of the actions points towards Africa before World War II, where the narrative oscillates between a conversation between the warrior god of iron Ogun, and the river goddess Oshun, while some characters are either fleeing the involuntary conscription of young boys to the Allied force, or negotiating the dilemma between African heritage and European education. With each act the play shifts towards the more contemporary Caribbean as the picture of Carnival is changed by the beginning of consumerist performance for the American soldiers in Trinidad. As Shango Irene and Kanga reminisce about the battle for Carnival, when the "Red House burn with the rage of the people" (Gibbons: 2012, 197), they also admit that even though nobody won, they resiliently persisted shouting "No! Thousands of we with one voice" (198). As the play closes with other, more organized Steelband performers fundraising for a proposed UK tour, Kanga, Shabba, and Pa Priest revive the traditional Orisha performance Ogun Ayan, with the vigorous fiery dance of Ogun with Shango. This hopeful return is a necessary contrast to the religious and spiritual resistance explored in *Shepherd*, the first work of Gibbons's trilogy.

Shepherd: Shouters Prohibition Ordinance

Gibbons plans *Shepherd*, the second of his *Love Trilogy* (though composed first), as a cyclical celebration of life and mourning for death. Deeply suggestive of suppression and loss, the play establishes a flock of worshipers led by the Shepherd praying after the demise of a Sister Dora from their congregation, and simultaneously preparing Clarisse for the impending birth of her son. The setting of the play signifies the austere minimum of a Spiritual Baptist community with the "faded black flag" (Gibbons 2012, 96) of mourning, mounted simply on a bamboo pole. Apart from it, there is but an altar with a Bible, some stones and candles, suggesting a necessity for quick flight if discovered by the authorities. Moreover, the absence of drumming except on two occasions for the entire duration of the play, stresses the necessity for secrecy imposed by the Shouters Prohibition Ordinance.

> [...] Leaders
> are killed, but we do not
> mourn, sons are gone but we come
> not in mourning; we come
> [...] to sing the bullets' song, to crack
> the loudspeaker's brittle fact to
> riddle with truth the tyrant's tight
> fist [...] (Gibbons 2012, 97)

A certain discomfort regarding the Spiritual Baptists, commonly (and somewhat derogatorily) dubbed Shouters, owing to their practice of shouting out chants with loud claps, dancing, and singing, was recorded in media as early as 1890s. This was when the French Catholics and British Protestants of the twin islands noticed that their efforts towards social and religious dominance through conflict had made it possible for more Afro-centric religious orders to find their way in the communal psyche (Fadeke Castor 2013, 480). Thus, there was a temporary truce among the two dominant religious sects as the British administration sought to stamp out any "African" presence in the religious practices of the region, culminating in the Spiritual Baptists Ordinance of 1912 in St. Vincent and the Shouters Prohibition Ordinance of 1917 that "outlawed person from holding flowers or a lighted candle in their hands at a public meeting, ringing bell or wearing a white head tie, and from any form of shaking of the body" (Frances Henry quoted in Fadeke Castor 2013, 481). The Ordinance did not attract wide dissension as there was a deep-seated bias against the "action" involved in Baptist rituals, different from the enforced sobriety of the then middle-class ethos:

> The prejudice implicit in the Shouters Prohibition Ordinance has been attributed prim fact that the possession phenomenon [...] whereby the personality of the devotee is displaced by what is believed to be the Spirit of the Holy Ghost, [caused one] to sing, shout, dance, stamp, prophesy

or cure. [...] To a public striving for "respectability," as manifested in the social and cultural mores of the white colonial power, the Baptist form of worship appeared particularly repugnant. (Marjorie Thorpe quoted in Butler, 2002)

There was an additional clause put in a Summary Conviction Offenses Ordinance dated May 19, 1921, which specifically targeted the "African" religious practices including Obeah, Bongo, and drumming after 10 p.m. The Shouters Prohibition Act, coming into effect November 28, 1917, not only prohibited the religious sect from convening and worshiping freely but it also imposed an administrative sanction allowing breaking and entering any household under reasonable suspicion of Shouters activity, including initiation, with a financial penalty of two hundred and forty dollars, a ridiculously high fine for the time. The ordinance states:

Police may enter, without warrant, house or place where Shouters' meeting is being held 7. (1) It shall be lawful for any party of members of the Police Force, of whom one shall be a Gazetted Police Officer or Subordinate Police Officer, without a warrant to enter at any time of the day or night, any house, estate, land, or place in or on which such Gazetted Police Officer or Subordinate Police Officer may have good ground to believe or suspect that s Shouters' meeting is being held or where he may have good ground to believe or suspect that any person or persons is or are being kept for the purpose of initiation into the ceremonies of the Shouters, and to take the names and addresses of all persons present at such Shouters' meeting or Shouters' house. ("Shouters Prohibition Ordinance Trinidad 1917" 1917)

This led the Baptists and the other quasi-African religious orders literally to the "bush," or the forests where the congregations secretly convened to worship. The protests lasted from the 1930s led by Uriah Butler and later by Elton George Griffith in the 1940s, till 1951, when the Ordinance was finally repealed. This series of persecutions lent a sense of secrecy and resistance to the rituals of the Baptists, changing the site and even the nature of their rituals to maintain the cover.

The opening chorus of the play implies a celebration of sacrifice and dissent in the face of oppression, as the hope of the congregation rests in "a child to be raised" among the sterility of a barren church site. As a result, the Shepherd urges the Pilgrim to silence: "Don't talk! Don't talk! Less your voice whisper the waves moan I hearing each and every season"

(Gibbons 2012, 105), as the only way to survive is to seek cover in the bushes, in the abandoned shores and to make their shouts blend with the nature around. As the congregation mourns "[t]hings have changed. There are no more warriors" (106), the Seer foresees decades of trouble (118) and the congregation survives with memories of "[…] blood. Dogs. The whip. And the fire" (122). The Prover's words point at the persecution as "revolt was squashed" and the leaders are hunted (128), and yet the Shepherd's long sermon brings forth the "hope of new birth":

> Yet we survived the bush, and the boots that broke our drums and trampled our offerings underfoot, and the raids by men whose faith was the office they wore, not their colour, and the keepers of peace with their complaints and the owners of land with their lawsuits and the owners of Christ with their curses. We survived them all, putting behind us the days of the bush. (151)

Though the religious scenario in the post-millennium Trinidad has changed considerably, Spiritual Baptists and Shango cults have long been associated with the idea of the oppressed and the rhetoric of protest. Stephen Glazier suggests that the advent of the Spiritual Baptist religion arises from a need among the deprived to form a religious community, like most Afro-Caribbean religions (Glazier 1993, 2). Glazier writes:

> It is important to recognize that in many respects, anthropologists and sociologists have failed to come to terms with contemporary Caribbean religions. When scholars, such as anthropologist I.M. Lewis, use the Spiritual Baptists and Shango to illustrate general theories of religion and protest or religion and deprivation, they often base their interpretations on data collected thirty of forty years ago. Many changes have taken place in both Caribbean religions and Caribbean societies over the past forty years. Frequently, these changes have been ignored in the academic study of Caribbean religions. (Glazier 1993, 1)

However, Glazier also admits to the change that has been wrought across most ethno-religious communities in the Caribbean, largely conditioned by European and American incursions. Though a predominantly working-class Black religion, of late Spiritual Baptism has also attracted membership from other ethnic communities of the Trinbagoian society. Though there have been allegations of imitations between the two religious cults—Spiritual Baptists and Shango—owing to certain similarities in their rituals, both carry their share of ethno-historic narrative as descendants from Africanized Christianity, as alternates to the forbidden traditional African forms of worship. Thus, many religious anthropologists have commented that both Shango and Spiritual Baptists are "cover" to traditional African rituals. However, the Spiritual Baptists' presence in urban residential areas has led to more and more aggressive restrictions.

Conclusion

While the Canboulay riots were more immediate and disruptive, directly precipitating from the 1881 prohibition, the Prohibition Ordinances of 1912, 1917, and 1921 created a long-lasting suppression of Afro-centric religious practices, permanently changing the character of Shango, Spiritual Baptist, and to a certain extent Rastafarianism. One can wonder whether there is a possibility of surviving a cultural catastrophe, when the immediate effect of the onslaught has disintegrated the essential core of a performance. For both *I Lawah* and *Shepherd*, the ordinances and prohibitions are absolute. While *I Lawah* offers a swift literal clapping out against a compelling injunction, *Shepherd* survives more gradually, as religion and rituals prove to be simultaneously resilient and yet slow to revive from the ban. The obvious efforts at "salting the earth" are resisted in degrees. Gibbons's justification for anthologizing the three plays may be an attempt to record the evolution of resistance against prohibitive policies imposed by an oppressive state mechanism. As recorded in history, Spiritual Baptist practices survive and flourish after the ordinance is repealed, but it takes decades for the shouts and claps to find their way back. The fiery Canboulay resists the ban vigorously, and yet as *Ogun Ayan* shows, it changes its face to accommodate the growing consumerist demands.

While Gilbert and Tompkins define Caribbean performance as a new cultural articulation created in the amalgamation of disparate fragments of the cultures in residence, there is an expectation for spectacle and energy, where the near ritualistic actants of the performance not only affect their own "physical welfare and alter their own emotional consciousness, as well as those of their audience" (Gilbert and Tompkins 1996, 62). And yet, in Gibbons's theater, Caribbean cultural existence, uniquely participatory in its externalization, is articulated in the "new theatre," strangely resonant of Louis Regis's idea of the "third theatre," as a declining form, where recurrent epistemic violence creates deep fissures, callously smoothed out by policymakers. The catastrophe is not always arbitrary and isolated like the Canboulay ban but can be a result of gradually increasing bigotry, suddenly erupting into a series of religious and racist intolerance. Gibbons's plays are commentaries on how the enforced middle-class propriety changed the ethical fiber of the performance (both cultural and religious) in popular perception, with any deviation from colonial policies of respectability, strictly persecuted. While in *I Lawah*, the disaster is immediate and recognized clearly, and hence can be successfully contested, *Shepherd* articulates the aftermath of the catastrophe more gradually, thus making any dissent longstanding and offering an alternative time scale for the thinking of resistance. In this sense, we are left to consider whether the final play of the trilogy and its cyclical return is a hopeful model for forms of resistance or an inevitable pattern of necessary accommodation.

Notes

1. Though not directly pertinent, a continuing effect of colonial disaster can be traced in the slowly disappearing oral folk song traditions in the Eastern cultural pockets of India. The aggressive colonial policies in these indigenous belts had prioritized the majoritarian linguistic and cultural tropes, deliberately sidelining folk song traditions like *bhadu, tusu, jhumur, gajan*, etc., with charges of viscerality, violence, and obscenity. As a result, even three-quarters of a century after Independence, these communities speak and perform in languages not ethnically their own, with the folk traditions on the brink of disappearance.
2. Shannon Dudley quotes Anna Maria Alonso in describing the long-lasting effect of such prohibitive colonial policies in post-1962 Trinidad where the creativity, profanity, ebullience, and defiance of Carnival are neutralized, thereby essentially killing it (2003, 13).
3. For more on Trinidad's jamette Carnival traditions, see: https://nationalarchivestt.wordpress.com/2016/01/08/the-carnival-of-the-underworld-trinidads-jamette-carnival/.
4. The practice of masquerading and reveling in revealing and eye-catching costumes during the Carnival parade has attracted mass objectification and censure. This is considered one of the most obvious instances of spatio-temporal permissiveness, characteristic of a Carnival.

5. The role of women in healing the wounds of catastrophe offers scope for further research. However, attempts can be made to connect my earlier study on the experience of cultural hybridity and resilience of female performers in the face of patriarchal confrontation throughout the postcolonial Caribbean.

WORKS CITED

Basu, Shrabani. 2022. *Gendered Identity and the Lost Female: Hybridity as a Partial Experience in the Anglophone Caribbean Performances*. Palgrave Macmillan.

Butler, Gary R. 2002. Personal Experience Narratives and the Social Construction of Meaning in Confrontational Discourse. *The Journal of American Folklore* 115 (456): 154–174. https://www.jstor.org/stable/4129217.

Dudley, Shannon. 2003. Creativity and Control in Trinidad Carnival Competitions. *The World of Music* 45 (1): 11–33. https://www.jstor.org/stable/41700086.

Elder, J.D. 1988. Cannes brûlées. *TDR* 42 (3): 38–43. https://www.jstor.org/stable/1146678.

Fadeke Castor, N. 2013. Shifting Multicultural Citizenship: Trinidad Orisha Opens the Road. *Cultural anthropology* 28 (3): 475–489. https://www.jstor.org/stable/43898484.

Gibbons, Rawle. 2012. *Love Trilogy*. Trinidad and Tobago and Jamaica: Canboulay productions & Arawak publications.

Gilbert, Helen, and Joanne Tompkins. 1996. *Post-colonial Drama: Theory, Practice*. Politics: Routledge.

Glazier, Stephen D. 1993. Funerals and Mourning in the Spiritual Baptist and Shango Traditions. *Caribbean Quarterly* 39 (3/4): 1–11. https://www.jstor.org/stable/40653856.

Lynn, Thomas J. 2010. Catastrophe, Aftermath, Amnesia: Chinua Achebe's 'Civil Peace'. *Peace Research* 42 (1/2): 73–88. https://www.jstor.org/stable/23607877.

Regis, Louis. 2017. Rawle Gibbons and the Theory and Practice of the Third Theatre. *Caribbean Quarterly* 63 (2–3): 183–202. https://doi.org/10.1080/00086495.2017.1352269.

Rivera, Danielle Zoé. 2020. Disaster Colonialism: A Commentary on Disasters beyond Singular Events to Structural Violence. *International Journal of Urban and Regional Research* 46 (1): 126–135. https://doi.org/10.1111/1468-2427.12950.

Romaine, Barbara. 2007–2008. Evolution of a Storyteller: the "Ḥakawātī" Against the Threat of Cultural Annihilation. *Al-'Arabiyya* 40/41: 257–263. https://www.jstor.org/stable/43195702.

"Shouters Prohibition Ordinance Trinidad 1917." 1917. Obeah Histories. https://obeahhistories.org/shouters-prohibition-ordinance/.

"The Carnival of the Underworld—Trinidad's Jamette Carnival." 2016. National Archives of Trinidad and Tobago. https://nationalarchivestt.wordpress.com/2016/01/08/the-carnival-of-the-underworld-trinidads-jamette-carnival/.

Urban, Ken. 2001. An Ethics of Catastrophe: The Theatre of Sarah Kane. *PAJ: A Journal of Performance and Art* 23 (3): 36–46. https://www.jstor.org/stable/3246332.

CHAPTER 9

Interrogating Disaster Through Apocalyptic Narratives in Dominican Theater

José Emilio Bencosme Zayas

On November 4, 2022, Santo Domingo, the capital of the Dominican Republic, experienced one of its worst floods of the twenty-first century. The National Meteorological Office (Onamet) reported that in just three hours more than 50% of the average monthly total rainfall had deluged the city (Diario Libre 2022). The story repeated itself in mid-November 2023 when a storm took the life of 34 people due to structural damage caused by a record rainfall that exceeded the previous year's disaster (Hoy 2023). Images of cars crushed by the fallen walls of an underpass in one of the main avenues circulated all over social media and major news outlets. Dominican cartoonist Poteleche published a cartoon on November 22, 2023, showing how the population of Santo Domingo had developed a new response stemming from the trauma caused by these episodes: people begin to run for their lives as soon as clouds appear in the sky (De los Santos 2023).

J. E. Bencosme Zayas (✉)
Santo Domingo, Dominican Republic
e-mail: je@emiliobencosme.com

© The Author(s), under exclusive license to Springer Nature Switzerland AG 2025
C. Stevens and J. D. Rossini (eds.), *The Coloniality of Catastrophe in Caribbean Theater and Performance*,
https://doi.org/10.1007/978-3-031-85791-1_9

The increase in flooding and other natural disasters across the Caribbean confirms Mathew Lawrence and Laurie Laybourn-Langton's assertion that "ours is the age of environmental breakdown, a new era of mounting instability brought about by human destruction of the natural world" (Lawrence and Laybourn-Langton 2021b, 6) and that "the environmental crisis is fundamentally a crisis of politics" (Lawrence and Laybourn-Langton 2021a, 32). In her essay on the impact of Hurricane Matthew in Haiti, Laura Wagner states that disasters "lay bare the vulnerabilities in a society," and adds that "[d]isasters make places more susceptible to other disasters, like a house with a cracked and crumbling foundation" (Wagner 2023, 58). In effect, this mirrors the fear that if one major environmental event were to happen in the Dominican Republic, the countryside and particularly the city of Santo Domingo would not be able to withstand it. While the country has experienced constant economic growth in the past two to three decades, climate resilience action in the Dominican Republic has not been a political priority, despite an increased awareness of the country's vulnerable geographic situation in the context of global warming. Economic interests have prevailed and have been reinforced when cataclysmic events like natural disasters and war have occurred. Surprisingly, theater practitioners in the Dominican Republic have scarcely broached the experience of political and environmental destruction caused by humans in the Caribbean.

Two exceptions, *Siete días antes del tsunami* [Seven Days Before the Tsunami] by Manuel García-Cartagena and *Un romance andaluz* [An Andalusian Romance] by Frank Disla lay bare the coloniality of disaster by highlighting how colonial oppression has contributed to bringing about catastrophic events. García-Cartagena and Disla's plays provide a space for understanding the ongoing impact of these issues on marginalized Dominicans through their use of metaphor, symbolism, blurring of fiction and reality, and acknowledgement of the audience as a character. On the one hand, *Siete días antes del tsunami* critiques capitalism's role in catastrophic events and underscores how systemic social problems, such as colonial relationships and profit-seeking through disaster, produce inequality, violence, and abuse among ordinary people. On the other hand, *Un romance andaluz* imagines a post-war scenario where, as we experience the end of the world, memories of armed conflicts arise and subaltern people navigate between participating in or rejecting the violence that the United States generates in its relationship with developing countries.

Nelson Maldonado-Torres defines "crisis" as a state of affairs that requires a decision, "disaster" as a moment when a decision has already been taken and the outcome revealed, and "catastrophe" as a dramatic turn of events that calls for thinking (Maldonado-Torres 2019, 333–336). For Maldonado-Torres, each of these definitions points to imperial values and histories that have produced the coloniality of disaster and have shaped "a multilayered and interconnected catastrophic reality" (Maldonado-Torres 2019, 339). However, Maldonado-Torres also understands that "thinking about catastrophe in the Caribbean leads to countercatastrophic responses such as decolonial thinking and decolonial aesthetics and poetics" (Maldonado-Torres 2019, 340). Similarly, in their scholarly work about islands, Jonathan Pugh and David Chandler argue that islands "have become important liminal and transgressive spaces [...] from which a great deal of Anthropocene thinking is drawing out and developing alternatives to hegemonic, modern, 'mainland' or 'one world' thinking" (Pugh and Chandler 2021, 43). The opposition between thought framed by colonial modernist values and non-hegemonic decolonial ideas is indeed central to the creative endeavors of the late twentieth and early twenty-first centuries in the Caribbean. Writers, visual and performance artists, spoken-word artists, and theater artists like García-Cartagena and Disla are re-politicizing their practices after the depoliticization experienced under neoliberal governments of the post-Cold War order. The possibility of communicating easily and rapidly through mass media and social media platforms has brought about an awareness of shared Caribbean problems such as racialization, economic dependency, exploitative tourism, migration, extractivism, and climate awareness. The plays analyzed in this essay partially respond to a need to develop new countercatastrophic aesthetics and poetics. In my view, Disla and García-Cartagena create doomsday scenarios to imply hope in the future through negation; their plays operate in *via negativa* to motivate action and question the current world order that could allow these catastrophes.

In *Siete días antes del tsunami*, or *El tsunami*,[1] Manuel García-Cartagena creates a tale about the end of the world on the shores of Hispaniola, the island shared by the Dominican Republic and Haiti. This dark comedy establishes the persistence of colonial racism, dehumanizing neglect, and capitalist exploitation in a series of unrelated scenes exploring issues in contemporary Dominican society including media, immigration, health care, and trade. The unifying thread is the conflict between the divine figures Anaisa and Yemaya regarding Ogun's decision to wipe out the island of Hispaniola and the awareness of the forthcoming disaster.

The play opens with an oracle who addresses the audience directly by breaking the fourth wall and suggesting that no one should be looking for moral lessons in a theater venue. Throughout the play, the constant use of this convention by several characters blurs the line between fiction and reality and provokes estrangement in the reception of the dialogues. The direct address interventions raise the question of whether they are directed to the internal universe of the play or to the extended reality that it ironically portrays. For example, the oracle states:

> Háganse de cuenta, pues, que yo no les he dicho nada, y vean y escuchen de qué manera las potencias que dirigen cada uno de nuestros actos se disputan entre ellas la suerte de cada uno de nosotros. Total, en nuestra época, a nadie en su sano juicio se le ocurriría esperar obtener lecciones de moral en una sala de teatro.
> [So, pretend that I've told you nothing, and see and hear how the powers that direct each of our actions dispute among themselves the fate of all of us. Nowadays, no one in their right mind would think of looking for moral lessons in a theater auditorium]. (García-Cartagena 2009)

There are two possible readings of the powers that control our fate. In the first, aligned with the structure of the play, "the powers" are the spirits that govern its internal universe, namely, Yemaya, Anaisa, and Ogun. These figures are part of the syncretic religions of Santería in Cuba and Vudú in the Dominican Republic. In Santería the divine spirits are known as orishas, while in Dominican Vudú they are known as misterios or loas. Yemaya is the orisha that represents the sea, and she is known as the mother of all orishas; Ogun is the orisha of metal, craftmanship, and war; and Anaisa is the misterio of love that brings happiness and good fortune to her followers. The syncretic religions of the Caribbean have played a crucial role in affirming identities marginalized by the institutionalized power of the State. The second possible reading is that "the powers" are the hegemonic structures in contemporary society. In this reading, the character of Ogun represents the impending destruction. By locating him outside the archipelago, in the mainland of the United States, the play turns him into a tyrant connected to the modus operandi of colonial powers that unleash hurricanes and floods over the Caribbean. Through the character of Ogun, García-Cartagena equates war with natural disasters. When Teatro Guloya performed the play in 2011, the memories of the destruction caused by an earthquake in Haiti were fresh and even though the Dominican Republic had not suffered any major natural disasters since Hurricane George in 1998, both sides of the island experienced the constant weakening of an already deprived State. In *El tsunami* evidence of a State that can provide security to its people is almost non-existent. These concerns in the universe of the play also resonate with the abandonment that Puerto Rico suffered six years later in dealing with the impact of hurricanes Irma and María.

The figures of Anaisa and Yemaya are idiosyncratically characterized in the play as defender and betrayer of the people, respectively. Anaisa is described as flirtatious and provocative, keeping the feminine and sexual energy that most people identify her with; but this passivity does not correspond to her profile in Dominican popular religiosity. On the other hand, Yemaya is shown as a messenger of Ogun and her motherly traits are almost completely erased by her disregard of the Dominican people. Her only concern is that Anaisa leaves the island and joins them in *lo paise* (the United States). In the words of Yemaya, salvation from disaster can only come through migrating to the mainland:

> Cuéntame, ¿te pusite la pila, como te dije que hiciera? Eprime a eso maldito, prima. Sácale el jugo. Total, si no se lo saca, tú se lo sacan otro con má fe y má caro, te lo digo yo. [...] Date prisa, prima, llénate lo borsillo, coge un avión y dipué arranca pacá, que aquí é que tá dio.
> [Tell me, did you get cracking, like I told you to? Squeeze those damn guys, cousin. Squeeze the last drop of juice out of them. In any case, if you don't do it, someone else will with more conviction and more money, I'm telling you. [...] Hurry up, cousin, fill your wallet, take a plane and get going, because here is where it's at]. (García-Cartagena 2009)

The idea that the United States is Paradise relates to the American Dream and the long-held notion that the prosperity that is denied to us in our own countries will come in the territories that created colonial domination in the Caribbean. The perception singled out by Yarimar Bonilla and Marisol LeBrón that Puerto Ricans "position migration to the United States as a salvation [...] rather than another form of disastrous uncertainty" can also apply to the Dominican reality in this context (Bonilla and LeBrón 2019, 12). Yemaya exhorts Anaisa to extract the most from the people who believe in her, replicating colonial relationships of exploitation. Yemaya's detachment from common people portrays the competitive nature of capitalist ideology in which foreign powers are only in developing nations to extract profits without caring for the lives of the people who live in those nations. It also reflects on how the extractive nature of this ideology takes commodities, financial resources, and people out of their territories and, in doing so, exacerbate catastrophes.

Yemaya serves as the messenger and enabler of destruction while Anaisa serves as the protector of the island. Yemaya is already conditioned by colonial thinking, she is living the good life with Ogun, far from the problems and conflicts of the Caribbean region. She does not care about the destruction and, on the contrary, she believes in extracting as many resources as possible from the people on the island. Anaisa, on the other hand, has maintained her faith in her people and is not willing to leave them behind and save herself.

In her first and last lines in the play, Anaisa evidences a complicated relationship with Dominicans by calling them both vermin (*alimañas*) and my children (*misijo*). From her words we can grasp that the underlying motive for the disaster is the criminal and sinful behavior of the majority of the citizens of the Dominican Republic: "no queda un solo crimen anotado en el catálogo mundial de la ignominia humana que no haya sido cometido en estas tierras" [there is not a single crime in the world catalog of human ignominy that has not been perpetrated in this country] and the inability to live together: "¡Tanta vese que le dije que se dejaran de pendejá y que aprendieran a viví junto!" [I told them to stop being so stupid and to learn to live together] (García-Cartagena 2009). Through the voice of Anaisa, García-Cartagena compares the Dominican Republic to Sodom and Gomorrah. The contradictory nature of Anaisa's speech operates as a wake-up call to the audience since she acknowledges the wrongdoings of our nation but implores for a more harmonious coexistence. She says that Ogun is tired of the unruly behavior of the masses of Dominicans that attempt migration by sea in dangerous *yolas* (rustic wooden boats) to become beggars in another country: "¡Esos pendejos están tan hartos de vivir en su país que se meten como quinientos en una yola para ir a mendigar a un país ajeno!" [These idiots are so fed up with living in their own country that they put some five hundred people on a boat to go and beg in a foreign country] (García-Cartagena 2009). By adopting this anti-immigration discourse, Ogun becomes associated with the actions of colonial powers. This orisha of war enters the realm of apocalyptic metaphors by being both the primordial orisha that opens new paths and the destructive force that annihilates the island of Hispaniola.

In addition to the framing of the play by the characters associated with Santería deities, García-Cartagena also includes a series of unrelated scenes with a range of characters from Dominican society. For the purpose of this essay, I only focus on three of the five scenes that are not related to the Santería deities. Each scene can be interpreted as different days that lead us to the final storm and as playing out how the colonial ethos and neoliberal ethos affect common people as well. For example, in the first scene after Anaisa's introduction, we can see the racist and colonial relationship that La Señora Ganzúa, the Spanish-born magazine director has with Cosito, her assistant. She reprimands Cosito for not doing his work and allowing too many images of Black people in her magazine, asserting that she does not want to see more "monkeys," and that the Dominicans are lazy and that the newspapers in the country are trash. Cosito is not submissive, but he does not vehemently challenge his boss after all the slurs and her attempt to strangle him. La Señora Ganzúa asserts her power both through verbal and physical violence. Cosito's liberation is only possible through convincing La Señora Ganzúa of the threat posed by the nearing tempest. Their relationship is asymmetrical and representative of the exploitative nature of colonialism. After this revelation, in a gesture of self-preservation, La Señora Ganzúa leaves the country since the storm threatens her economic goals and exerting power over Cosito is not a priority for her. By doing this, La Señora Ganzúa applies the extractive recommendation of Yemaya: take all you can and leave.

As previously mentioned, the State, as an institution that can provide protection to its population, appears to be absent in the lives of the characters portrayed in the play. While this complete abandonment of the people amid the disaster portrays despair, it also enables revenge. Midway through the play, in a scene set in the waiting room of an expensive doctor, Tato Bizco and Anita Lasará are two ghosts that return to the world in exchanged bodies. Their dialogue suggests that they both had accidents and have returned for follow-up visits with the doctor. Anita Lasará appears in the waiting room after having been in a car accident, but she faints when she hears the news of the tsunami. Tato Bizco is purposely visiting the doctor to avenge the death of his sister who did not receive timely medical attention because she did not have medical insurance or money to cover the costs. It seems that Tato Bizco is on a vendetta to kill all the doctors who are complicit by medical negligence in the death of his sister. The need for revenge when the world is about to end is the ultimate manifestation of despair. For Tato Bizco, salvation is personal and so is revenge, therefore the death of the doctors in the impending natural disaster could not be left to chance. The scene ends with Anita Lasará and Tato Bizco expressing evangelical devotion in a search for salvation as they face the end of the world. In the current context in the Dominican Republic despair is manifested through the thought that there are only individual solutions to collective problems, which is congruent with the concepts of the neoliberal ethos. In a Weberian approach, this ethos can be linked to the rise of evangelical groups in the Dominican Republic because, even if they create a sense of community, they view salvation as individual and not collective; also, since there is no State, justice is absent from this world and can only be executed by God.

Just before the final scene, in which the day of judgment arrives, the play presents Don Plin and Don Plon, two small-business owners taking advantage of the chaos to inflate the price of essential items and food. Don Plin is a hardheaded businessperson who sees nothing wrong with profiting from the misery ensuing from the destruction, while Don Plon is a faint-hearted man with a slight moral conscience. Don Plin's view is that businesses are not for the weak and that they are made to exploit the paying customer:

> DON PLIN: Plon, eto é negosio. ¿Tú mentiende? Ne-go-sio. ¿Y pa qué son lo negosio? Pa jodé al que paga. Y punto. Apunta ahí, Cundía: Dosciento cincuenta peso el cartón de huevo.
> DON PLON: ¿Cómo? ¿Y no eran dosciento...?
> DON PLIN: Eso era ahorita, Plon. Ya subieron. Te toca a ti ahora: ¿A cómo vendemo la leche? Vé a bucá la lata y tírala y déjate de pendejá.
> [DON PLIN: Plon, this is business. Do you understand? Busi-ness. And what is business for? To screw the payer. That's it. Write it down, Cundía: Two hundred and fifty pesos for a carton of eggs.
> DON PLON: What? Wasn't it two hundred...?
> DON PLIN: That was just now, Plon. They've already gone up. It's your turn now: How much do we sell the milk for? Go get the can, sell it, and stop being a fool.] (García-Cartagena 2009)

Don Plin is adamant in his focus on making a profit. Don Plon questions some of Don Plin's actions, out of some sort of moral remorse because people are dying. But, in the end, Don Plon yields to Don Plin's pressure and prices the milk to increase the profits for the sellers. This scene poses the moral questioning of an economic system that embraces the concepts of freedom and markets at its core but ends up creating an abusive model based on greed. Business is not made amongst equals in a society but between people who hoard and consumers who are seen as fools who should only accept the conditions enforced on them. Abusive practices are not only an imposition from foreign powers but are reproduced inside the fabric of a society in crisis.

The play ends with Yemaya executing Anaisa with Ogun's machete. Yemaya tries in vain to convince Anaisa to leave the island and forget about the people she has been protecting. Yemaya's fear of Ogun's wrath is stronger than her compassion for her cousin and she ends up complying with the mission of killing Anaisa. Instantaneously, the storm, the screams, and the sounds of waves stop. We return to the realm of the spirits and experience the conclusion of time and the plausible salvation of humanity. If time stops and then starts again, a new era begins. The end of the world is always a promise of a new beginning.

There is a parallel between the communal violence of the human realm and the intra-familial violence among spirits. We either create a renewed sense of community that rejects colonial structures or we experience the destruction that these structures will impose on us. The destructive force of Ogun severs the link between Anaisa and Yemaya in the same way in which global capitalism is destroying the bonds to our kin. This kinship is not a reference to the idea of a nuclear family but to an extended Caribbean family that has been divided by colonialism. For example, exchanges between Cuba, Puerto Rico, and the Dominican Republic are limited by the imposition of political systems that limit communication between us and destroyed the Antillean ideology framed by people like Ramón Emeterio Betances, Gregorio Luperón, Eugenio María de Hostos, and José Martí and present in the region during the late nineteenth century and early twentieth centuries. The play does not explicitly suggest a new Antillean spirit, but the metaphor of Anaisa and Yemaya as cousins who are fighting amongst themselves suggests the remnants of these ideas. Furthermore, to resist this destructive force and heal the bonds that are being severed, the scenes denote, through a via *negativa* approach, that we must learn to work together (both nationally and regionally) to create a system in which exploitation, speculation, and revenge are not the norm.

Whereas *Siete días antes del tsunami* imagines a divided Dominican Republic prior to the end of the world, *Un romance andaluz* starts with the end of the world and is consistent with apocalyptic narratives that always imagine that there would always be enough survivors who will resist the cataclysm to foster a new beginning. As Maria Manuel Lisboa observes, "apocalypse [...] usually tends to be not an absolute wipe-out, merely a clearing of the decks in the anticipation of a new beginning" (Lisboa 2011, 8). What happens after the end of the world is the starting point of Frank Disla's play, a solo performance with seven independent scenes in which the last phrase of each scene is a reference to the title of the next one. The symbolism of the number seven alludes to the creation and destruction of the world in their biblical connotations. God created Earth in seven days in the book of Genesis and destroyed it when the seven seals were opened with the second coming of Christ.

The biblical references in the play are almost exclusively to the Book of Revelations. For example, the first two scenes after the introduction, *Mar de vidrio mezclado con fuego* [Sea of Glass Mixed with Fire] and *Perdurable olor a muerte y escombro* [Lingering Smell of Death and Debris], refer to Revelations 15 and 16, which contain images that speak of the anticipation and the execution of God's wrath against the wicked through the unleashing of the seven angels carrying the seven plagues. These scriptural indicators, present throughout the play, are explicitly recalled in the last scene *Las siete trompetas apocalípticas* [The Seven Apocalyptic Trumpets], fostering a cyclical sense of creation and destruction.

From the start of the play, Disla combines the military concept of the theater of war, the geographic region where war operations are happening, with the staging of a theater play that portrays the armed confrontation between warring parties. The opening image is a metaphor for both desolation and isolation; the space conveys the complete destruction of war, and the sole survivor of said destruction is separated from the outsiders who enter the space. Actor Uno welcomes spectators as they enter this abandoned space with a tone of warning similar to the oracle's in García-Cartagena's play, reminding us that we are in a theater, where conflict is key to dramatic structures and is also characteristic of war:

> La acción es bélica. Del conflicto ni hablar, este ha sido siempre eterno. Las épocas suceden arrastrándolos como polvareda helada de cometas. Parte intrínseca de ellas mismas. Roces hirientes, los conflictos, sin los cuales no existimos. El lugar no importa. Han venido aquí, a este recital dramático, a divertirse, fin primordial del teatro.

[The action is bellicose. Conflict isn't worth mentioning; it's eternal. The epochs follow one after the other, pulled along like the frozen dust of comets, an intrinsic part of themselves. Conflicts, wounding clashes, without which we don't exist. The place doesn't matter. You have come here, to this dramatic performance, to have fun, the primary purpose of the theater]. (Disla 2016, 22)

Actor Uno's opening remarks also allude to Theodor Adorno's provocative claim that writing poetry after Auschwitz would be an act of barbarism. What, then, are his intentions in providing an artistic performance? If art and poetry are just a recollection of nauseating rhetoric and trite metaphor when compared to the bodies of soldiers, women, and children affected by war, what is the purpose of telling these stories? I would argue that along with the existential question of deciphering the meaning of life and the history of violence and peace evoked by Actor Uno, the underlying reason is the preservation of memories and remembering, as in re-membering, placing together the dislocated and dismembered bodies of war.

The metatheatrical and performative aspect of Actor Uno's presence is key to the notion of the body that remembers and operates in different layers of reality. First, Actor Uno works as a blank character inside a fictional doomsday scenario. He is the container of multiplicities and the body that brings back the bodies of real people who suffered the pains of war by portraying their prejudices, traumas, and physical disabilities. But he is also the fictional body that refers to other fictions that construe humanity in its common narratives. In Actor Uno we have a fragmented body that goes from fiction to reality and rejoins them in a single entity. The audience follows the story through the unifying body of Actor Uno.

When Actor Uno introduces his story, he explains that when destruction came over the city during rehearsals, all his theater colleagues disappeared but he survived because his mother entrusted a dragon to safeguard him from any harm. Since his mother used to tell him fantasy stories, this metaphor implies that our first memories and our imagination can save us from destruction. This emotional and mental realm operates as a tool for resistance. Actor Uno's train of thought and the memories that he brings forth operate as catalyzers to this question of the meaning of life when everything has been lost to destructive forces. He uses tropes that compare the destruction coming from angels with the destruction caused by humans. This is consistent with Maria Manuel Lisboa's assertion that when the enactment of destruction "fell under the control not of God or nature but of human agency [...] it acquired cosmic possibilities" (Lisboa 2011, 105). When Actor Uno toasts to the memory of the fallen he talks about the permanence of the smell of death and debris. Here "the fallen" is not a metaphor or just an abstraction because with the advent of war and destruction we are shown that humanity has collapsed either by physical death or by the crushing of our spirit.

Death is present in the play not only in terms of the disappearance of the body but also through the afflictions of the spirit. Disla, touching the realms of documentary theater, brings real-life stories into the fictional space. The cases of Wilkin Cuello González, a Dominican veteran physically disabled in the Iraq War, and Manuel Vieites, an Argentine veteran of the Malvinas War with Britain, serve as anchors to reality in this metatheatrical play. Their stories tell of a trauma that, on the one hand, show how imperial interests sell dreams of incorporation to their nations to the afflicted bodies of oppressed nations, and, on the other, portray the dehumanization of war and the miserable feelings experienced by veterans.

Disla's play opens the debate on the creation of heroic figures. The veterans from Latin American countries, like Wilkin Cuello González, are not considered heroes in the imperial territories for which they fought. They become anonymous heroes. While liberation figures are heroes in their countries of origin they are also vilified and considered enemies because they dared to oppose the global powers. *Un romance andaluz* offers a nuanced vision of the complexities of the heroic. The imperialist aggressor glorifies their soldiers in the very same way that the resisting forces exalt their combatants. The text poses the question of whether war can ever be a heroic activity even if the moral reason for violence falls on the resisting countries' side. Actor Uno, speaking as Vieites, asks "¿Quién soy? ¿El soldado aguerrido que despedían antes de tomar el avión, o la lacra humana en la que me transformaron cuando llegué?" [Who am I? The battle-hardened soldier they fired before I boarded the plane, or the human scum they turned me into when I arrived?] (Disla 2016, 29). The existential question of "Who am I?" implies that Vieites has lost his identity and cannot see himself as a person after the war. Vieites's monologue is full of despair. In his dreams he either dies or kills and he concludes by saying that his children deserve a father, and his grandchildren do not deserve a grandfather that only thinks about suicide. This monologue is followed by the point of view of a soldier called Dusty, who experiences constant guilt for killing a child carrying a grenade. Both Vieites and Dusty suffer from the lingering effects of the disaster in their daily lives after war. As both testimonies suggest, war creates trauma that stays in the minds and bodies of the people who experience it. The scene ends with the remembrance of events like the Holocaust, the US military interventions in the Dominican Republic, the Vietnam War, the coup in Chile, and the memory of 9/11. But this remembrance unfolds as a fiction and as a denial of what happened because "Las gestas universales, las grandes conflagraciones son fruto de la imaginación" [Universal battles and great upheavals are the fruit of the imagination] (Disla 2016, 29). This last statement contests the notion of the real by establishing that reality is constructed from imagination. The preservation of memory and imagination are key elements to the potential survival of humanity. War is a repeated story that indicates our lack of imagination.

The last scene of the play ponders the simple ways in which any conflict can arise and precipitate the end of the world. Actor Uno, as Juan Pérez, explains how two guys started a bacchanal that unleashed the apocalypse in Perth Amboy, New Jersey. Juan Pérez is an ordinary person, a nobody who witnesses the seven angels bring forth destruction. He concludes that wars start *con cualquier pendejada* [with any kind of bullshit] and that he takes refuge in *la palabra* [the word]. This is a reference to the Word of God but, left uncapitalized, it refers to how language arts can be a path to salvation in human terms. This is sustained when Actor Uno concludes: "esta no es una profesión de hambre, es de sueños, los de todos, traspaso la imagen de la realidad, con un gesto soy capaz de recrear el mundo" [this isn't a profession of hunger, it's a profession of dreams, everyone's dreams; I go beyond the image of reality, with a gesture I am capable of recreating the world] (Disla 2016, 49). Disla's play chronicles our time in line with Maria Manuel Lisboa's claim that "Stories of apocalypse ultimately narrate us. [...] there is no deity, force of nature or machine that can break us, only we ourselves" (Lisboa 2011, 105). Throughout *Un romance andaluz* there is a sense that the guilt of being alive belongs to us since we are responsible for our own destruction, but the dramatist proposes that we should use the playfulness of art to confront the violence we have created.

Close to the end of each of the plays analyzed here we are reminded of the impact of premillennialism and the belief in the Rapture that pervades

Dominican Republic's evangelical tradition. When Tato Bizco in García-Cartagena's play and Juan Pérez in Disla's play invoke their religious affiliation, they are pointing to the social perception of these religious practices and how these have grown and permeated Dominican society in the last decades (El Caribe 2022). The rise of the evangelical movement responds to variables such as the need to create communities of support as a response to the absence of the State. The vacuum and despair of modern society are being filled by promises of the afterlife. The end of the world for evangelical Christians might be a fulfilment of God's contract with humanity but it also creates otherness between believers and non-believers. Pastors in the Dominican Republic, for example, have linked themselves to nationalistic right-wing movements that want to displace the syncretic religions rooted in our culture and reject everything that is considered Haitian or Black, like Dominican Vudú. Although evangelicalism serves to foster a sense of community, its politics end up being a reproduction of coloniality.

Whether it be a natural disaster or war, both plays reveal the human hand in producing disaster. While García-Cartagena has created a story in which destruction comes from an act of God, Disla establishes a play in which devastation was unleashed by humans in the theater of war. Each scene in *El tsunami* portrays a fragmented society in which daily activities and relationships are tainted by personal interest and oppressive structures of power. As in global warming, humanity triggers its own demise which comes through an external, non-human environmental force. *Un romance andaluz* tells us the other side of the story in which the conflict between peoples produces total annihilation. In both cases, the failure to organize collective responses is what enables damnation. Without minimizing the reproduction of the structures of domination in Dominican society, destruction in both plays is executed by a colonial power that enables catastrophe in the global sphere that, in turn, permeates all interactions. In this sense, García-Cartagena and Disla embrace the concept that our imagination, as a tool of resistance and survival, is the option that is given to us to envision a different society in which humans can live in harmony with ourselves and the environment. Although there is no organized artistic movement that incorporates these principles, the last decade has encouraged discourses that interrogate imperialism and colonialism in artists like Aniova Prandy, Ernesto Rivera, and Yéssica Montero; curators like Yina Jiménez Suriel and Luis Graham Castillo; writers like Michelle Ricardo, Johan Mijail, and Yaissa Jimenez; and theater-makers like Ingrid

Luciano and Isabel Spencer. Most of them, to echo Maldonado-Torres, are creating countercatastrophic narratives that resist the coloniality of catastrophe, while cultivating cooperation and new ways of thinking.

Note

1. This is the shortened title used for marketing purposes in the production directed by Claudio Rivera at the Teatro Guloya, a theatre group and performance venue based in Santo Domingo, Dominican Republic in 2011.

Works Cited

Bonilla, Yarimar, and Marisol LeBrón. 2019. Introduction. In *Aftershocks of Disaster: Puerto Rico Before and After the Storm*, ed. Yarimar Bonilla and Marisol LeBrón. Chicago: Haymarket Books.

De los Santos, Rafael. 2023. Caricatura de Noticiero Poteleche 22 noviembre 2023. *Diario Libre*, November 22. https://www.diariolibre.com/opinion/noticiero-poteleche/2023/11/21/caricatura-noticiero-poteleche-22-noviembre-2023/2529651. Accessed 25 November 2023.

Diario Libre. 2022. En tres horas cayó más del 50 % de las lluvias esperadas en noviembre. *Diario Libre*, November 4. https://www.diariolibre.com/actualidad/nacional/2022/11/04/en-tres-horas-cayo-mas-del-50--de-lluvias-de-noviembre/2130917. Accessed 25 November 2023.

Disla, Frank. 2016. *Un romance andaluz*. Santo Domingo: Editora Nacional.

El Caribe. 2022. Los evangélicos crecen en República Dominicana. *El Caribe*, July 28. https://www.elcaribe.com.do/panorama/pais/los-evangelicos-crecen-en-republica-dominicana/. Accessed 27 November 2023.

García-Cartagena, Manuel. 2009. *Siete días antes del tsunami*. Unpublished manuscript.

Hoy. 2023. Disturbio superó al "diluvio" del 4 de noviembre de 2022. *Hoy*, November 19. https://hoy.com.do/disturbio-supero-diluvio-del-4-de-noviembre-de-2022/. Accessed 25 November 2023.

Lawrence, Mathew, and Laurie Laybourn-Langton. 2021a. How We Win. In *Beyond the Ruins: The Fight Against Environmental Breakdown*, ed. Mathew Lawrence and Laurie Laybourn-Langton. Verso.

Lawrence, Mathew, and Laurie Laybourn-Langton. 2021b. Introduction. In Lawrence et al., *Beyond*.

Lisboa, Maria Manuel. 2011. *The End of the World: Apocalypse and Its Aftermath in Western Culture*, 1st ed. Open Book Publishers. https://doi.org/10.2307/j.ctt5vjt0h.8.

Maldonado-Torres, Nelson. 2019. Afterword: Critique and Decoloniality in the Face of Crisis, Disaster, and Catastrophe. In *Aftershocks of Disaster: Puerto Rico Before and After the Storm*, ed. Yarimar Bonilla and Marisol LeBrón. Chicago: Haymarket Books.

Pugh, Jonathan, and David Chandler. 2021. There Are Only Islands After the End of the World. In *Anthropocene Islands: Entangled Worlds*, 1–40. London: University of Westminster Press. https://doi.org/10.2307/j.ctv1v3gqxp.4.

Wagner, Laura. 2023. After the Storm: Hurricane Matthew, Haiti, and Disaster's Longue Durée. In *The Power of the Story: Writing Disasters in Haiti and the Circum-Caribbean*, ed. Vincent Joos, Martin Munro, and John Ribó, 50–61. New York City: Berghahn Books. http://www.jstor.org/stable/jj.2775917.6.

CHAPTER 10

Sensing Catastrophic Realities in Diasporic Puerto Rican Theater

Megan Bailon

Scenes in *La otra orilla* (1996) [The Other Shore] by Teatro Pregones and *Yemaya's Belly* (2004) by Quiara Alegría Hudes—both works by Puerto Rican creators—evoke extreme weather and ecological events. After an opening scene of dialogue and a song in *La otra orilla*, the stage lights begin to mimic lightning, turning red and menacing, and the characters are thrown by the wind of the storm, reeling around the platform in the middle of the stage. The minimal set functions at times as the site of departure and place of arrival and at other times as a raft tossed by the waves, invoking three common tropes in Puerto Rican theater about migration to the US mainland in a way that collapses the typical progressive temporality of the migration journey. This initial disorienting event sets the tone for the rest of the play. In a similarly destabilizing fashion, a parallel scene in *Yemaya's Belly* takes place as two characters on a raft

M. Bailon (✉)
Chicanx/e and Latinx/e Studies Program, University of Wisconsin-Madison, Madison, WI, USA
e-mail: bailon@wisc.edu

© The Author(s), under exclusive license to Springer Nature Switzerland AG 2025
C. Stevens and J. D. Rossini (eds.), *The Coloniality of Catastrophe in Caribbean Theater and Performance*,
https://doi.org/10.1007/978-3-031-85791-1_10

are overtaken by a storm that sweeps one of them into the ocean depths. The stage notes indicate that the next scene takes place *"through layers and layers of blue"* (Hudes 2008, 40), where a possible drowning scene is presented to the audience via an oneiric sequence of memories.

As I consider these works from the perspective of the aftermath of Hurricane Maria, their meaning is overdetermined by all that has passed in Puerto Rico in the last several years—hurricanes that hit in the wake of an ongoing economic crisis, blackouts, a migratory exodus from the island, ensuing political crises, subsequent earthquakes, a pandemic, and a continuing cycle of storms. And while Hurricane Maria and the events of the last several years have been sensational, scholars have aptly highlighted their mundanity; as Yarimar Bonilla states, "[…] The most deeply felt catastrophe is not the arrival of hurricanes, earthquakes, or even the looming threats of climate change but the slowly accruing effects of raciocolonial governance" (Bonilla 2020, 147). Taking a cue from Bonilla and others in response to the contemporary moment in Puerto Rico, I examine these plays within their historical context to invite further consideration of these "accruing effects" and accumulating catastrophes, and of the role that theater and performance, as embodied and multi-sensory art forms, have long had in working to interrogate and unmask them.[1]

This chapter examines how *La otra orilla* and *Yemaya's Belly* aesthetically and thematically problematize the language of "crisis" by presenting multilayered portrayals of Caribbean migration explicitly situated within a (neo)colonial and neoliberal reality. In these two plays, I am interested in the way that rhetoric around various Caribbean migration "crises" obscures the accruing effects of postcolonial economic governance practices based on extraction, intervention, unequal notions of interdependence, and displacement. Both plays, which were created in a diasporic context, were first staged at the turn of the twenty-first century in the wake of compounding examples of Caribbean migration by sea that have long been articulated in the United States as discrete "crises": the "Cuban rafter crisis," the "Haitian refugee crisis," and the uptick in yola travel across the Mona Passage between the Dominican Republic and Puerto Rico.[2] While both plays respond to these "crises" thematically by featuring migrants from vaguely defined Caribbean islands traveling in precarious vessels to the United States, I explore how the aesthetic dimensions of each play question contemporary articulations of crisis as temporally and spatially confined phenomena that can be diagnosed, solved, and overcome within existing political and ethical frameworks.

The two plays use a multi-sensory aesthetic approach that relies on both Caribbean poetics and Yoruba cosmology to denaturalize the Western temporal, spatial, and epistemological confines of the "crises" they depict as they stage (im)migration stories as catastrophes that are entangled in the colonial legacies of the Caribbean. I argue that the plays immerse audiences in the everyday sensorial reality of colonialism and neoliberalism within the region, prompting them to think beyond the acuteness and temporally constrained language of crisis as they are invited to reevaluate and reimagine their sensory engagements with the world as ethical practices.

My analysis follows the distinction that Nelson Maldonado-Torres makes between crisis and catastrophe to capture both the compounding nature of the concerns that are central to the plays in question and the way that these concerns defy Western liberal solutions. Writing in the wake of Hurricane Maria about Puerto Rico, Maldonado-Torres explains, "like crisis, which calls for a diagnosis, catastrophe calls for thinking; unlike crisis, however, catastrophe challenges all existing cognitive frameworks" (Maldonado-Torres 2019, 336). This view of catastrophe is compatible with Rob Nixon's theorization of slow violence where environmental catastrophes "overspill clear boundaries in time and space" (2013, 7) rather than happening in a sudden turn of events and remaining restricted to their purely ecological impacts. Moreover, framing these plays in terms of "catastrophe" rather than "crisis" distinguishes the Caribbean lived realities at the center of both plays from Lauren Berlant's concept of "crisis ordinariness," which does account for a cumulative sense of crisis but frames it in terms of a "cruel optimism" that clings to liberal democratic dreams of upward mobility (Berlant 2011, 149). As Bonilla has pointed out, the fantasies that Berlant emphasizes in her argument are those of a limited few within the global North and, in postcolonial societies, have been increasingly unsustainable to the point of ridiculousness (Bonilla 2020, 156–157). It is precisely this nonsensical nature of the fantasy of migration as the key to the "American Dream" amidst compounding catastrophes—what Maldonado-Torres refers to as "a multilayered and interconnected catastrophic reality" (Maldonado-Torres 2019, 339)—that both *La otra orilla* and *Yemaya's Belly* highlight. In Claudia Aradau and Rens Van Munster's work, catastrophe as "the limit of knowledge and radical unknowability" (Aradau and Van Munster 2011, 5) is further connected to the sensorial as it carries the connotation of being "a form of partition of the sensible in which modalities of knowledge are renegotiated" (87). It is this way that catastrophe partitions off, acknowledges, and explores the limitations of prevailing methods of problem-solving and sensory relationships that I see as central to the aesthetics of both *La otra orilla* and *Yemaya's Belly*.

The plays foreground the long-term development and effects of contemporary capitalism before denaturalizing it on a sensory level, effectively seeking to reorient audiences' relationship to it. In both plays, these sensory experiences are put in direct conversation with the geopolitical and economic realities that make sea migration a necessity for some, providing a reminder of how contemporary capitalism engages a fully embodied response with ethical implications. Benjamin L. McKean describes the way that the machinations of the global economy—based since at least the 1970s in neoliberal theory—"can play as a source of orientation to the world" (McKean 2022, 9). Drawing on Foucault's concept of governmentality, McKean articulates the role of neoliberal economic theory as "orienting" people to perceive global institutions as legitimate by highlighting an individual freedom to choose while also guiding "people to particular perceptions and action" (2022, 21). When read alongside Sara Ahmed's phenomenological definition of orientation as "registering the proximity of objects and others" and shaping "not only how we inhabit space, but how we apprehend this world of shared inhabitance" (Ahmed 2006, 3), we might understand how the governing economic theory of contemporary capitalism both directs people in support of its own perpetuation in a fully embodied way and also determines the orientation of people toward others with whom they share geopolitical space. Candice Amich helps to further articulate the sensory component of contemporary capitalism as "a perceptual regime that disciplines time and space" via what she labels as "the neoliberal sensorium" (Amich 2020, 4). In explanation of how this disciplining of the senses unfolds, Amich argues that the project of neoliberalism relies on community being "sensible […] only to the extent that it is profitable and manageable" (2020, 4). By shifting focus from crisis to catastrophe—a shift away from Western views of temporality and of relationships within geographical space—the plays disrupt this disciplining of the senses and reorient audiences toward those displaced under contemporary capitalism.

Both plays stage (im)migration crises through the sea-based journeys of the main characters onstage, drawing on a more extensive tradition of Hispano-Caribbean theater featuring migration journeys on makeshift vessels.[3] When analyzed together, a multi-sensorial framing becomes evident in their familiar stories of sea migration. In *La otra orilla*, the loose plot follows the journey of a male and female character as they seem to embark on a journey across the ocean. They travel past ships brought to life via the sound effect of a blaring horn, through a cacophony of thunderstorms, and arguments over the feasibility of the choice to make the journey.[4] By the end it is unclear whether the characters have arrived at their destination, the journey is more metaphorical than real, the platform on the stage is a raft or an urban rooftop or some other more symbolic location, and if the characters are alive or dead. While the plot remains ambiguous, the aural components are used to both conjure and question the sensorial regime that requires the migration of the bodies onstage. In *Yemaya's Belly*, there is a similar sense of ambiguity around the characters' arrival to the continental United States. The coming-of-age story follows Jesus (who later changes his name to Mulo), a twelve-year-old boy who is displaced from his rural village after losing his family in a wildfire.[5] After losing his home and family to the fire, he begs a new young friend, Maya, to take him on one of her habitual trips across the sea to the United States. The final third of the play is the disorienting story of this journey which ends with their arrival to their destination still pending and, in similar fashion to *La otra orilla*, leaving the audience wondering about the characters' fate. In this play, where neocolonialism and neoliberalism are experienced through taste, touch, smell, and sight, the similar ambiguity around the question of arrival centers the audience's attention on the implications of everyday sensorial realities.

The temporal and spatial ambiguity that results from the aesthetic choices of the creators of *La otra orilla* and *Yemaya's Belly* also shift the focus of each work from the acute specificity of crisis to the larger postcolonial context that forms the basis for each play. Both plays exceed their original context of turn-of-the-twenty-first-century Puerto Rico. After the global economic crisis of the 1980s, the 1990s in Puerto Rico were characterized by rising unemployment, growing socioeconomic inequality, a slowing of outside investment due to anxiety about the impending end of special tax benefits for US corporations, and increasing out-migration (Rivera-Batiz and Santiago 1996). As Jorge Duany notes, by the 1990s, due to intensifying levels of migration to the mainland, the number of Puerto Ricans living on the mainland reached levels almost equal to the number of Puerto Ricans on the island (2000, 6). These economic dynamics connect to an extensive history of Puerto Rico as a "proto-neoliberal" (Villanueva 2015, 67) project where rhetoric of autonomy and self-determination have long clashed with the pursuit of cheap labor and disaster capitalism[6]—economic dynamics that were widely experienced across the Caribbean during this time. It is this pan-Caribbean concept of "being in the same boat" in the present that is tied to a colonial past also characterized by the transatlantic slave trade that sets the stage for these plays.[7]

The incorporation of both postcolonial Caribbean poetics and Yoruba ways of knowing are key to how sensory disruptions of colonialism and capital connect with temporal and spatial disruptions in these works. In *La otra orilla*, the sonic components of the play in particular draw on a colonial history grounded in the transatlantic slave trade using a symbolic system rooted in Yoruba culture. In *Yemaya's Belly*, more senses are engaged as syncretic religious cosmologies that include Yoruba religious practices inform not only the visual components of the play but also an aesthetics that engages the aural, tactile, and gustatory. As postcolonial theorist Édouard Glissant observes, Western concepts of temporality favor linear progress as they emphasize "setting out upon the fixed linearity of time, always toward a projection," finding legitimacy in the concept of "filiation" (Glissant 2010, 47). This concept that traces progress from a historical root in linear fashion is problematic for Caribbean identities that trace their origin stories back—at least in part—to the transatlantic slave trade which functioned as an uprooting and an interruption of filiation. Because both plays incorporate Yoruba cultural references, it is also relevant to note, as Alan West-Durán helpfully articulates, "African philosophical and religious thought, where there is a strong bond between the world of the living, the dead, and other spirits as well as the orishas that do not adhere to linear concepts of time" (West-Durán 2013, 199). If catastrophe exceeds established ways of diagnosing, resolving, and progressing beyond the issues of the present—the language of crisis—the plays' integration of a non-Western sensorium both acknowledges catastrophe and gestures toward a possible foundation for addressing it.

Aural Disruptions in *La otra orilla*

In *La otra orilla*, visible Yoruba symbolism is accentuated by other aural elements that suggest the embracing of non-Western sensory perceptions as a necessary precursor to an ethical reorientation. As the two main actors, Jorge Merced and Rosalba Rolón, appear stranded together on a "raft"—a slightly raised platform centered in the black box stage, actress Judith Rivera plays a third character who periodically embodies the role of the orisha Oyá. In Yoruba cosmology, Oyá is "the deity of the storm and hurricanes" (Karade 1994, 27). In the play's initial storm scene, having already climbed onto a box situated in the back corner of the raised platform, Rivera waves a red scarf over the scene in time with the crashing sound of minor notes that create thunder before the background is washed in a red light. The redness of this scarf calls to mind the orisha Oyá as well as Shangó who is associated with lightning (29). While colors are often used in theater to symbolic effect, it is the active role of Rivera's character in this scene that ritualizes a sense of divine intervention and puts one in mind of the syncretic nature of color symbolism in everyday Caribbean realities. For example, syncretized Yoruba and European religious traditions associate red with the Cuban figures of Santa Barbara, who is associated with Shangó, and La Virgen de la Candelaria, who is associated with Oyá (Falola and Akinyemi 2016, 34). In this way, the visual and aural vocabulary in the play situates the audience within an everyday reality inflected by non-Western sensory elements.

Overlaying these visual components the use of music results in temporal and geographical disruptions at an aural level. When Merced and Rolón first enter the stage, they are both dressed in garments that make a clear reference to the mid-century style of "the Great Migration" of Puerto Ricans to the mainland as they stand upstage and wave a good-bye toward the audience.[8] In the only other song number in the piece, jíbaro guitar melodies accompany nostalgic lyrics about an old bridge in a sunny, fragrant setting that recalls the internal wave of migration that accompanied Puerto Rico's mid-century transition from a rural to an manufacturing-based economy.[9] However, these visual and aural references to Puerto Rican cultural specificity are quickly submerged in a more ambiguous temporal and geographical context. For example, in one scene, Merced's character draws multiple histories of migration together stating, "Consigo un pasaje en avión, en bote, en yola...en pie" [I will get there on a plane, a boat, an improvised Dominican boat...on foot]. Another scene features a shift from spoken dialogue to dialogue sung as a bolero accompanied by the live band in downstage left, situated just outside the overlapping spotlights that draw focus to centerstage. As Lawrence La Fountain-Stokes (2008, 192–193) has highlighted in reference to a different work by Teatro Pregones, the bolero is a traditional Puerto Rican musical form connected with memory, which gives the effect of a blurring of lines between present and the past invoked by the nostalgic melody. However, the culturally-specific melody quickly fades into the ambient tones that recur throughout *La otra orilla* and provide broader symbolism to reinforce the affective force of the work—from the eerie to the menacing to the playful. If, as Patricia Herrera and Marci R. McMahon emphasize in their "sonic manifesto," "Latinx theater artists make difference audible and use sonic strategies to claim space, citizenship, and belonging" (Herrera and McMahon 2019, 242), these moments of Puerto Rican cultural specificity that always disperse into spatial and temporal ambiguity reverberate with the dispersed, everyday, and accreting experiences of coloniality throughout the archipelago.

On top of these sometimes subtle sensory elements, the disjointed and at times absurd dialogue situates the aural and visual elements in the context of an ethical dilemma for the audience. A blue wash of light that envelops the stage and backdrop for most of the play leaves the audience to contemplate whether they are simply having trouble distinguishing between ocean and horizon or if the characters are already lost in the depths of the ocean. As this blue wash blurs the audience's perception of whether characters are sinking or floating toward their destination, the characters offer up the phrases, "Solo hay silencio" [There is only silence] and "Solo hay vacío" [There is only emptiness] into the audience sitting in darkness beyond the stage lighting. While positioning the characters as hearing "silence" calls the audience's attention to the ethical question of what is heard and unheard in this play, references to a void prompt the audience to think of the broader Caribbean poetics related to space and time outlined in Édouard Glissant's history of the "abyss." For Glissant, this concept recalls the layers of Caribbean history symbolized by the belly of the slave ship, the depths of the sea, and the void of memory that follows from this history. Describing the new forms of relation based not on linear histories but rather on the common experiences of the abyss, Glissant states, "Relation is not made up of things that are foreign but of shared knowledge. This experience of the abyss can now be said to be the best element of exchange" (Glissant 2010, 8). This symbolism of the abyss evoked in the dialogue, music, and visual vocabulary challenges the usefulness of the concept of "crisis" in connection with the migration "crises" being staged in this play as resolvable aberrant deviations from the linear progression of time. Instead, *La otra orilla* situates the so-called migration "crises" from the 1990s within the depths of a postcolonial and catastrophic lived reality. An aurality based on sound effects, music, and dialogue introduces broader questions about the visibility and audibility of these everyday embodied experiences that exceed specific and sensationalized instances of (im)migration across the sea.

Reclaiming the Senses in *Yemaya's Belly*

Like in *La otra orilla*, in *Yemaya's Belly*, the unsettling of fixed temporality and spatiality provides the backdrop for a reorientation of the senses in the face of catastrophe. The choice of Yemaya—the mother of all orishas and divinity of all oceans—as the orisha that frames the play not only emphasizes the island setting but also contributes to the play's obscuring of the island's specific geographical and temporal location.[10] In spite of the fact that multiple reviews available online reference Cuba as the name of the island at the center of the story, geographical space is ambiguous in the published version.[11] The setting is: "The ocean. It may be miles away, a distant whisper. Or we may be underwater [...]" (Hudes 2008, 198). And the first scene begins in "a mountain farming town on an island" (199) according to the stage directions. This complements the connotation of Yemaya as a global deity. Her presence also adds depth to the spatiality of the play—disrupting both linear and lateral movement—in the scene where Mulo, after setting sail with Maya toward the United States, seems to fall off of his raft and plummet into the ocean. As Mulo falls through a "hotel underwater" (235) in the oneiric scene mentioned above where he is a rich businessman who has profited off his design of a new flavor of Coke and where he interacts with various characters from his hometown, he encounters Yemaya in the deepest moment. From these depths she admonishes Mulo, "Remember me like you remember your ancestors" (237), affirming a connection between the spatial and temporal disruptions in the play.

Temporal disruptions in the plot are accentuated using lighting to show a disjointed and non-linear progression from scene to scene. For example, in the first scene, the entire plot is compressed—both in spatial and temporal terms—into a few minutes of narration. The story that Jesus tells in this first moment of dialogue is one about a boy whose father will not give him a penny, so he runs away and spends the night in a coconut tree, and, on a high wind that comes up in the night, flies over the ocean to the "house of the President of America" where he receives a penny to buy a sugar cookie (199). This disruption of linearity via narrative compression and dispersion is then further enhanced using lighting across the seventeen scenes as the lighting shifts from sunrise to, after an unspecified amount of time, night, then "dark morning" (215), sunrise, a week-long time jump, midnight, sunrise, a time jump of "several days" (238), and, finally, "bright sun" (241). Within this progression, after beginning in linear fashion with the dawning of the sun, time is, in different moments, stretched or compressed or lost in ambiguity. And while ending in full sun does suggest a general symbolism of recognition or enlightenment, any organization around a linear progression initiated by the first scene's sunrise remains unfulfilled. Yemaya's presence as a character further emphasizes this disruption with her call to memory quoted above. As Eric Mayer-García notes, Yoruba-influenced theater traditions emphasize "how we keep company" with the past (2022, 529), and, in this sense, Yemaya functions to mark the layering of temporality as the cumulative effect of colonial violence within the play.

It is within this broader context of temporal and spatial disruption that a sensory tension is established between contemporary capitalism and a postcolonial reimagining of sensory engagements with the world. Colonial and capitalist relationships frame the play from the beginning as the first scene, which in turn frames the entire work, refers to flag colors and export products that connect the United States to much of the Caribbean archipelago. The protagonist Jesus begins a story by saying, "Red white and blue / Sugar and gin / My story begins" and ends this initial monologue with "Red white and blue / Sugar and rum / My story is done" (Hudes 2008, 199). In addition to referencing Yoruba color symbolism as *La otra orilla* does, the colors named here are not only those of the US flag but also those of, among others, the Puerto Rican, Dominican, and Cuban flags, suggesting that the temporal and geographical disruptions have implications for how Caribbean nationhood and belonging are understood throughout the play. By invoking sugar, rum, and gin—export products related to the colonial histories of various Caribbean islands, the play emphasizes the intertwined histories of colonialism and capitalism within the archipelago, challenging notions of national sovereignty and always already framing local and individual stories within a more dispersed geopolitical context.

In *Yemaya's Belly*, these histories churn in the background of Jesústurned-Mulo's coming-of-age story and ultimate sea migration. On a structural level, this play—in which the central male protagonist moves from a rural mountain town to the city before setting sail for the continental United States—reproduces not only a common migration trope in Puerto Rican theater but also real-world patterns of development that have unfolded throughout the Caribbean archipelago where agricultural economies based on colonial export products like sugar and coffee transitioned to manufacturing export economies—a trend that many attribute at least in part to the Reagan-era Caribbean Basin Initiative (CBI).[12] In the play, the fallout of this economic transition involving the progressive implementation of neoliberal economic policies is entangled with colonial and environmental histories. The rural mountain town where Jesús grew up is destroyed by a wildfire whose casualties include his parents—a verisimilar plot device that corresponds to a Caribbean reality where most vegetation, including the palm forests referenced throughout *Yemaya's Belly*, belongs to fire-prone ecosystems that are increasingly vulnerable to the "slow violence" of drought and rising temperatures (Robbins et al. 2008, 529). In the play, the characters connect this environmental reality with one of economic dependence, saying, "Who do they think they are to come and tell us the fire was a good thing? [...] It's an excuse not to give us any aid" (Hudes 2008, 227). In the Caribbean, plantation economies had already established the patterns of mass production of crops for export alongside the importation of European food staples (Thompson 2019, 10–11); the CBI encouraged the neoliberal continuation of this model by encouraging reduced crop diversity and a shift in household diets to include processed imported foods (Miller 2023, 88). Two of the main props used in the play—a bottle of Coke and cans of Spam—are representative of the island's reliance on imported products from the United States. Such globalized consumer products can be considered "invasive" (Etherington 2022, 41) in the way that they materialize the integration of US empire into the intimate spaces and daily lives of US territorial possessions.

While these enmeshed issues appear at a thematic level in the play, they are also staged as embodied and sensory-rich rituals. In her stage directions that parallel her perception of Lukumí rituals and theater as "bodies in the dark, breathing in communion" (Hudes 2022, 265), Hudes emphasizes: " [...] *A ritual involves a body and an object, together in a moment of possession. Rituals are crude, physically exaggerated. They make the body raw*" (Hudes 2008, 198). In the moment where Jesús tries Coke for the first time, the stage directions emphasize his multi-sensory, erotic, and ritualized experience where the cold burns his hand

and his tongue visibly licks and tastes the rim of the bottle before he gulps down the contents (211). The Coke is both dangerous and alluring but is ultimately experienced as pleasurable (222). Later in the play, Jesús and Maya's conversation about Spam highlights repeats this ritual and dominates sight, smell, touch, and taste:

> MULO: Does it sting when you eat it?
> MAYA: No. For the tenth time.
> MULO: Does it have little air bubbles?
> MAYA: Here you go. Smell it first. [*He smells the meat.*]
> MULO: Does all American meat smell like that? (231)

In the play, and in line with Amich's concept of the "neoliberal sensorium," US global consumer products are reframed as "possessing" the characters, shaping and distorting their reality.

In contrast to this ritualized and embodied experience of neoliberalism, the touch of another prop—a duck feather—disrupts linear time in a way that ultimately highlights a possible formula for reorienting the senses. The first ritual moment of the play involves Yemaya appearing to Jesús's Uncle Jelin and engaging him in a ritual involving a duck feather—a typical offering associated with Yemaya (Hudes 2008, 207).[13] As Anne García-Romero highlights in her analysis of ritual in *Yemaya's Belly*, this feather from Yemaya sets the play's other rituals in motion (García-Romero 2016, 155). I would further emphasize the way that the play follows Jesús's relationship with this feather as a capitalistic one that is at first extractive, possessive, and transactional. Jesús first "snatches the duck feather"; then, he declares, "It's mine anyway", when it is gifted to him; finally, he trades it for his first Coke (Hudes 2008, 206–209). In contrast, in the final ritual of the play, Jesús-now-Mulo retrieves the feather from between Maya's breasts in a sensual scene where he "*puts the feather to his nose and smells it*" (241). While this scene speaks to Mulo's sexual awakening, it is also a precursor to the scene where Mulo and Maya perform their mothers' funerals, with Mulo declaring, "We don't have their bodies but this feather stands for them instead" (242). Confirming García-Romero's assertion that the play creates a sacred space that "is not some lofty, faraway place, but a location that is sensual and earthy" (García-Romero 2016, 155), this transformation of Jesús/Mulo's relationship with the feather highlights how the sensory reclamation that occurs in the play goes hand-in-hand with the temporal disruptions that reorient characters away from transactional ways of knowing through an embodied acknowledgement of the coexistence of the past and present.

Conclusion: Beyond Existing Cognitive Frameworks

It is worth noting that in both cases the sense of deferred or pending arrival is not necessarily an implied tragedy and leaves listeners space for what Mayer-García calls "a postcolonial sense of futurity" (2022, 529). This concept highlights how inhabiting a transcultural space marked by both Western linear and Yoruba cyclical time forms the possible basis for the ability to see a potential future beyond the limitations of the present.[14] In *La otra orilla*, a not-unhopeful ending clashes with an initial sense of hopelessness. At around the fifteen-minute mark of the play, the sound of a loud ship horn indicates the invisible presence of a passing ship. "¡Eh! ¡Estamos aquí!" [We are here!], the two main characters onstage begin to yell, gesticulating wildly at the ship while facing the audience who is thus positioned as the interlocutor of their cries for help. The sound builds to a climax before fizzling out as the characters proclaim, "Es inútil" [It's useless], and, "Resignación" [Resignation]. This situating of the audience in the problematic position of being the ones who choose not to hear and see the plight of the migrants represented on the stage reinforces a theme that persists throughout the play. The hopelessness of the situation is underscored by the play's production in Spanish for a Spanish-speaking audience, which leaves a viewer wondering if those being hailed by the dialogue—the economic and political decision-makers with the power to intervene in the events portrayed onstage—have the linguistic ability to hear this ethical challenge. Despite the hopelessness of exchanges like this one throughout the play, the play ends with the characters declaring, "No debamos perder de vista el horizonte […]. Tiene que haber algún lugar para nosotros" [Let's not lose sight of the horizon […]. There has to be a place for us]." In a similar future-affirming fashion, with hope for a possible rescue and reference to another beginning, the final statement by Mulo in *Yemaya's Belly*, "It's land" (243), acknowledges the possibility of landing on solid ground. While linear progress toward arrival—the goal of real and staged migration journeys as well as a sense of overcoming and moving past a temporary crisis—remains uncertain in both plays, there is a sense of an awakening awareness of catastrophe as the necessary basis for thinking beyond "existing cognitive frameworks" (Maldonado-Torres 2019, 336).

In conversation with the multi-sensory components explored throughout this chapter, these endings that ask audiences to dwell on questions of visibility and audibility as catalysts to understanding future possibility reflect an ethical positioning of audiences that, taking its cue from Yoruba cosmology, emphasizes an embodied approach to knowledge. Yoruba traditions—in conversation with Glissant's exploration of filiation—are key to understanding the non-Western approaches to both temporality and spatiality in the works. In *La otra orilla* and *Yemaya's Belly*, theater puts past and future into conversation with present migration "crises," reorienting audiences' attention toward the ethical dilemmas that characterize the catastrophic reality underlying the specific moment of crisis experienced by the characters featured onstage. In the plays, creators capture the sensorium of postcolonial and neoliberal realities while also asking audiences to consider how other forms of embodied engagement might destabilize or alter the way these regimes discipline the senses. This shifts thinking from how to restore the progress disrupted by a moment of crisis and toward the ritualized and sustained everyday actions necessary to address a catastrophic reality.

Notes

1. For a detailed analysis of how disasters like Hurricane Maria unmask racialized and otherwise unequal social dynamics that accrue over time due to postcolonial governance strategies, see Bonilla (2020, 148).
2. For an example of this language of crisis in relation to Cuban rafters in the mid-1990s, see the "Cuban Raft" entry on the National Museum of the American Latino website. For an example in relation to Haitian refugees in the early-1990s, see the language in the Haitian Refugee Protection Act of 1992, H.R. 3844, 102nd Congress (1991–1992). In his comprehensive work *Undocumented Dominican Migration*, Frank Graziano details the sensationalized media campaigns sponsored by the US Embassy to discourage travel in *yolas*—or makeshift boats—in the early 2000s (Graziano 2013, 89–90). Also see Stevens (2019).
3. See Ybarra (2017) and Stevens (2019) for other detailed and incisive readings.

4. I accessed the 1996 recorded staging of *La otra orilla* at the Hemispheric Institute Digital Video Library.
5. My analysis is based on the 2008 published acting edition of Hudes's *Yemaya's Belly*. After being developed in a Brown University workshop in 2002, the play was first presented in a professional production in 2004 (Hudes 2008, 197).
6. For an analysis of how US power brokers have historically applied the tropes of neoliberalism to Puerto Rico long before the 1973, which is commonly acknowledged as the origin point for neoliberalism, see Villanueva (2015).
7. With the phrase "being in the same boat," I am thinking of works such as Ana Lydia Vega's short story collection *Encancaranublado y otros cuentos de naufragio* (1982) ["Encancaranublado" and other shipwreck stories] and Mayra Santos Febres' poetry collection *Boat People* (2005) that use the metaphor of sea travel to highlight a pan-Caribbean postcolonial reality.
8. Rolón's character is dressed in a black skirt suit with a scalloped white lapel, black almond-toe pumps, and a black pillbox hat with some gray gauze piece attached. Merced's character is wearing a dark gray three-piece suit with black oxfords, a maroon scarf, and a gray fedora. The clothes look like they could have been cut from black-and-white mid-century images visualized in, for example, the photo collection Pioneros II: Puerto Ricans in New York City 1948–1998 (Sánchez-Korrol and Hernández 2010).
9. Operation Bootstrap was a top-down economic development plan of modernization and industrialization that was carried out in Puerto Rico to shift the island's economy from a previously agrarian one. It depended heavily on the efficient redistribution and control of the Puerto Rican population through encouraged migration to the US mainland.
10. For further exploration of Yemaya's global significance, see Falola and Akinyemi (2016, 506–507) and Karade (1994, 27).
11. In their invocation of a Cuban context, reviews tend to reference similarities to Cuban youth Elián González's migration story—which became a transnational controversy and custody battle from 1999–2000—or to contextualize the play in relation to President Obama's historic visit to Cuba in 2016. See Horowitz (2005), Lemieux (2017), See (2005), and Wilson (2017).

12. The Caribbean Basin Initiative refers to the Reagan administration's economic policy toward the Caribbean centered around a piece of legislation—the Caribbean Basin Economic Recovery Act of 1983, which gave certain Caribbean countries duty free access to US manufacturing and agricultural markets (Schrank 2008, 145–146). Additionally, the policy offered foreign assistance for the development of new infrastructure meant to attract foreign investment (145).
13. For an analysis of the relationship between Yemaya and the symbol of the duck, see Beliso De-Jesus (2013).
14. Mayer-García combines "postcolonialism" with José Esteban Muñoz's articulation of "futurity" as that which is both latent in and surpasses the failings of the present (Mayer-García 2022, 541–542).

Works Cited

Ahmed, Sara. 2006. *Queer Phenomenology: Orientations, Objects, Others*. Durham: Duke University Press.

Amich, Candice. 2020. *Precarious Forms: Performing Utopia in the Neoliberal Americas*. Evanston: Northwestern University Press.

Aradau, Claudia, and Rens Van Munster. 2011. *Politics of Catastrophe: Genealogies of the Unknown*. New York: Routledge.

Beliso-De Jesús, Aisha M. 2013. Yemayá's Duck: Irony, Ambivalence, and the Effeminate Male Subject in Cuban Santería. In *Yemoja: Gender, Sexuality, and Creativity in the Latina/o and Afro-Atlantic Diasporas*, ed. Solimar Otero and Toyin Falola. Albany: State University of New York Press.

Berlant, Lauren G. 2011. *Cruel Optimism*. Durham: Duke University Press.

Bonilla, Yarimar. 2020. Postdisaster Futures. Hopeful Pessimism, Imperial Ruination, and *La futura cuir*. *Small Axe* 62: 147–162.

Duany, Jorge. 2000. Nation on the Move: The Construction of Cultural Identities in Puerto Rico and the Diaspora. *American Ethnologist* 27 (1): 5–30.

Etherington, Bonnie. 2022. Reckoning With the Oceanic Territoriality of 'Uncle SPAM': Processed Meats and Resurgent Seeds in Craig Santos Perez's Poetics of the Militarized Pacific. *Native American and Indigenous Studies* 9 (2): 38–65.

Falola, Toyin, and Akintunde Akinyemi. 2016. *Encyclopedia of the Yoruba*. Bloomington: Indiana University Press.

García-Romero, Anne. 2016. *The Fornes Frame: Contemporary Latina Playwrights and the Legacy of Maria Irene Fornes*. Tucson: University of Arizona Press.

Glissant, Édouard. 2010. *Poetics of Relation*. Translated by Betsy Wing. Ann Arbor: University of Michigan Press.

Graziano, Frank. 2013. *Undocumented Dominican Migration*. Austin: University of Texas Press.

Herrera, Patricia, and Marci R. McMahon. 2019. ¡Oye, Oye! A Manifesto for Listening to Latinx Theater. *Aztlán: A Journal of Chicano Studies* 44 (1): 239–248.

Horowitz, Jane. 2005. Going With Her Gut Instincts: 'Yemaya's Belly' Playwright Lets Each Story Shape a New Dramatic Structure. *The Washington Post*, November 21. https://www.washingtonpost.com/archive/lifestyle/2005/11/22/going-with-her-gut-instincts/d141428a-1136-420c-9d3d-3463b854acd8/.

Hudes, Quiara Alegría. 2008. *Yemaya's Belly*. New York: Dramatists Play Service Inc.

Hudes, Quiara Alegría. 2022. *My Broken Language: A Memoir*. William Collins.

Karade, Baba Ifa. 1994. *The Handbook of Yoruba Religious Concepts*. Weiser Books.

La Fountain-Stokes, Lawrence. 2008. Trans/Bolero/Drag/Migration: Music, Cultural Translation, and Diasporic Puerto Rican Theatricalities. *Women's Studies Quarterly* 36 (3/4): 190–209.

Lemieux, Katy. 2017. Yemaya's Belly Asks Whether the American Dream Is Good, or Even Real. *The Dallas Observer*, March 2. https://www.dallasobserver.com/arts/yemayas-belly-asks-whether-the-american-dream-is-good-or-even-real-9237275.

Maldonado-Torres, Nelson. 2019. Afterword: Critique and Decoloniality in the Face of Crisis, Disaster, and Catastrophe. In *Aftershocks of Disaster: Puerto Rico Before and After the Storm*, ed. Yarimar Bonilla and Marisol LeBrón. Chicago: Haymarket Books.

Sánchez-Korrol, Virginia and Pedro Juan Hernández. 2010. *Pioneros: Puerto Ricans in New York City 1892–1948*. Arcadia Publishing.

Mayer-García, Eric. 2022. Esu's Crossroads and Ogun's Crossing Over: Intercultural Creativity and Postcolonial Futurity in the Theater of Femi Euba. *Atlantic Studies* 19: 526–545.

McKean, Benjamin L. 2022. *Disorienting Neoliberalism: Global Justice and the Outer Limit of Freedom*. Oxford University Press.

Miller, Donna. 2023. Climate Change and Globalization: Food Security in the Caribbean. *Caribbean Quilt* 7 (1): 86–91.

National Museum of the American Latino. n.d. "Cuban Raft." Accessed March 18, 2024. https://latino.si.edu/exhibitions/presente/immigration-stories/cuban-raft.

Nixon, Rob. 2013. *Slow Violence and the Environmentalism of the Poor*. Cambridge: Harvard University Press.

Rivera-Batiz, Francisco, and Carlos E. Santiago. 1996. *Island Paradox: Puerto Rico in the 1990s*. Russell Sage Foundation.

Robbins, A. Marcus J., Claus-Martin Eckelmann, and Maya Quiñones. 2008. Forest Fires in the Insular Caribbean. *Ambio* 37 (7–8): 528–534.

Santos Febres, Mayra. 2005. *Boat People*. San Juan: Ediciones Callejón Inc.

Schrank, Andrew. 2008. Sugar's Political By-Product: The Caribbean Basin Initiative. *Globalizations* 5 (2): 143–150.

See, Rich. 2005. A CurtainUp DC Review: Yemaya's Belly. *CurtainUp*, November 18. http://curtainupcom.siteprotect.net/yemayasbelly.html.

Stevens, Camilla. 2019. *Aquí and Allá: Transnational Dominican Theater and Performance*. Pittsburgh: University of Pittsburgh Press.

Teatro Pregones. 1996. Video of play *La otra orilla*. Teatro Pregones Collection, Hemispheric Institute Digital Video Library, New York University, New York, NY. http://hdl.handle.net/2333.1/jsxksn9b.

Thompson, Merisa S. 2019. Still Searching for (Food) Sovereignty: Why Are Radical Discourses only Partially Mobilised in the Independent Anglo-Caribbean? *Geoforum* 101: 90–99.

Vega, Ana Lydia. 1982. *Encancaranublado y otros cuentos de naufragio*. Editorial Antillana.

Villanueva, Victor. 2015. Puerto Rico: A Neoliberal Crucible. *Journal of Cultural Economy* 8 (1): 62–74.

West-Durán, Alan. 2013. What the Water Brings and Takes Away: The Work of María Magdalena Campos Pons. In *Yemoja: Gender, Sexuality, and Creativity in the Latina/of and Afro-Atlantic Diasporas*, ed. Solimar Otero and Toyin Fabiola. Albany: State University of New York Press.

Wilson, Lindsey. 2017. A Feather-light Plot Drowns This Dallas Theater Company's Poetic Play. *Culture Map: Dallas*, March 13. https://dallas.culturemap.com/news/arts/03-13-17-yemayas-belly-cara-mia-theatre-co-review/.

Ybarra, Patricia. 2017. *Latinx Theater in the Times of Neoliberalism*. Evanston: Northwestern University Press.

CHAPTER 11

PROMESA, Anti-colonial Drag, and Diasporic Puerto Rican Trans Revolution

Lawrence La Fountain-Stokes

How can over-the-top queer and trans theatrical experiences challenge the nefarious impact of US imperialism in the Caribbean and envision bridges of solidarity between Puerto Ricans and Nuyoricans? Mara Vélez Meléndez's play *Notes on Killing Seven Oversight, Management and Economic Stability Board Members* addresses the contemporary collapse of self-governance in Puerto Rico and the catastrophe of colonialism through a parodic, dream-like drag show centered on killing seven members of the Puerto Rico Oversight, Management and Economic Stability (PROMESA) Board who, despite their having been appointed and not democratically elected, have controlled the archipelago's economy since 2016.[1] The play, which received extensive and mostly positive press

---

L. La Fountain-Stokes (✉)
Department of American Culture and Department of Romance Languages and Literatures, University of Michigan, Ann Arbor, MI, USA
e-mail: lawrlafo@umich.edu

© The Author(s), under exclusive license to Springer Nature Switzerland AG 2025
C. Stevens and J. D. Rossini (eds.), *The Coloniality of Catastrophe in Caribbean Theater and Performance*,
https://doi.org/10.1007/978-3-031-85791-1_11

coverage, was presented for the first time at Soho Rep in New York City in 2022 in collaboration with The Sol Project under the direction of David Mendizábal and was described as "Mara Vélez Meléndez's Off-Broadway debut" and as "a drag show about decolonizing places and people."[2] According to press materials, the protagonist, Lolita (Christine Carmela), a Puerto Rican transgender character inspired by the revolutionary Lolita Lebrón, "in the name of la Revolución, finds herself in the Wall Street office of the Puerto Rico Oversight, Management and Economic Stability Board with glamour, glitter, and a gun."[3] In 2024, the play had its West Coast premiere at the Moxie Theatre in San Diego, California, under the direction of Andréa Agosto, in collaboration with Diversionary Theatre, where it was also described as a "drag fantasmagoria" (Coddon 2024).[4]

Notes on Killing is structured around Lolita's interactions with the gay, cisgender Nuyorican Receptionist (Samora la Perdida), who stages seven drag performances in which they parodically rehearse killing each of the board members. The play follows the absurdist tradition of Samuel Beckett's *Waiting for Godot*, Myrna Casas's *Absurdos en soledad*, and Pedro Pietri's *The Masses Are Asses*, positing social critique through complex dialogues and actions, the meanings of which are potentially unclear. The play works against the invisibilization of brown trans subjects that Francisco J. Galarte (2021) has critiqued; highlights Puerto Rican transloca subjectivities (La Fountain-Stokes 2021a); and opens a creative space for what Andrea Bolivar (2018) identifies as spaces of being "a *fantasía*" for transgender Latinas.

Inspired by the theater of the absurd, by camp and queer theatrical and performance practices, and by Hannah Arendt's *On Revolution* (Olujobi 2022, 14–23), Vélez Meléndez proposes feminist, queer, and trans revolutionary solutions to American colonial exploitation in place since the 1898 invasion of Puerto Rico by US troops during the Spanish-American War. This exploitation became intensified after the fiscal collapse of 2008 and especially after the impact of Hurricanes Irma and María in 2017, the earthquakes of 2020, and the COVID-19 pandemic that same year.[5] This period has also been marked by radical mass anticorruption activism, most notably in the summer of 2019, which led to the ouster of then governor Ricardo Rosselló Nevares.[6]

By centering a Puerto Rican transgender character (Lolita, interpreted by a trans actress) and a gay Nuyorican cisgender character performing in drag (the Receptionist, interpreted by a gender nonconforming performer) who states that they are "from the Bronx" and speak "*limited* Spanish" (Vélez Meléndez 2022b[1], 20, emphasis in the original), the play makes a major intervention on the American stage and in Caribbean diasporic theater while challenging dominant cisgender patriarchal heterosexual conceptions of puertorriqueñidad. It builds upon other transloca and dragtivist queer and trans Puerto Rican precedents (La Fountain-Stokes 2021a)[7] and allows for a conversation between island (or archipelago) and diaspora as a means to critique the power of the Board, known in Spanish as "la Junta de Supervisión Fiscal." *Notes on Killing* is notable as a work by an island-born-and-raised, now diasporic transgender Puerto Rican playwright who draws on her personal experiences (Solís 2022; Vélez Meléndez 2022a) and has collaborated with a Puerto Rican, Nuyorican, Diasporican, and Latinx LGBTQ+ cast and production team, including a TNB2S+ (transgender, non-binary, and Two-Spirit+) Latine (Ecuadorian Puerto Rican) director.[8]

In this chapter, I analyze *Notes on Killing* in the context of scholarship regarding Puerto Rican colonialism, disaster capitalism, and cultural resistance. I see this production as expanding Diana Taylor's notion of the "repertoire" as a series of embodied performance practices, for example, those of the Puerto Rican television astrologer Walter Mercado (Taylor 2003, 110–132), and as an example of what David Román presents as performances that, in their use of drag, reflect directly on politics and society in the United States (Román 2005, 78–108). I draw from José Esteban Muñoz's concept of "terrorist drag" (Muñoz 1999), Kareem Khubchandani's (2023) decolonial drag, and my own work on transloca performance (La Fountain-Stokes 2021a) to better contextualize Vélez Meléndez's radical exploration of drag and trans performance and identity.

In its parodic and over-the-top-expression, Vélez Meléndez's play is different from other theatrical and artistic responses to the Puerto Rican financial collapse and to natural disasters, such as the collective play *¡Ay María!* presented across the island in late 2017 (Bonilla and LeBrón 2019, 38–60), the Whitney Museum of American Art exhibit *no existe un mundo poshuracán: Puerto Rican Art in the Wake of Hurricane Maria* (Guerrero 2023), and Cecilia Aldarondo's masterful documentary *Landfall* (Aldarondo 2020). As a trans piece, its closest referent is Roque

---

[1] Vélez Meléndez, Mara. 2022b. Notes on Killing Seven Oversight, Management and Economic Stability Board Members. New York: Soho Rep.

Raquel Salas Rivera's *The Tertiary/Lo terciario*, a Marxist-inspired bilingual poetry collection by a Lambda-Literary-Award-winning transgender Puerto Rican author who explicitly critiques the Fiscal Supervision Board, calling them out by name (Salas Rivera 2018, 73).

Notes on Killing stages a dramatic collision between queer Ridiculous variants of theater of the absurd and Puerto Rican traditions of decolonial political theater that envision national liberation but have markedly excluded matters of sexual difference; these two radically different traditions have historically not intersected, except perhaps in the work of the queer Puerto Rican performer and filmmaker José Rodríguez Soltero. While John Vaccaro's Play-House of the Ridiculous and Charles Ludlam's Ridiculous Theatrical Company offered a direct, openly-gay affront to conservative bourgeois sexual mores, they did not include sustained attention to matters of race, ethnicity, or US imperialism in the Caribbean. Vélez Meléndez's play is closer to the work of contemporary queer performers (including Taylor Mac) that Sean F. Edgecomb (2017) identifies as "neo-Ridiculous." As a result, *Notes on Killing* disconcerts and delights audiences for varying reasons, having to do with individuals' different life experiences and varying political concerns.

Colonial Extractivism/ Vulture Capitalism and Rage

As a rewriting of Ibsen's 1896 *John Gabriel Borkman* (Solís 2022), Vélez Meléndez's play shares a critique of the nefarious impact of capitalism, namely of corrupt banking. While Ibsen's play is in the realist mode and focuses on individual actions and their impact on a family—according to one scholar, the protagonist of this play is "modern drama's prototype of the fallen capitalist speculator" (Korte 2015, 151)—*Notes on Killing* offers a structural critique of US government complicity in colonial exploitation as well as a critique of individual financial actors, many of them Puerto Rican, specifically the seven board members whose biographies are shared on stage, before they appear transformed into parodic over-the-top drag characters. The granularity of this critique (its individualization) serves to humanize the abstraction of a fiscal control board whose impact is felt collectively in Puerto Rico by most of the population. The comparison between Ibsen and Vélez Meléndez serves to highlight the pernicious effects of capitalism as a centuries-long economic modality of accumulation of wealth, while also highlighting the particularities of twenty-first-century colonial governance in Puerto Rico (Image 11.1).

As a semi-didactic play meant to raise awareness about contemporary politics, *Notes on Killing* begins with basic contextual information regarding PROMESA, including how this word (the name of a US government bill, signed into law by an ostensibly progressive Democratic president) cynically translates into "promise." As Lolita plays with a gun on stage, she talks about her father, a pro-independence nationalist surveilled by the CIA (Delgado 2025)—or perhaps by the FBI (Navarro 2003)—, and the impact of the news in 2016 about the government's more than $70 billion in debt:

> LOLITA: Dad was ... doing his thing and the Puerto Rican Governor was on the news talking about the huge debt held by the island and how the debt was "unpayable." (Vélez Meléndez 2022b, 14)

We then learn that Lolita's father "died of a heart attack the next day," shortly before President Barack Obama signed the PROMESA Bill into law. As Lolita indicates,

Image 11.1 Christine Carmela as Lolita in the Soho Rep production of Mara Vélez Meléndez's *Notes on Killing Seven Oversight, Management and Economic Stability Board Members*, New York City, 2022 (Image courtesy of Soho Rep)

LOLITA: Not long after, these United States of America, in all their imperial and colonizing grandeur, sign a bill titled the Puerto Rico Oversight, Management and Economic Stability Act.
P-R-O-M-E-S-A
PROMESA
The bill imposes an UNELECTED board of seven "experts on economy" with deciding power over finances, budgets, essential services
Classic board stuff
They restructure … and guarantee the payment a debt created by irresponsible politicians, politicians that haven't been held accountable for STUPID decisions
Anyway
The people on the island are being held accountable
And this Board is out there making sure that happens
Single-handedly proving the enduring colonial status of the island of Puerto Rico under the United States of America (Vélez Meléndez 2022b, 15)

Given this context, Lolita poses one of the play's key political questions: whether the use of violence is justified in contexts of oppression. She asks: "Do we hesitate to kill our leaders because we're tired?," "or… are we tired because we keep hesitating to kill our leaders?" (Vélez Meléndez 2022b, 16). As a dream fantasy of revenge, *Notes on Killing* becomes an honor play (in the mode of a farce) in which an aggrieved Puerto Rican trans daughter seeks to avenge her dead father and a collapsed colonial nation. Simultaneously, it becomes a space where a genderqueer Nuyorican drag performer (the Receptionist) vindicates their mother in their own process of decolonization, which entails narrating family stories as part of a process of overcoming the shackles of restrictive gender binarism.

Soho Rep's inclusion of a fragment of Hannah Arendt's essay *On Revolution* in its *Supplement* publication invites audience members to critically reflect on the current situation in Puerto Rico as part of a longer history of financial exploitation and on the revolutionary ability or inability to transform society through violent actions (Arendt 2022). In her reading of Marx's analysis of the French Revolution, Arendt highlights the subversive potential of disempowered social groups and how they possess radical revolutionary abilities, but also questions their long-term efficacy. Arendt offers a critical reading of Marxist and liberal democratic thought (Wellmer 1999), stating that "suffering, once it is transformed into rage, can release overwhelming forces" (Arendt 2022, 19).

It is precisely this rage that Lolita and the Receptionist tap into, a rage that builds on the history of revolutions in Puerto Rico and elsewhere, such as the 1868 Grito de Lares, the 1950 Jayuya Revolt, and the 1954 United States Capitol shooting by Lolita Lebrón, Rafael Cancel Miranda, Andrés Figueroa Cordero, and Irvin Flores Rodríguez. It is also a rage comparable to that which motivated the Verano del 19 mass protests in 2019 or to what Marisol LeBrón (2021b) has called *coraje* or "a decolonial feminist politics of rage in Puerto Rico"; to the rage highlighted by Frantz Fanon, whether it is speaking against racism in *Black Skin, White Masks* (Fanon 2008) or against colonialism in *The Wretched of the Earth* (Fanon 1963); and to the rage (articulated as anger) against sexism, racism, and homophobia expressed by the diasporic Caribbean queer feminist writer and activist Audre Lorde (1981) in her landmark essay "The Uses of Anger." It is also transgender rage, what Susan Stryker describes as "how to harness the intense emotions emanating from transsexual experience—especially rage—and mobilize them into effective political actions" (1994, 237), as well as what the Argentine trans activist and theorist Marlene Wayar (2021) calls "furia travesti."

The current financial and humanitarian crisis in Puerto Rico has been amply documented. Naomi Klein's *The Battle for Paradise: Puerto Rico Takes on the Disaster Capitalists* informed Soho Rep's production and appears in their *Supplements* volume, including Klein's critique of colonialism and its impact on the psyche of the people of the archipelago, including Puerto Rico, Vieques, and Culebra. As she states:

> The deepest scars may be even harder to see. Colonialism itself is a social experiment, a multilayered system of explicit and implicit controls designed to strip colonized peoples of their culture, confidence, and power. With tools ranging from the brute military and police aggression used to put down strikes and rebellions, to a law that once banned the Puerto Rican flag, to the dictates handed down today by the unelected fiscal control board, residents of these islands have been living under that web of control for centuries. (Klein, in Olujobi 2022, 30)

Meanwhile, Ed Morales, in *Fantasy Island: Colonialism, Exploitation, and the Betrayal of Puerto Rico*, describes the financial, education, and infrastructure crisis, highlighting the role of art as a conveyor of social resistance, seeing it as "faithful to Puerto Rican culture and tradition carrying with it a political component, just as seeking recognition counteracts the invisibility assigned to them by the exploitative mechanisms of colonial capital" (Morales 2019, 258). Rocío Zambrana, in *Colonial Debts: The Case of Puerto Rico*, expands this analysis, centering the impact of neoliberalism and disaster capitalism. According to Zambrana, the people most affected by Hurricane María in 2017 were trans individuals who no longer had access to hormone therapies and faced discrimination in the refuge centers, as well as the islands' population of people experiencing domestic abuse who saw crimes against them increase dramatically (Zambrana 2021). The deliberate nature of these crises is further registered by José Atiles (2024) in *Crisis by Design: Emergency Powers and Colonial Legality in Puerto Rico*.

The bibliography on the Verano del 19 mass protests also brings the crisis of colonial governance into focus, including how queerness forms part of this social critique and radical revolutionary impetus, whether it is by taking a stand "against Muerto Rico" (LeBrón 2021a), decrying the 4,645 deaths provoked by the hurricane's aftermath and governmental ineptitude (Powers Guimond 2020) or exploring the "poetics of devastation and insurgency" (Rodríguez Castro 2022). Similarly, Arnaldo Cruz-Malavé (2022) showcases the queer performativity of mourning, for example as embodied by voguers dancing at the Resistencia Ball, showcasing how queer, trans, and gender-nonconforming bodies challenge institutional state power through a politics of abjection and joy.

Feminist, Queer, and Trans Revolutions

Of course, the particularity of Vélez Meléndez's play is the way it combines a trenchant critique of the coloniality of catastrophe (described by Klein as the systematic disinvestment that became intensified in 2006 with the flight of American corporations after the repeal of tax incentives, which then led to a total collapse of the Puerto Rican economy in 2008 and to massive layoffs in 2013) with the history of feminist, queer, and trans resistance highlighted by artists such as Cecilia Aldarondo (2020) and Salas Rivera (2018). This appears most notably in *Notes on Killing* through the invocation of the figure of Lolita Lebrón (1919–2010), best known for participating in an attack on US Congress in 1954 on behalf of the independence of Puerto Rico that injured four American legislators. While Sandra Ruiz (2019) has analyzed Lebrón's political performance as part of what Ruiz calls "Ricanness," a decolonial aesthetic and political strategy built on challenging abjection and affirming ontological being, Jon Rossini (2024) has analyzed multiple representations of Lebrón by diasporic Puerto Rican playwrights in the US, focusing primarily on Migdalia Cruz's *Lolita de Lares* (1995) and Desi Moreno-Penson's *Beige* (2016), while also offering some comments on Vélez Meléndez.[9] These analyses highlight the centrality of gender and women's participation in revolutionary movements, as much as they highlight a history of Puerto Rican armed resistance to US imperialism.[10] We could say they echo Arendt's analysis of the rage of the dispossessed, also bringing together the political critique of individuals such as Pedro Albizu Campos (1893–1965), perhaps the best-known antiimperialist leader in Puerto Rico, with the broader antiimperialist critique of Fanon.

Vélez Meléndez's play centers the revolutionary figure of Lolita Lebrón, borrowing her name and visuals—the dress she wore in her 1954 attack, with its distinctive details: "a grey skirt suit with three lines across the chest: one navy, another indigo and the third one white" (Vélez Meléndez 2022b, 16–17)—but repurposes and expands her politics to address queer and trans concerns, a subject that was quite anathema to the ultra-Catholic, family-centered Nationalist politics espoused by leaders such as Albizu Campos and Lebrón, who never positioned themselves in support of the LGBTQ+ civil rights struggle. Here, Lebrón would seem to be standing in for other, more visible, Puerto Rican queer and trans revolutionary leaders such as the Stonewall veteran and Young Lords member Sylvia Rivera (La Fountain-Stokes 2021a, 2021b). Yet Vélez Meléndez is not the only trans Puerto Rican artist who references Lebrón: the globally-recognized rapper Villano Antillano opens her 2022 debut album *La sustancia X* with the song "Precaución, esta canción es un hechizo" in which the transfemme non-binary singer and composer not only references the nationalist leader ("A mí no me apuntes, tú no me señales / Siempre defensiva, tiro con puñales / Porque como la Lebrón estoy buscando congresales" [Don't point at me, don't point me out / Always defensive, I throw daggers / Like Lebrón, I'm looking for congressmen]) but even includes a fragment of Lebrón's recorded voice presenting a speech in 2005 (Rivera 2018).

One of the most notable aspects of Vélez Meléndez's play is the way it offers parallels between a national revolution of self-determination (the insistent affirmation of the need for Puerto Rican independence and the undesirability of statehood and of the current "freely associated state" or commonwealth status) and an individual revolution regarding gender identity (the meanings of being transgender or nonbinary, fighting against the oppression of patriarchal, heterosexist, cisgender domination). One of the ways in which this is articulated is through the Receptionist's struggles with identifying a new name. We learn their former, legal one, Eduardo, which they have abandoned but which nevertheless still appears on their government identification, but during most of the play, the Receptionist will insist that they have not chosen a new one. Lolita (also not her name, but the name she has chosen in the PROMESA office on Wall Street as her nom de guerre) keeps suggesting names such as Andrea and Cathy to no avail. In fact, it is not until the end of the play that the Receptionist claims the name Lolita for herself when answering a phone call. As such, "Lolita" becomes a symbol of everywoman in a transfeminist gesture that bridges revolutionary legacies (whether it is Lolita Lebrón or the nineteenth-century poet and patriot Lola Rodríguez de Tió, who penned the revolutionary lyrics of the national anthem) with the legacy of queer and trans revolution, for example, that of Sylvia Rivera, Marsha P. Johnson, and Christina Hayworth, a Stonewall veteran who established the first LGBTQ+ pride parade in Puerto Rico in 1991. It also echoes the legacy of Antonio Pantojas, who was a committed, pro-independence leftist drag performer and actor, as well as my own dragtivist practice as Lola von Miramar (La Fountain-Stokes 2021a, 21–25).[11] Here, the name "Lolita" conjures Susan Stryker's "transgender rage," Marlene Wayar's "furia travesti," and Sylvia Rivera's "street transvestite action revolution," as an embodiment of autochthonous diasporic Puerto Rican transfeminism: an inclusive, radical feminism that does not exclude transgender subjects (Garriga López 2019).

Transloca Drag Disruption

Notes on Killing is eminently an extended drag show that uses the parodic feminization and cartoonish representation of PROMESA board members (including as a flamboyant bishop and as an over-the-top drag king) as a strategy of critique. The political potential of drag is fully realized in the seven embodiments, following the tradition of Theatre of the Ridiculous and its neo-Ridiculous inheritors, while also bringing to life Román's, Muñoz's, and Khubchandani's analysis of the political potential of drag by artists of color as a type of subversion. Following Taylor (2003), the language and physical embodiments of routine (or rather fabulous) drag performances become a rich source of resistance and historical memory: a repertoire that activates emotions in the audience and that is identified as a site of cultural continuity, creativity, and innovation.

In his book *Performance in America*, Román analyzes politics and society in the United States, highlighting Miss Visa Denied, the Malaysian immigrant drag queen protagonist of Chay Yew's 1998 play *A Beautiful Country*, who is "meant to be, according to the program, 'a metaphor of [the] duality experienced by most immigrants: a person caught between two continents, two cultures, two languages, and two homes'" (Román 2005, 93). In uncharacteristic fashion, the character is performed by three actors, which "suggests not simply duality but multiple fragmentation" (Román 2005, 96). For Román, building on Muñoz's "queer acts" and Lisa Lowe's "immigrant acts," Miss Visa Denied becomes an embodiment of "queer immigrant acts" that "acknowledge the alternative forms of sociality and community that these interrelated and collective efforts render positive" and that, much like Vélez Meléndez's play does, "make possible transnational queer subjects, transforming the social and public worlds in which these individuals travel" (Román 2005, 104).

Muñoz's conceptualization of "terrorist drag" is also useful to analyze *Notes on Killing*. In *Disidentifications*, Muñoz analyzes Vaginal Davis's work, proposing a modality of drag performance that destabilizes, disorients, and challenges white supremacy, capitalism, and heteropatriarchy, and which is diametrically opposed to mass-commercialized, corporate-sponsored drag. As the scholar indicates, it is "a queerer modality of drag that is performed by queer-identified drag artists in spaces of queer consumption" (Muñoz 1999, 99). For Muñoz, Davis's punk inspired, civil-rights-struggle-inflected, highly irreverent performances engage radical over-the-top aggressive camp strategies. Muñoz's careful discussion of why Angela Davis (and not the Black Panthers) served as a role model for Vaginal Davis is especially pertinent to understand Vélez Meléndez's play (and why her Lolita is based on Lolita Lebrón and not Nationalist Party president Pedro Albizu Campos):

> Unable to pass as heterosexual black militant through simple counteridentification, Vaginal Davis instead disidentified with Black Power by selecting Angela and *not* the Panthers as a site of self-fashioning and political formation. Davis's deployment of disidentification demonstrates that it is, to

employ Kimberle William[s] Crenshaw's term, an *intersectional strategy*. (Muñoz 1999, 99, emphasis in the original)

Building on Félix Guattari's discussion of the theatrical group the Mirabelles, Muñoz argues for "the potential political power of drag," a political drag that "is about creating an uneasiness, an uneasiness in desire, which works to confound and subvert the social fabric." Muñoz thus sees Vaginal Davis's performance as effecting "counterpublic terrorism" that embodies "a radical impulse toward cultural critique" (1999, 99–100).

This mode of radical critique that subverts mass-commercialized, corporate-sponsored performance also centers Khubchandani's analysis of "decolonial drag" and the radically over-the-top drag performances that spectators witness in *Notes on Killing*. Khubchandani's co-authored book (penned in unison with his drag persona of LaWhore Vagistan) proposes drag "marked by its histories of dissidence," a drag that is "not in subservience to and in collusion with colonial aesthetics and knowledge forms" (Khubchandani 2023, 17). As LaWhore Vagistan asks, "can we perform decolonial critiques through drag without losing the fun, play, and pleasure drag is known for?" (Khubchandani 2023, 17). The answer, as Vélez Meléndez's play demonstrates, is yes (Image 11.2).

Image 11.2 Christine Carmela as Lolita and Samora la Perdida as the Receptionist in the Soho Rep production of Mara Vélez Meléndez's *Notes on Killing Seven Oversight, Management and Economic Stability Board Members*, New York City, 2022 (Image courtesy of Soho Rep)

It is in this context that the appearance of Andrew G. Biggs, José R. González, Carlos M. García, Arthur J. González, David A. Skeel Jr., Ana J. Matosantos, and José Carrión III (the seven original members of the Fiscal Supervision Board, all played by the Receptionist) transformed into the drag parodies of Andrea Baggs, Joséphone Ramonita González, Karlos Grace, Artritis Jay Gonzuela, Bishop Avid Silk, Anita Saintkiller, and Yoseph N. Carry-On attains its political force, its absurdist tone, and its entertainment value. This is done through musical choice, wardrobe, dance choreographies, and dialogue, as well as through the elaborate death scenes, which involve fake guns, machetes, and carefully effected stage combat. This is how the Cambridge University and London School of Economics graduate Andrew G. Biggs (a former Social Security Analyst at the Cato Institute and current senior fellow at the American Enterprise Institute) becomes the over-the-top Andrea Baggs, a girl boss wearing bright, colorful clothes, who appears to the tune of the Spice Girls's "Spice Up Your Life" to discuss cash flow and to accuse Lolita of being a terrorist (Vélez Meléndez 2022b, 29–37), while the San Juan-born José R. González (Chief Executive Officer and President of Federal Home Loan Bank of New York, former CEO and President of Santander BanCorp and of Santander Securities Corporation, and a graduate of Yale and Harvard) becomes Joséphone Ramonita González to the tune of Olga Tañón's "El frío de tu adiós" to talk about loans, bonds, and interest, appearing dressed as a judge, later revealing a dress with the Puerto Rican flag beneath her judicial gown (Vélez Meléndez 2022b, 45–53). In both cases, we witness the radical disjuncture of technocratic financial discourse being used to justify colonial violence but articulated through drag performance: a disconcerting, hilarious, but also perverse twist, which is resolved through the dramatic staging of death.

One of the Receptionist's most unusual and striking drag performances is that of Carlos M. García transformed into the drag king Karlos Grace, "a little Cutie McHottie" who enters to the sultry rhythm of the American R&B singer and songwriter Ginuwine's "Pony" (Vélez Meléndez 2022b, 60–61). As Lolita indicates, García, who was born and raised in Mayagüez, Puerto Rico, is the CEO of Bay Boston Managers LLC, a former Senior Executive Vice President of Santander Bank, and the former CEO of the Government Development Bank for Puerto Rico, or as Lolita states, "another traitor" (Vélez Meléndez 2022b, 60). Meanwhile, according to the stage notes, Karlos Grace is "a hunky, flirty piece of male drag" who "makes his entrance and gives LOLITA a lap dance" while insisting that he is "Karlos with a K" (Vélez Meléndez 2022b, 61). Karlos discusses statehood and flirts with Lolita, presenting the possibility of romance. While Lolita still goes on to kill him, the inclusion of a seductive Latino drag-king character presents an interesting twist in the plot, signaling a multiplicity of desires and the potential for male impersonation as a type of gender-nonconforming camp, as Muñoz discusses in relation to Carmelita Tropicana's performance of the suave Cuban ladies' man Pingalito Betancourt (Muñoz 1999, 128–135).[12]

The fourth drag performance is brief but entertaining: it consists of the Receptionist as the Fordham University School of Law graduate and U.S. Trustee Arthur J. González turned into the elderly Artritis Jay Gonzuela, who walks in with the assistance of a walker looking "old, but fabulous and almost regal" to the rhythm of Dolly Parton's "Nine to Five." Lolita kills her almost immediately, leading the Receptionist to die "fabulously, taking their time" (Vélez Meléndez 2022b, 68–69).

The final three drag performances are quite complex. The fifth is that of the Receptionist as David A. Skeel, who becomes Bishop Avid Silk to the rhythm of Madonna's "Like a Prayer" (Vélez Meléndez 2022b, 76). Here, the S. Samuel Arsht Professor of Corporate Law at the University of Pennsylvania Carey Law School who taught previously at the Temple University School of Law and clerked for the Honorable Walter K. Stapleton of the U.S. Court of Appeals becomes an over-the-top prosperity gospel preacher who "floats in from the door wearing fabulous clerical robes and carrying a religious scepter" (Vélez Meléndez 2022b, 76). The bishop and Lolita discuss religion and profit, religion and politics in Puerto Rico, religion and cisgendered heteronormativity, and molestation, as part of Lolita's trenchant critique of the Church and of the collusion of right-wing Christianity and the pro-statehood movement, including a discussion of conversion therapy (Vélez Meléndez 2022b, 82). The parody is built as a response to Skeel's book *True Paradox: How Christianity Makes Sense of Our Complex World*, and to the way the University of Pennsylvania corporate law professor neatly ties together capitalism and religion, which then gets translated into extractive colonial governance in Puerto Rico that entails draconian austerity measures (such as the privatization of public goods and the closure of schools and hospitals) as well as the systematic impoverishment of the population, a perverse situation that the University of Pennsylvania PhD recipient and poet laureate of Philadelphia Roque Raquel Salas Rivera has also fiercely critiqued (Salas Rivera 2018, 73–74).

The only woman member of the original Financial Oversight and Management Board for Puerto Rico, Ana J. Matosantos, gets a slightly different treatment. Born and raised in Puerto Rico, educated at Stanford, and a California resident, in *Notes on Killing* Matosantos becomes Anita Saintkiller, described as "fabulous, intimidating, awe-inspiring, magnanimous and breathtaking all at the same time" and appearing on stage to the rhythm of Céline Dion's "Where Does My Heart Beat Now?" (Vélez Meléndez 2022b, 85). While Lolita identifies her as "also a traitor" (Vélez Meléndez 2022b, 85) and mentions her butch appearance—in fact, Matosantos was subject to homophobic attacks in Puerto Rico as an openly lesbian woman (Metro Puerto Rico 2017)—their interaction seems slightly different. Alas, Saintkiller goes on to describe all Puerto Ricans as martyrs and proposes to "destroy that island to shreds," "sell it to the highest bidder," and "get rid of everybody and start over" (Vélez Meléndez 2022b, 87), and Lolita shoots her. In this play, Saintkiller (Matosantos), in spite of her progressive pedigree and of being Puerto Rican, is portrayed as benefitting from hegemonic femininity, in other words, as "actively complicit in reproducing a matrix of domination" (Hamilton et al. 2019).

Finally, the last drag performance is that of the chairman of the board José Carrión III, a Puerto Rican University of Pennsylvania graduate and insurance broker who becomes Yoseph B. Carry-On, a "shadowy circus ringleader" who appears to the sound of "Closer" by the American industrial rock band Nine Inch Nails "carrying the WHOLE Board, the whole show on my shoulders" (Vélez Meléndez 2022b, 94). In fact, before Carry-On appears, the Receptionist turns into the previous six characters in quick succession as part of a roll call, highlighting their artificiality and mutability, as if partaking of Luis Rafael Sánchez's well-known 1984 play *Quíntuples*, where two actors play six roles of the Puerto Rican Morrison family, a traveling troupe of actors (Stevens 2002). It is Carry-On who most clearly represents the financial interests of the wealthy Puerto Rican economic class and of the historic creole bourgeois elite, what the scholar Joaquín Villanueva has called "the Criollo bloc" (Villanueva 2022). For Carry-On's death duel, Lolita eschews her fake gun and plastic machetes appear, leading to a dramatic stage combat scene that includes sparks. In the context of Puerto Rican national liberation struggles, machetes have extremely strong symbolism, as they are reminiscent of countryside peasants or jíbaros as well as of the Fuerzas Armadas de Liberación Nacional (FALN), better known as Los Macheteros (the

Machete Wielders), which is why the workers' street and community theater collective Papel Machete, who have a critical cantastoria against PROMESA, also references them in their name.[13]

Carry-On's betrayal of Puerto Ricans, and his singlehanded focus on exploitation and profit, make him a particularly nefarious character. The circular nature of these characters' appearances—as zombies, revenants, or living dead, who return from the grave and/or are replaced by others just like them—ultimately posits the machinations of the US government, of Wall Street, and of Puerto Rican elites as embroiled in what Chris Harman has labeled "zombie capitalism." For Harman, "twenty-first century capitalism as a whole is a zombie system, seemingly dead when it comes to achieving human goals and responding to human feelings, but capable of sudden spurts of activity that cause chaos all around" (Harman 2010, 12).

Conclusion

In *Notes on Killing Seven Oversight, Management and Economic Stability Board Members*, Mara Vélez Meléndez invites us to think about what it means to decolonize disaster capitalism through drag and trans performance, specifically by presenting Puerto Rican and Nuyorican trans and gender-nonconforming protagonists performing grotesque drag parodies meant to mock, fun, entertain, and horrify, making some spectators laugh and others cringe. The play highlights coloniality, catastrophe, and the world-making capacity of theater in the Caribbean and its diaspora, but in a rather unusual way for a Puerto Rican play set and first staged in New York City. Here, trans revolution is actualized and drag becomes a radical tool of critique, a strategy of translocal performance, in which madness (locura) combines with translocality, whether it is through the travails of a diasporic Puerto Rican trans revolutionary (Lolita) or of a Nuyorican nonbinary genderqueer drag queen performer (the Receptionist) who by the end also becomes Lolita.

This solidarity and coming together, the bridging of cisgender and trans differences and of Puerto Rican and Nuyorican specificities in favor of a collective, utopian, radical vision, echoes Joan Micklin Silver and Julianne Boyd's 1983 musical revue *A... My Name Is Alice*, specifically its use of humor to negotiate differences among women, where all become Alice (Bennetts 1984), as much as the sense of female solidarity, collectivity, revolution, and humor in Dolores Prida's 1977 musical

Beautiful Señoritas, which includes portrayals of beauty queens, cabaret performers, a midwife, *guerrilleras* (women guerrilla fighters), and nuns (Sandoval-Sánchez 1999, 150–161), but clearly distances itself in its parodic embrace of violence, coming closer, perhaps, to the apocalyptic, dystopian environment of José Rivera's *Marisol* (1992) and to Migdalia Cruz's (at times) dark vision of humanity. The uniqueness of Vélez Meléndez's play resides in its timely engagement with a very serious topic through camp humor and violence, which she approaches through the lens of what she calls "Wonderland," a twisted transloca lens, in a utopian, almost absurd, irreverent way (Vélez Meléndez 2022a).

Notes on Killing, a disturbing and uncomfortable play to some critics because of its use of guns and multiple stagings of mock killings (Barbour 2022), which has also been perceived as "a bit overzealous" and "unwieldy" and "like too much and too little all at the same time" (Reiter 2024), forces mainstream audiences to tackle uncomfortable topics that many Americans routinely ignore, particularly the effects of American imperialism, decolonial Puerto Rican trans rage, and the potential use of violence to combat American antidemocratic governance in its colonies. As part of a group of radical queer and trans Puerto Rican cultural productions that also includes Aldarondo's *Landfall* and Salas Rivera's *The Tertiary/Lo terciario*, Vélez Meléndez tackles the coloniality of Puerto Rican catastrophe from a profoundly provocative LGBTQIA+ stance.

Notes

1. On PROMESA, see Atiles (2024), Klein (2018), Morales (2019).
2. For reviews and analysis of the New York staging, see Barbour (2022), Rossini (2024), Snook (2022), Solís (2022), Soloski (2022).
3. On Lolita Lebrón, see Arroyo (2014), Power (2017), Rossini (2024), Ruiz (2019), Soto Vega (2018).
4. Also see Dixon (2024), Reiter (2024).
5. See Bonilla (2020), Bonilla and LeBrón (2019), Klein (2018), Morales (2019), Zambrana (2021).
6. See Atiles (2024), Cruz-Malavé (2022), LeBrón (2021a), Powers Guimond (2020), Rodríguez Castro (2022).
7. The cast and creative team cite *Translocas* as an inspiration and resource for the play (Olujobi 2022, 46–61).

8. See Vélez Meléndez et al. (2022). Mendizábal is a member of Breaking the Binary Theatre, which uses the acronym TNB2S+ for transgender, non-binary, and Two-Spirit+. See https://www.btbnyc.com/overview.
9. Also see Montes Ireland (2023).
10. Also see Jiménez de Wagenheim (2016).
11. On Antonio Pantoja, see La Fountain-Stokes (2021a, 9), Laureano (2007).
12. Also see Halberstam (1998, 231–266).
13. On Papel Machete's Cantastoria PROMESA, see https://papelmachete.com/announcement/p-r-o-m-e-s-a/.

WORKS CITED

Aldarondo, Cecilia, dir. 2020. *Landfall*. Troy, NY: Blackscrackle Films.
Arendt, Hannah. 2022. *On Revolution*. In Olujobi, 14–23.
Arroyo, Jossianna. 2014. Living the Political: Julia de Burgos and Lolita Lebrón. *CENTRO Journal* 26 (2): 128–155.
Atiles, José. 2024. *Crisis by Design: Emergency Powers and Colonial Legality in Puerto Rico*. Redwood City: Stanford University Press.
Bennetts, Leslie. 1984. How Evolution Helped "Alice." *New York Times*, May 7. https://www.nytimes.com/1984/05/07/arts/how-evolution-helped-alice.html.
Barbour, David. 2022. Theatre in Review: *Notes on Killing Seven Oversight, Management, and Economic Stability Board Members*. *Lighting and Sound America*, May 31. http://www.lightingandsoundamerica.com/news/story.asp?ID=CUE6R2.
Bolivar, Andrea. 2018. We Are a *Fantasía*: Violence, Belonging, and Potentiality in Transgender Latina Sexual Economies. Ph.D. diss., Washington University in Saint Louis.
Bonilla, Yarimar. 2020. The Coloniality of Disaster: Race, Empire, and the Temporal Logics of Emergency in Puerto Rico, USA. *Political Geography* 78: 102181. https://doi.org/10.1016/j.polgeo.2020.102181.
Bonilla, Yarimar, and Marisol LeBrón, eds. 2019. *Aftershocks of Disaster: Puerto Rico Before and After the Storm*. Chicago: Haymarket Books.
Coddon, David L. 2024. Puerto Rican Nationalist's Story with a Drag Twist. *San Diego Union-Tribune*, May 3, 10.
Cruz-Malavé, Arnaldo. 2022. Dancing in an Enclosure: Activism and Mourning in the Puerto Rican Summer of 2019. *Small Axe* 26 (2) (68): 1–23.

Delgado, José A. 2025. La CIA operó desde Puerto Rico durante la década de 1970, según documentos y fuentes cercanas. *El Nuevo Día*, January 8. https://www.elnuevodia.com/corresponsalias/washington-dc/notas/la-cia-opero-desde-puertorico-durante-la-decada-de-1970-segun-documentos-y-fuentes-cercanas-a-esa-agencia-de-espionaje/

Dixon, David. 2024. Moxie's 'Notes on Killing...' Intelligently Explores Colonialism and Gender. *San Diego Story*, May 20. https://sandiegostory.com/moxies-notes-on-killing-intelligently-explores-colonialism-and-gender/.

Edgecomb, Sean F. 2017. *Charles Ludlam Lives!: Charles Busch, Bradford Louryk, Taylor Mac, and the Queer Legacy of the Ridiculous Theatrical Company*. Ann Arbor: University of Michigan Press.

Fanon, Frantz. 1963. *The Wretched of the Earth*. Translated by Constance Farrington. New York: Grove Press.

Fanon, Frantz. 2008. *Black Skin, White Masks*. Translated by Richard Philcox. New York: Grove Press.

Galarte, Francisco J. 2021. *Brown Trans Figurations: Rethinking Race, Gender, and Sexuality in Chicanx/Latinx Studies*. Austin: University of Texas Press.

Garriga López, Claudia Sofía. 2019. Transfeminism. In *Global Encyclopedia of Lesbian, Gay, Bisexual, Transgender, and Queer (LGBTQ) History*, ed. Howard Chiang, 1619–1623. Gale Virtual Reference Library. Farmington Hills, MI: Charles Scribner's Sons.

Guerrero, Marcela, ed. 2023. *No existe un mundo poshuracán: Puerto Rican Art in the Wake of Hurricane Maria*. New York: Whitney Museum of American Art and Yale University Press.

Halberstam, Jack. 1998. *Female Masculinity*. Durham: Duke University Press.

Hamilton, Laura T., Elizabeth A. Armstrong, J. Lotus Seeley, and Elizabeth M. Armstrong. 2019. Hegemonic Femininities and Intersectional Domination. *Sociological Theory* 37 (4): 315–341. https://doi.org/10.1177/0735275119888248.

Harman, Chris. 2010. *Zombie Capitalism: Global Crisis and the Relevance of Marx*. Chicago: Haymarket Books.

Jiménez de Wagenheim, Olga. 2016. *Nationalist Heroines: Puerto Rican Women History Forgot, 1930s–1950s*. Princeton: Markus Wiener Publishers.

Khubchandani, Kareem. 2023. *Decolonize Drag*. New York: OR Books.

Klein, Naomi. 2018. *The Battle for Paradise: Puerto Rico Takes on the Disaster Capitalists*. Chicago: Haymarket Books.

Korte, Christine A. 2015. The Manifesto as Genre in Ibsen's *John Gabriel Borkman*. *Nordlit* 34: 151–160.

La Fountain-Stokes, Lawrence. 2021a. *Translocas: The Politics of Puerto Rican Drag and Trans Performance*. Ann Arbor: University of Michigan Press.

La Fountain-Stokes, Lawrence. 2021b. The Life and Times of Trans Activist Sylvia Rivera. In *Critical Dialogues in Latinx Studies: A Reader*, ed. Ana Y.

Ramos-Zayas and Mérida M. Rúa, 241–253. New York: New York University Press.

Laureano, Javier. 2007. Antonio Pantojas se abre el traje para que escuchemos el mar: Una historia de vida transformista. *CENTRO Journal* 19 (1): 330–349.

LeBrón, Marisol. 2021a. *Against Muerto Rico: Lessons from the Verano Boricua.* Cabo Rojo: Editora Educación Emergente.

LeBrón, Marisol. 2021b. Policing *Coraje* in the Colony: Towards a Decolonial Politics of Rage in Puerto Rico. *Signs: Journal of Women in Culture and Society* 46 (4): 801–826.

Lorde, Audre. 1981. The Uses of Anger. *Women's Studies Quarterly* 9 (3): 7–10.

Metro Puerto Rico. 2017. Ana Matosantos: "Yo soy puertorriqueña, soy gay, soy muy orgullosa de mi identidad." *Metro Puerto Rico*, July 18. https://www.metro.pr/pr/noticias/2017/07/18/ana-matosantos-puertorriquena-gay-orgullosa-identidad.html.

Montes Ireland, Heather. 2023. Decolonization Is Imminent: Notes on Boricua Feminism. *Feminist Formations* 35 (1): 18–29.https://doi.org/10.1353/ff.2023.a902063

Morales, Ed. 2019. *Fantasy Island: Colonialism, Exploitation, and the Betrayal of Puerto Rico.* New York: Bold Type Books.

Muñoz, José Esteban. 1999. *Disidentifications: Queers of Color and the Performance of Politics.* Minneapolis: University of Minnesota Press.

Navarro, Mireya. 2003. New Light on Old F.B.I. Fight: Decades of Surveillance of Puerto Rican Groups. *New York Times*, November 28. https://www.nytimes.com/2003/11/28/nyregion/new-light-on-old-fbi-fight-decades-of-surveillance-of-puerto-rican-groups.html.

Olujobi, Ife, ed. 2022. *The Supplements: Notes on Killing Seven Oversight, Management and Economic Stability Board Members.* New York: Soho Rep.

Power, Margaret. 2017. 'If People Had Not Been Willing to Give Their Lives for the Patria or There Had Not Been the Political Prisoners, Then We Would Be Nothing'. Interview with Lolita Lebrón. *Radical History Review* 128: 37–45. https://doi.org/10.1215/01636545-3857754.

Powers Guimond, Christopher. 2020. *4645.* Cabo Rojo: Editora Educación Emergente.

Reiter, ErinMarie. 2024. Review: *Notes on Killing Seven Oversight, Management and Economic Stability Board Members* at Moxie Theatre. *Broadway World San Diego*, May 21. https://www.broadwayworld.com/san-diego/article/Review-NOTES-ON-KILLING-SEVEN-OVERSIGHT-MANAGEMENT-AND-ECONOMIC-STABILITY-BOARD-MEMBERS-at-MOXIE-Theatre-20240521.

Salas Rivera, Jose. 2018. Lolita Lebron su mensaje lo dice todo video por Jose Rivera Sábado 17 de de Septiembre, 2005. YouTube, January 2 https://youtu.be/1Y3s0ObDCP4?si=cai-IyvwT21ym4_5.

Rodríguez Castro, Malena. 2022. *Poéticas de la devastación y la insurgencia: María y el verano del 19*. Cabo Rojo: Editora Educación Emergente.

Román, David. 2005. *Performance in America: Contemporary U.S. Culture and the Performing Arts*. Durham: Duke University Press.

Rossini, Jon D. 2024. *Pragmatic Liberation and the Politics of Puerto Rican Diasporic Drama*. Ann Arbor: University of Michigan Press.

Ruiz, Sandra. 2019. *Ricanness: Enduring Time in Anticolonial Performance*. New York: New York University Press.

Sandoval-Sánchez, Alberto. 1999. *José, Can You See?: Latinos On and Off Broadway*. Madison: University of Wisconsin Press.

Snook, Raven. 2022. Notes on Killing... Is a Radical Drag Comedy about Puerto Rico. *Time Out*, June 1. https://www.timeout.com/newyork/theater/notes-on-killing-seven-oversight-management-and-economic-stability-boardmembers

Solís, José. 2022. Asked to Adapt a Classic Play, This Writer Rethought Her Life. *New York Times*, June 3. https://www.nytimes.com/2022/06/03/theater/mara-velez-melendez-soho-rep.html.

Soloski, Alexis. 2022. 'Notes on Killing' Review: For These Puerto Ricans, Promises Never Kept. *New York Times*, May 30. https://www.nytimes.com/2022/05/30/theater/notes-on-killing-review.html.

Soto Vega, Karrieann M. 2018. *Rhetorics of Defiance: Gender, Colonialism, and Lolita Lebrón's Struggle for Puerto Rican Sovereignty*. PhD diss.: Syracuse University.

Stevens, Camilla. 2002. Traveling Troupes: The Performance of Puerto Rican Identity in Plays by Luis Rafael Sánchez and Myrna Casas. *Hispania* 85 (2): 240–249.

Stryker, Susan. 1994. My Words to Victor Frankenstein Above the Village of Chamounix: Performing Transgender Rage. *GLQ* 1 (3): 237–254. https://doi.org/10.1215/10642684-1-3-237.

Taylor, Diana. 2003. *The Archive and the Repertoire: Performing Cultural Memory in the Americas*. Durham: Duke University Press.

Vélez Meléndez, Mara. 2022a. In Wonderland. In Olujobi, 4–11.

Vélez Meléndez, Mara. 2022b. *Notes on Killing Seven Oversight, Management and Economic Stability Board Members*. New York: Soho Rep.

Vélez Meléndez, Samora La Perdida, David Mendizábal, Christine Carmela, and Javier Antonio González. 2022. An Octopus Garden: In Conversation. In Olujobi, 62–86.

Villanueva, Joaquín. 2022. The Criollo Bloc: Corruption Narratives and the Reproduction of Colonial Elites in Puerto Rico, 1860–1917. *CENTRO Journal* 34 (2): 27–50.

Wayar, Marlene. 2021. *Furia travesti: diccionario de la t a la t*. Buenos Aires: Paidós.

Wellmer, Albrecht. 1999. Hannah Arendt on Revolution. *Revue Internationale de Philosophie* 53 (208) (2): 207–22. http://www.jstor.org/stable/23955552

Zambrana, Rocío. 2021. *Colonial Debts: The Case of Puerto Rico*. Durham: Duke University Press.

CHAPTER 12

Beyond Catastrophe: Teresa Hernández and the Puerto Rican Performative Body in the New Millennium

Priscilla Meléndez

The social, ideological, and political factors that have shaped Caribbean identity today have also pigeonholed it within an imaginary that is alternately idealized and chaotic. In *Sea and Land: An Environmental History of the Caribbean,* historians Stuart B. Schwartz and Matthew Mulcahy highlight the modern vision of this region as both utopian and dystopian:

> European migrants who ventured to the Caribbean in the early modern era encountered a world of simultaneously great promise and peril [...]. Islands and surrounding mainland territories with climates of "eternal spring," lush tropical vegetation, and a seemingly endless promise of profit, and perhaps even redemption, created Edenic expectations among many colonialists. But if the attractions of the region seemed promising, a paradise, its perils,

P. Meléndez (✉)
Department of Language & Culture Studies-Hispanic Studies, Trinity College, Hartford, CT, USA
e-mail: priscilla.melendez@trincoll.edu

© The Author(s), under exclusive license to Springer Nature Switzerland AG 2025
C. Stevens and J. D. Rossini (eds.), *The Coloniality of Catastrophe in Caribbean Theater and Performance,*
https://doi.org/10.1007/978-3-031-85791-1_12

particularly in the form of various natural disasters, made life there usually uncomfortable, risky, and at times deadly. (Schwartz and Mulcahy 2022, 187)

In recent decades the vicissitudes suffered in this region and caused by natural disasters have far overshadowed the utopian image of the Caribbean, provoking serious economic crises, social instability, and incessant waves of migration. Events such as the 2010 earthquake in Haiti; the droughts in parts of Guatemala, Honduras, and Nicaragua between 2015 and 2019 (Masters 2019); the landslides in the Dominican Republic; Hurricanes Irma in Cuba and María in Puerto Rico (both in 2017); the earthquakes in Puerto Rico two years later; the pandemic that began in 2020; and the eruption of the La Soufrière volcano in Saint Vincent in 2021, to mention but a few, have significantly damaged life and well-being across the entire region. But even more disconcerting is that these natural disasters are intertwined with those of human manufacture: the repression campaigns of the Daniel Ortega government in Nicaragua; the 2019 resignation of Puerto Rico's governor Ricardo Roselló pressured by the protests of a community exhausted by government mediocrity; the assassination of President Jovenel Moïse in Haiti in the summer of 2021; and the death of Haitian migrants—mainly women and children—near the coast of Puerto Rico in May 2022. All this without mentioning the current invasion of those who acquire real estate in the Caribbean area as a mechanism to evade paying taxes in their own countries. In the case of Puerto Rico, and soon after hurricane María, the *New York Times* described the predatory attitudes of these citizens: "Dozens of entrepreneurs, made newly wealthy by blockchain and cryptocurrencies, are heading en masse to Puerto Rico this winter. They are selling their homes and cars in California and establishing residency on the Caribbean island in hopes of avoiding what they see as onerous state and federal taxes on their growing fortunes, some of which now reach into the billions of dollars" (Bowles 2018).

Considering these Caribbean *misfortunes* (that evoke those *infortunios* of Puerto Rican sailor Alonso Ramírez that were published in 1690 by Mexican intellectual Carlos de Sigüenza y Góngora) it is evident that in the current millennium the balance between the utopian and dystopian has tilted toward the disastrous. However, and amidst this dire perception of the region, the coexistence between opposite views of the Caribbean in general and of Puerto Rico in particular highlights other binary structures such as text and context, the aesthetic and the political, the hyperbolic and the insignificant, monologue and dialogue, those with a voice and the voiceless, among others. That is, by referring to this region as a univocal entity ("the Caribbean") but also as a conglomerate of continental and insular peoples with diverse cultural, ethnic, linguistic, and political roots, we point to their concurrent singularity and multiplicity and to their persistent cultural richness, even when surrounded by horrific events that can be paralyzing.

In his 1980 collection of essays *El país de cuatro pisos y otros ensayos*, published in English as *The Four-Storeyed Country and Other Essays*, Puerto Rican critic and short-story writer José Luis González (1926–1996) highlighted the utopian view of Caribbean unification amidst individuality, promoting the respective national independence of all Caribbean peoples as a prerequisite for achieving a confederation that would fairly integrate the economic, political, and cultural structures of the region (González 1980, 42–43). In the 1980s, but from a more literary and irreverent standpoint, the Puerto Rican writer Ana Lydia Vega also offered a sardonic vision of that tension between Caribbean unity and diversity in her story "Encancaranublado" (1983) ["Cloud Covered Caribbean"] where a dystopian event—a shipwreck—takes center stage. In Vega's story a Haitian man trying to emigrate to Miami on a flimsy boat encounters a Dominican man in the middle of the ocean who lives on the same island, only in a "different" part, who is heading in the same direction looking for a better life and equally hungry. Despite the similarities in the lives of these two men, the reader confronts the painful reality that these characters can barely communicate with each other since they speak different languages, Kreyòl and Spanish. This hurtful irony becomes more acute when the two men adrift are forced to accept another castaway, this time a Cuban who also wishes to go to Miami to escape poverty and lack of opportunities. But as we reach the end of Vega's story a Black Puerto Rican appears, not on a miserable boat, but on a commercial ship flying the Stars and Stripes. Faced with this sudden appearance, one can only imagine the benefits provided by his "envied" American citizenship: mobility, employment, access to First-World wealth, civil rights, and the enjoyment of democratic structures. However, the falsehood of these "privileges" is exposed when the destiny of this Black *boricua* becomes indistinguishable from that of his Haitian, Dominican and Cuban brothers with whom he tragically shares more than expected, that is, forced migration, poverty, discrimination, and the consequences of racism. His American citizenship, acquired by Puerto Ricans in 1917 through the Jones Act, does not protect him or other Puerto Ricans from misery but on the contrary—as will be demonstrated through the performative work of Teresa Hernández—creates a long-lasting history of social, economic, and moral dysfunction.

This dire picture is exacerbated in the new millennium as catastrophes in Puerto Rico continue to batter the island at all levels. During a period of stagnation of the economy that had never recovered from the 2008 recession and that exacerbated the long standing debt carried by the public sector, in September 2017 Puerto Rico experienced a Category 4 hurricane that devastated most of the island and laid bare the fragility of a society living for centuries under colonial power and subject to the decisions of a financial oversight board and government outside its territory (Meléndez 2022, 132).[1] In July of 2019, this same population that had suffered the effects of the policies of a mediocre government's response to the hurricane was able to create a united front that peacefully yet determinedly took to the streets and toppled the pro-statehood governor Ricardo Rosselló. But just as civil society was becoming stronger and Puerto Ricans were coming to terms with their extremely precarious economic and political situation, several strong earthquakes shook the island in December 2019 and January 2020, creating an even grimmer picture. To everyone's astonishment, tragedy would strike again when only two months later the world was immersed in the unprecedented COVID-19 pandemic.

Is it possible to imagine any good coming out of this sequence of horrific events? Surprisingly, we find in Arcadio Díaz Quiñones's "Foreword" to the collection of essays *Aftershocks of Disaster: Puerto Rico Before and After the Storm* (2019) a reference to a conversation between the Puerto Rican political anthropologist Yarimar Bonilla and Canadian author and filmmaker Naomi Klein that sheds a hopeful light on the overwhelming darkness: "Klein and Bonilla shared the conviction that *disasters open up new possibilities for critical thinking and for art* as a form of intervening in politics and imagining a radically different society" (Díaz Quiñones 2019, xiii; emphasis mine).[2]

In what follows, I will reflect on the performative projects of Teresa Hernández (b. 1964)—solo performer, multifaceted dancer, body artist, producer of multimedia spectacles, cultural manager, and *provocateur*—, and on her work *Mimeologías* created in four iterations: 2002, 2006, and two versions in 2017.[3] Through the fictional science of studying *mimes* (gnats), the audience sees on stage one of many of Hernández's performative identities, *el mime*, who, in the Puerto Rican and Dominican "entomology world," is an undesirable tiny mosquito-like insect that can die easily. In her own words:

> El personaje del **Mime** surge en mi práctica de improvisación de movimiento de un sentirse invisible para las estructuras culturales de una comunidad teatral que se inclinaba a estéticas y prácticas conservadoras. La hibridez en mi trabajo como actriz, bailarina, performera que escribe y produce sus piezas busca otras narrativas y maneras de estar en el universo escénico. (Hernández n.d.b)
> [*El mime* stems from my practice of improvisation on movement from a feeling of being invisible to the cultural structures of a theater community leaning toward conservative practices and aesthetics. The hybridity of my work as actress, dancer, and performer who writes and produces her own work looks for other narratives and ways of being in the scenic universe. (Hernández 2022b, 78)]

As will be demonstrated, Hernández's critical and experimental art opens up artistic possibilities amidst social and political disaster, explicitly in Puerto Rico and implicitly in the Caribbean. That is, while Hernández's creative expressions centering on the body denounce, suffer, and poke fun at the chaos of an island enveloped by dysfunctionality and tragedy, it also echoes the possibility that a singular, daring, and apparently minuscule voice can make audible and visible the common struggles among the castaways that literally and metaphorically populate the Caribbean waters and islands. As Hernández herself clarifies, "Mis temáticas cuestionan los imaginarios nacionales-coloniales, el patriarcado, la violencia cotidiana, la industria de la seguridad, los rostros del poder. Problematiza[n] los cánones del arte y reivindica[n] el espacio personal como uno micropolítico." (Hernández 2022a, 209) ["My topics question the national/colonial imaginaries, patriarchy, daily violence, the security industry, the faces of power. They interrogate the canons of art and claim personal space as something micropolitical" (Homar and pastrana santiago 2023, 182)].[4] I argue that the work Hernández produces is emblematic of a corporeal space of creativity, movement, reflection, and denunciation that underscores Puerto Rico's complex identity at the intersection of performance, dance, love, life, violence, and death. In *Mimeologías* we see Hernández carrying out her solo performance as part of an exploration of the self while also characterizing the proliferation of voices and

Image 12.1 Teresa Hernández as El mime in *Mimeologías* (*Photo Credit* Antonio Ramírez)

bodies (physical, political, social, artistic) that can be empowered but also animalized and destroyed on stage.[5] As will be underscored, the dehumanizing element comes to life on various levels, and the most overt is through the protagonist *el mime* [the gnat]. Ironically, this character wears in the first iteration "a raincoat, high heels and his hair pulled to the back" (Hernández 2022b, 72) and in the last a "black pencil skirt, short silver jacket, black beret, and rings with eyes in both hands" (Hernández 2023, 75). *El mime* takes center stage in a lavish display of identities: my mime-1, my mime-2, my mime-3, he, she, it, I (Images 12.1 and 12.2).

Hernández herself states: "La animalidad y/o el ser 'cosa' son estadios que investigo en mi insaciable deseo de dejar de ser para encontrar otras esencias desde donde mirar, estar, accionar" (Hernández 2022a, 210)

Image 12.2 Teresa Hernández as El mime in *Mimeologías* (*Photo Credit* Antonio Ramírez)

["Animality and/or being as 'thing' are stages that I scrutinize in my insatiable desire to cease being in order to find other essences from which to observe, be, act" (Homar and pastrana santiago 2023, 184)]. This dual identity between humanness and animality leads to another binary between selves where the emphasis on the "I" (Teresa on stage) creates a twofold *mime* where the term itself is composed of two linguistic and political identities: the Spanish possessive "mi" and its English translation "me." As is well known, Spanish has been unsuccessfully targeted by those who promote Puerto Rico's annexation to the US and has been a contentious topic in the realm of education, politics, and cultural identity. With sagacity, Hernández places the action of *Mimeologías* in PRUSA, a country whose name is also dual, playful, contradictory, and ironic, since it unites the acronym of the occupied country (PR-Puerto Rico) with the acronym of the occupier (USA).

Influenced by artists and teachers connected to the world of dance, choreography, and experimental projects—Petra Bravo, Awilda Sterling-Duprey, Maritza Pérez, and Viveca Vázquez—, Hernández embraces what has been called a workshop process where, in connection with a social commitment, artists create their own style, establish their particular voice and artistic ideology, inventing/improvising their repertoire (Aponte-González 2006). Reflecting on her work within emerging platforms, Hernández summarizes her craft:

Por el momento describo mi práctica como una interdisciplinaria: se sostiene entre los lenguajes del cuerpo en movimiento, la escritura, la actuación, el espacio y el vídeo. Integro diversos elementos: vestuario, pelucas, objetos cotidianos, mobiliarios y diferentes materiales plásticos que responden a mis obsesiones del momento. Estos se yuxtaponen y se confrontan en un espacio liminar donde las nociones de precariedad son exploradas y celebradas. (Hernández 2022a, 209)
[At the moment, I describe my practice as transdisciplinary: it is supported by the languages of the body in motion, writing, acting, space, and video. I integrate various elements: costumes, wigs, everyday objects, furniture, and different visual materials that respond to my obsessions of the moment. These are juxtaposed and confronted within a liminal space where notions of precariousness are explored and celebrated. (Homar and pastrana santiago 2023, 183)]

By focusing on the power and versatility of a single body through movement, choreography, dance, and visible costume changes, Hernández creates a compelling intimacy with the audience that deflates the excesses and distractions of an overstuffed stage. But above all, it allows us to center our gaze on the particularities of the body made up of members (legs, arms, head) that act in harmony but also express their individual functions and identities.[6] Rígel Lugo has pointed out with great insight: "El teatro de Teresa es un trabajo sobre el cuerpo, o más bien un cuerpo de trabajo que trabaja a través del cuerpo" [Teresa's theater is a work on the body, or rather a body of work that works through the body] (Lugo 2012).[7] In *Mimeologías*, for example, the audience constantly deals with sameness and repetition as in a ritual and also as a strategy to combat the obliviousness of the inhabitants of PRUSA. That is, a *mime* who barely speaks and who supposedly stays the same inevitably changes with the passing of time: "*Ejecuta 'mi mime-1' casi igual que en la primera ocasión, pero no exactamente. El mime está diferente: han pasado cuatro años (no se olvide)*" (Hernández n.d.b) ["*He performs 'my mime-1' almost identical to the first time, but not exactly. El mime has changed: it has been four years (do not forget)*" (Hernández 2022b, 73)].

A closer look at a single object—a cigarette—exemplifies how her work constantly evolves and how it takes on a life of its own within a sociopolitical context. The protagonist asks for a cigarette from a member of the audience and walks out smoking and coughing, but only after clarifying that the cigarette is imaginary. Nevertheless, the cough and hoarse voice of *el mime* is described as that of a heavy smoker (Hernández 2023, 73), which is underscored by the fact that the second segment begins with the coughing of *el mime* in the bathroom and the statement that "Fumar está prohibido dentro de la sala. *(Tose)*" (Hernández, n.d.b.) ["Smoking is not permitted inside the theater. (*Coughs.*)" (Hernández 2022b, 73)]. In the fourth iteration of this performance fifteen years later, *el mime* is still coughing, "as if his throat is going to burst" (Hernández 2023, 75), suggesting that the 1990s governmental prohibition of smoking in public spaces has not yielded the desired results of deterring people from engaging in this practice. Would education have worked better than prohibition?

The emphasis of the singularity of the body on stage is precisely one of the features of Hernández's transdisciplinary production. This relates to Louis Catron's understanding of monodrama in his book *The Power of One: The Solo Play for Playwrights, Actors, and Directors* (2000). He underscores that the roots of *solo performance* are found in prehistoric times, that is, long before the beginning of theater as a formal organization (Catron 2000, 8). But above all, Catron invites us to imagine a bridge between these prehistoric events and the postmodern and experimental artist who appears alone on stage, as Hernández frequently does:

> A prehistoric tribe gathers around a flickering fire to watch a shaman who becomes, alternately, god, hunter, and savage beast of prey. His ritual is, in a very real sense, a one-person performance that incorporates an organized story, characterization, theme gesture, magic, impersonation, dance-pantomime, and costume—the ingredients of theatre—in a traditional ceremony that teaches members of the tribe how to deal with the mysterious and often frightening unknown world that hunts the shadows beyond the fire's light. (2000, 5)

As part of this independent and somehow ritualistic production model, Hernández not only stands out for her ingenious creation of characters, but also because these stage identities either reappear and adapt to new contexts, or they begin to die. Hernández points out that the creation of these characters represents a substantial part of her work which clearly deals with the long-standing social and political problems of the island: "con mis mujeres-personajes-presencias exploro y expongo las ansiedades del Puerto Rico cotidiano, investigando transversalmente temáticas de género, sexualidad y clase" (Hernández 2022a, 210) ["Through my women/characters/presences, I explore and unmask the anxieties of everyday Puerto Rico, transversally probing issues of gender, sexuality, and class" (Homar and pastrana santiago 2023, 183)]. This practice is recognizable in the development of characters in most of her works: The Queen in *Control de acceso* (1995) [Controlled access], Nancy in *Coraje II* (2011) [Courage II], and *la mujer del cuchillo* (2019) [the knife woman], among other works.

For example, Hernández's performance *Control de acceso* tackles gated communities by confronting the audience with five sections that explore those that are inside and those that occupy the outside or marginalized spaces. The performance centers on expressions of racism by placing a blond Queen on stage who wishes to preserve racial purity in her reign, despises miscegenation, privileges French, English, and those with wealth and access to information while rejecting "the other" who occupies lower levels. Ironically, what the audience witnesses next is the presence of a member of that lower group: Teniente Cortés, a female security guard who is emblematic of the proliferation in Puerto Rico of gated communities where the outsider can only enter if invited and approved by those inside. Out there are drug dealers and criminals while inside we ironically see the corrupt elite represented by the Primera Dama [First Lady] and her less-than-mediocre operatic performance.

Clearly, issues of environmental destruction, machismo, classism, and sexism emerge in Hernández's works and become daunting as they seem unsolvable. But what seems unique within this dystopian panorama is this artist's capacity to confront the formidable disasters and use them to open —to take up the words of Díaz Quiñones — "new possibilities for critical thinking and for art as a form of intervening in politics and imagining a radically different society." In the book *Respect for Acting*, the German-American theater actress and teacher Uta Hagen reflects how the artist can be a catalyst for change:

> To rebel or revolt against the status quo is in the very nature of an artist. A point of view can result from the desire to change the social scene, the family scene, the political life, the state of the ecology, the conditions of the theater itself. Rebellion or revolt does not necessarily find its expression in violence. A gentle, lyric stroke may be just as powerful a means of expression. To portray things the way they are, to hold up a mirror to the society, can also be a statement of rebellion. (Hagen & Frankel 2008, 15)

Hernández's unconventional and rebellious work emphasizes both the friction and interdependence between politics and performance, which allows her to "live her country" while preserving her humor and ideology despite internal and external threats and pains ("Declaraciones impermanentes"). In many instances the spectator of her work witnesses the tensions emerging from opposite forces where the *solo performer* unfolds into diverse identities, the character's monologue intertwines with pseudo-dialogues directed to the audience, where silence is interrupted by verbosity, the private confronts the communal, the possibility of solidarity meets antagonism, and the search for freedom faces oppression. Hernández herself has stated: "El trabajo con los contrarios, así como el sentido de oposición marca el tempo de mis búsquedas" (Hernández 2022a, 210) ["The work with opposites, as well as the sense of opposition, marks the tempo of my explorations" (Homar and pastrana santiago 2023, 184)].

It should be recognized by now that the experimental, irreverent, and rebellious nature of Hernández's artistic enterprise seeks the unexpected, the surprising, the precarious, the uncomfortable, which leads her to define herself as an independent artist who, in her own words, "crea e interpreta conceptos escénicos al margen de las definiciones absolutas. Trabajo en ese espacio liminal entre el artificio, lo real y la contaminación de ambos" [creates and interprets scenic concepts outside of absolute definitions. I work in that liminal space between artifice, reality, and the contamination of both] ("Declaraciones impermanentes"). While unmasking and dismantling the historical and artistic restraints to which the Puerto Rican cultural body has been subjected, Hernández reflects sharply on art itself, on the relationship between artist and audience, on theory, and on the performative process, launching a severe criticism of the deterioration of the institutions that are expected to support those same enterprises. Hernández speaks ironically about the genesis of the "corporation" that she is forced to create to legitimize her art, and which as a response, she registers as "Producciones Teresa, no inc.":

> La burocracia administrativa en el ámbito de la cultura crecía vertiginosamente en esos tiempos y, se puso de moda el "incorporarse" como sello de validación para la producción cultural, lo que no necesariamente implicaba buscar profundidad o rigor en la investigación artística. Tomé distancia de esa "moda", coloqué mi nombre en minúscula y me proclamé como una no incorporada desde el ámbito de lo pequeño […].

[The administrative bureaucracy in the field of culture was growing rapidly at that time and "incorporating oneself" became fashionable as a seal of validation for cultural production, which did not necessarily imply seeking depth or rigor in artistic exploration. I distanced myself from that "fashion," I placed my name in lower case and proclaimed myself, from the standpoint of small things, as not incorporated [...] (Hernández, n.d.a)]

As a response to the persistently dysfunctional reality of the island, and in Hernández's attempt to combat the official and bureaucratic (as suggested in the allusion to the prohibition of smoking in public), many of her projects dismantle the idea of perfection, totality, and institutionalization, placing instead at center stage the small, the impermanent, and the precarious: "Mi estética busca una honestidad conmigo misma, privilegia el 'casi nada' y lo contrasta con la hiperbolización, el humor, el espacio dramático o trágico" (Hernández 2022a, 210) ["My aesthetic seeks honesty with myself, privileges the 'almost nothing,' and is contrasted with hyperbole, humor, dramatic or tragic space" (Homar and pastrana santiago 2023, 184)]. That is, already in 1999 Hernández is highlighting the freedom that smallness allows her by not having to submit to the monumental forces of artistic, social, or political power:

> *Me gusta lo pequeño porque me da espacio para equivocarme. Es pequeño porque no entra en espacios "establecidos u oficiales". Cómo hacer de eso algo de alcance, es la pregunta. Pero se escoge lo pequeño por homenaje a lo íntimo, porque me permite el hacer, la pregunta incansable, el gozo de la imaginación y el control de las concesiones. Mientras más grande, más concesiones; esa ecuación no me satisface.*
> [*I like smallness because it gives me room to make mistakes. It is small because it does not fit into "established or official" spaces. The question is how to make something significant. But I choose smallness as a tribute to intimacy because it allows me to act or perform, to tirelessly ask questions enjoy imagination, and to control which concessions I make. The bigger it is, the more concessions must be made; that equation does not satisfy me*]. ("Declaraciones impermanentes" in Hernández 2023, 55)

Given these statements that emphasize singularity and minimalism, the evolving piece *Mimeologías* "by/with" Teresa Hernández is a transdisciplinary work characterized by its adaptability to the changing times and political context represented in its already mentioned four iterations: 2002, 2006, and two versions in 2017. This eight-page work, published in English but not yet in its original Spanish, alternates the genealogical/autobiographical/stage direction narrative of the piece with the performative segments. That is, in the initial portion we are told what prompted the creation of the piece, when the play was first performed, where the action takes place, and, most importantly, who the protagonist is. Following this preface, *el mime* proceeds to utter short and enigmatic phrases, some of them repeated several times, and on certain occasions addressing someone in the audience: "¿Puedes darme ese cigarrillo que está allí debajo?... Es imaginario. Préndemelo. Gracias" (Hernández, n.d.b) ["Could you give me that cigarette down there?... It's imaginary. Light it up for me. Thank you" (Hernández 2022b, 73)].

From the beginning to the end of *Mimeologías*, the character/artist Teresa allows us to constantly see how the self is intertwined with the other through the use of pronouns that weave them together. That is, we see in the singular *mime* the coexistence of the pluralized "I" and the performed other. For example, *Mime*-1 initially appears in Hernández's work *Infarto: ¿un talent "shou"?* (2002), *mime*-2 in *Nada que ver: composiciones escénicas sobre el yo* (2006), *mime*-3 in *O(h)culta* (2017) and *mime*-4 in the project *Privada* (2017). This clash of pronouns where at times the voice is identified as "his," "my," or "I" highlights both the individual angle of Hernández's artistic vision, and her constant unfolding when executing all the roles she invents, assumes, and is. I argue then that this transformation of a single voice into multiple ones represents a polyphony of anti-establishment views that aim to confront crisis and catastrophe in an island that has experienced plenty of these.

But *Mimeologías* also suggests that this proliferation of problematic identities exists in a threatening artistic and economic environment that can derail the performative search for both self and other: "En su obsesiva investigación de su *mi-misma*, bajo la amenaza con ser disecada o desechada por el ojo absolutista del ARTE y por la perversa banalidad de los MERCADOS, Teresa escenifica algunos de sus Yo-es" (Hernández, n.d.b) ["In *her* obsessive research on *her my-self* (in Spanish, mi-misma) and threatened to be dissected or discarded by the absolutist eye of Art and the perverse banality of the Market, Teresa performs some of her Selves" (Hernández 2022b, 72)]. Hernández's characteristic use of opposition manifests here in the tension among multiple identities, empowering her to gravitate between border selves through the transformation of her body, the modulation of her voice, and the metamorphosis of space. *Mimeologías's* autobiographical voice talks directly about the challenging conditions that each new version of her work encounters. For example, she reminds us that the theatrical space where the 2006 performance took place—the teatro Yerba Buena located in Río Piedras—was closed in 2010 "by greedy, culturally insensitive profiteers" (Hernández 2022b, 73).

As the piece moves from one segment to the other, our attention falls on the multiple bodily identities of *el mime* that fluctuates from the micro (a creature that is too difficult to see because of its smallness, but extremely annoying because of its buzzing) to the macro (the stage *mime* is too large to miss, although in need of a microphone to be heard and to amplify his message). In *mi mime-2*, for example, the audience witnesses the transition from one iteration to the other:

Mi mime 2
(Entra al escenario con su acostumbrada sobriedad siniestra. Coloca el trípode con los letreros y el stand-micrófono. Ejecuta "mi mime-1" casi igual que en la primera ocasión, pero no exactamente. El mime está diferente: han pasado cuatro años (no se olvide). Luego de toser en el baño, entra música de secuencia. Sale del baño, cambia el letrero que anuncia: "mi mime-2". Trae un objeto tapado en la mano derecha. Se acerca al micrófono). (Hernández, n.d.b)
[my mime-2
(El mime enters with his characteristic sinister sobriety. He arranges the tripod with the signs, and the microphone stand. He performs "my mime-1" almost identical to the first time, but not exactly. El mime has changed: it has been four years (do not forget). After coughing in the restroom, the sequence music begins. He exits the restroom and changes the sign to announce: "my mime-2." He carries a covered object in his right hand. He approaches the microphone.) (Hernández 2022b, 73)]

Each iteration of *Mimeologías* weaves the personal with the political by centering on different topics within their respective historical moments—violence, fear, invisibility, commercialization, exclusion, war—and through different symbolic objects such as a cigarette, a small silver coffin-purse, a microphone, a sign, a haiku poem, and a camera. Additionally, what Hernández and the 4 *mimes* have in common is that they are all natives and residents of the enigmatic Caribbean country PRUSA. Clearly, the complex history and identity of this politically divided Caribbean island is the framework for the complex life of *el mime* who is not only the emblem of smallness but is seen as undesirable and associated with decay, in addition to the fact that *mimes* die easily (Hernández 2022b, 72).

As the artist/character Teresa searches for the imperceptible, the impermanent, and the insignificant, she speaks of her desire to move from the practice of modern pantomime toward the "insectology of performance and minimalism" (Hernández 2022b, 74). That is, the emphasis on smallness is Hernández's way of underlining her bitterness toward institutions that seek to silence and paralyze those who deviate from the norm and who, with determination, build their artistic identity in liminal, ambiguous, and uncomfortable spaces. To complicate matters even further, the physical spaces where these liminal identities are performed are being sold to the highest bidder by real estate companies as gentrification turns small urban theaters and alternative community spaces into Airbnbs. As part of what we could dub a "poetics of the small," *el mime*'s body movements and props—for example, the small silver coffin-purse *el mime* carries, or the Brechtian signs that announce each performance text (Hernández 2022b, 73)—become the center of communication. Nevertheless, what seems meaningful is that Hernández's attempt to speak through the small body of *el mime* results in hoarse and opaque speech, paralleling PRUSA's failure to speak independently, effectively, and loudly in sociopolitical terms.

Could it be then that PRUSA's economic, political, and social failures are represented in *el mime* that died in the first segment? In "mi mime-1," we are told that "Un mime ha fallecido. No todos los días muere un mime, aunque la gente piense lo contrario" (Hernández n.d.b) ["my mime-1 [...] A *mime* has died. Not everyday a *mime* dies, though some may think otherwise" (Hernández 2022b, 73)]. We not only hear the tragic news but realize that the "self"/*mime* is carrying a coffin-purse with three compartments. But for what or for whom are those three spaces? Should we assume then that *el mime*/and PRUSA is/are dead, and will soon be burried? Would it be absurdly reasonable to think that the purse carries in each of the three compartments the corpses of some of the island's failed institutions, mediocre leaders, or perhaps the corpses of what used to be PRUSA's three main political parties? Could this tripartite silver coffin-purse be carrying the dead bodies of the Popular Democratic Party (that supports the colonial *status quo*), the New Progressive Party (that claims statehood), and the Independence Party (who we think supports becoming a republic)? If so, that would be quite a funeral.

In an environment where colonialism prevails, that is, where the absence of individual and collective freedom, political mediocrity, class struggles, and racism are experienced, the uncertainty that emerges amidst recurrent crises leads to feelings of fear in "my mime-2," who is coughing and carries a covered object (Hernández 2022b, 73). Tensions increase when, underscoring fear and prohibition, *el mime* uncovers a camera and requests a member of the audience to photograph him as he poses in front of a pavilion: "*Incómodo recibe la foto*" (Hernández, n.d.b) ["*Visibly uncomfortable, he allows his picture to be taken*" (Hernández 2022b, 74).] In the context of Puerto Rico's colonial reality where freedom is debatable, does the nervousness of *el mime* being photographed suggest that he might be under surveillance, observed by official forces, or in some kind of danger? By entering a gated community, or by actively opposing the political establishment, or for no good reason, any resident of PRUSA can be targeted, underscoring the precariousness of life in this country.

In "my mime-3" (2017), the insect steps behind a Japanese-style screen as the text describes the artist's new interest in the expressiveness and austerity of the *haiku*, a three-verse poem that in this formal aspect might be (or not) ironically connected to the three compartments of the small silver coffin-purse (Hernández 2022b, 74). The last iteration, "Mimeology 4: The Calls," is charged with political references to PRUSA's dire situation by placing *de mime* on a stage that simulates a cage ("jaula-escenario, cárcel") and by alluding to a phone call by someone who speaks another language and is a spy, torturer, and tooth snatcher from Ukraine.

> La espía.
> Se lucra.
> De Ucrania
> Arranca dientes. [...]
> Que no te robe un solo diente. [...]
> La ruina nos reina.
> Cuidado con la reina que PROMETE. (Hernández, n.d.b)
> [The spy
> She profits.
> She is from Ukraine.
> A tooth snatcher. [...]
> Do not let her snatch your teeth. [...]
> Ruin reigns.
> Watch out for the PROMESA queen. (Hernández 2022b, 76–77)]

In case anyone misses the allusion to the woman from Ukraine, in a footnote to the manuscript the artist Teresa/*Mime* identifies the spy and tooth-snatcher as Natalie Jaresko, a US-Ukrainian citizen and Executive Director of PROMESA, "acronym for Puerto Rico Oversight, Management and Economic Stability Act (2016) imposed by the US Congress under President Barack Obama [...] to control Puerto Rican finances and push for the restructuring of the island's public debt" (Hernández 2022b, 76, note 4). The overt allusion in this fourth segment to the not-especially-promising PROMESA and its austerity policies that reduce and oppress PRUSA are directly connected to the economic and humanitarian crises being denounced. Closely linked to the false PROMESA project mocked by Hernández is the infamous Junta de Control Fiscal (Financial Oversight and Management Board for Puerto Rico), also established in 2016 by the US government with the alleged purpose of creating the basis for the country's economic development. *Mimeologías's* identity as an experimental and political performance in various chronological stages, frames its eccentric identity around false promises, ineffective communication, absence of a community, hypocrisy, and even death in an island marked by poverty, inequality, political corruption, and failing institutions.

As stated, the juxtaposition between a small body and a message that needs to be audible has become a reality when the mosquito gains access to a microphone, allowing everyone to hear what is being said (Hernández 2022b, 72). Maybe now, with the steady sound of the microphone, the members of the community will hear clearly and will dare to confront political and social marginalization, injustice, colonialism, and racism, inciting everyone to overcome their precarious reality. But maybe something more daring will happen: they/us will grab the microphone to speak out loud and clear, allowing the community to move beyond catastrophe by building a new Caribbean and a transformed Puerto Rico. *Mimeologías* is definitively not about an artist who sees herself as being on the margins, tiny, without relevance; rather, it is about denouncing marginality and identifying and welcoming smallness in a dignified way and with a mike in hand. Maybe Hernández will give life to many more mimes as she searches for answers and change: "Desde entonces allí, aquí, acá resido, una artista pequeña, no incorporada e insaciable en la búsqueda de preguntas como parte de mi práctica artística de treinta años, la cual no se cansa de transmutar" ["Since then there, here, I reside, a small artist, not incorporated and insatiable in the search for questions as part of my artistic practice [...], which never stops changing"] (Hernández, n.d.a).

Notes

1. The distinguished and versatile visual artist Antonio Martorell portrays the tragedy and trauma of this period in an emotionally powerful work titled "Números" [Numbers] (2018) in which he contradicts the governments under-counting of people killed by Hurricane Maria and its aftermath (Crimmins 2022). The piece is a large wall with lists of numbers to account for all the deaths that were not recognized by the government. It starts at one and goes up to the hundreds, each written in a unique calligraphy (Crimmins 2022). In his essay "My Cry into the World," Martorell again contests the blatant disinformation circulated by the government and "the governor of Puerto Rico, Ricardo Roselló... [who] stubbornly clung to the 'official' figure of 64 dead." The closest estimate has been approximately 3,000 deaths.
2. My 2022 essay "An Island in Crisis: Theater Groups and Social Change in Puerto Rico in the New Millennium" offers a synthesis of the disastrous events that took place in the last decades, how they derailed the thin possibility of a hopeful future, and how artists creatively confronted these crises. In that text, I examined the significant contributions of two theater collectives, *Agua, Sol y Sereno* and *Y No Había Luz* and how, amidst so many devastating events, the artistic community, and these two groups, were neither paralyzed nor silenced. With determination and hard work, they expanded their activism and reaffirmed their goals to bring about major social, physical, artistic, economic, and political transformations to the island (Meléndez 2022, 132–133).
3. I refer the reader to important writings on Hernández's artistic production: Lowell Fiet, *El teatro puertorriqueño reimaginado* (2004), who devotes a segment of his chapter on women playwrights in the new millennium to Teresa Hernández; and the more recent book by Beatriz Llenín Figueroa, *Affect, Archive, Archipelago* (2022), specifically to the chapter "Sea, Salt, Survive: Teresa Hernández's Multitudinously Small Art Overflowing Sea."
4. When quoting from Homar and pastrana santiago first offer the Spanish version from a not commercially available edition of the

text artistically assembled by Editorial Beta-Local (2022), and then from the recently published University of Michigan Press 2023 English-language edition. Homar and pastrana santiago include in their book reflections written by dancers themselves about their own artistic trajectory and craft. All quotations reproduce the style of the original.
5. The quotes from *Mimeologías* are from an unpublished Spanish manuscript provided to me by Teresa Hernández. All the translations of Hernández's piece are from Aurora Lauzardo's English version, *Mimeologies*, published in a special issue I edited in June 2022 titled "Contemporary Latin American and Latinx Theater" and published in the journal *Review: Literature and the Arts in the Americas*. All other translations are mine, except when indicated. All quotations reproduce the style of the original.
6. In Hernández's *Mimeologías*, the body/bodies on stage will perform multiple characters and the spectator will be challenged to identify her/his identity.
7. Michelle Clayton has highlighted the need to study in this region the national histories of dance with the goal of establishing a conversation between them, and a closer relationship among dance and different art forms such as music, film, visual arts, but particularly, literature. She notes that Latin American studies has recently seen the beginnings of a more sustained attention to dance in cultural criticism, in the discipline-crossing work of critics such as Florencia Garramuño, Mary Louise Pratt, and Vicky Unruh, not to mention illuminating studies of dance in local contexts that explore its historical interactions with literature and other art forms (Clayton 2022, 449). Unruh's essay "Choreography with Words: Nellie Campobello's Search for A Writer's Pose" is of particular significance since it explores the intersection between dance and literature in the works of a renowned Mexican woman artist of the first half of the twentieth century.

WORKS CITED

Aponte González, Mila. 2006. Interview with Teresa Hernández [Interview in Spanish]. Hemispheric Institute of Performance and Politics, October 18. https://hdl.handle.net/2333.1/fxpnvx8t.

Bonilla, Yarimar, and Marisol LeBrón, eds. 2019. *Aftershocks of Disaster: Puerto Rico Before and After the Storm*. Chicago: Haymarket Books.

Bowles, Nellie. 2018. Making a Crypto Utopia in Puerto Rico. *New York Times*, February 2. https://www.nytimes.com/2018/02/02/technology/cryptocurrency-puerto-rico.html.

Catron, Louis. 2000. *The Power of One: The Solo Play for Playwrights, Actors, and Directors*. Portsmouth, NH: Heinemann.

Clayton, Michelle. 2022. Tracking Dance in Latin American Literature. In *The Routledge Companion to Twentieth and Twenty-First Century Latin American Literary and Cultural Forms*, ed. Guillermina de Ferrari and Mariano Siskind, 447–455. New York: Routledge.

Crimmins, Peter. 2022. New Exhibition at Taller Puertorriqueño Takes a Deeper look at Puerto Rico's Struggles. WHYY, PBS, May 8. https://whyy.org/articles/taller-puertorriqueno-new-exhibition-puerto-rico-antonio-martorell-philadelphia/.

Díaz Quiñones, Arcadio. 2019. Foreword. In Bonilla and LeBrón, eds., *Aftershocks of Disaster*, ix–xiii.

González, José Luis. 1980. *El país de cuatro pisos y otors ensayos*. Río Piedras, P.R.: Ediciones Huracán.

González, José Luis. 2013. *The Four-Storeyed Country and Other Essays*. Translated by Gerald Guiness. Princeton, NJ: Markus Wiener Publishers.

Fiet, Lowell. 2004. Teresa Hernández. In *El teatro puetorriqueño reimaginado: Notas críticas sobre la creación dramática y el performance*, 322–331. San Juan, PR: Ediciones Callejón.

Hagen, Uta, and Haskel Frankel. 2008. *Respect for Acting*. Hoboken, NJ: John Wiley and Sons.

Hernández, Teresa. n.d.a. Bio de Producciones teresa, no inc. Unpublished manuscript.

Hernández, Teresa. n.d.b. *Mimeologías de/con Teresa Hernández* & Notas sobre el texto de *Mimeologías*. Unpublished manuscript.

Hernández, Teresa. "Declaraciones impermanentes." Unpublished manuscript.

Hernández, Teresa. 2022a. Habitar(se), escribir(se), mover(se): teresa hernández. In Homar and pastrana santiago, eds., *Habitar lo imposible*, 208–13.

Hernández, Teresa. 2022b. *Mimeologies*. Translated by Aurora Lauzardo. *Review: Literature and Arts of the Americas* 28: 72–77.

Hernández, Teresa. 2023. *quienes tajan mar: registro de una práctica artística andariega*. Edición Beatriz Llenín Figueroa. Toa Baja, PR: Editora Educación Emergente.

Homar, Susan, and nibia pastrana santiago, eds. 2022. *Habitar lo imposible: Danza y experimentación en Puerto Rico*. San Juan, PR: Editorial Beta-Local.

Homar, Susan, and nibia pastrana santiago, eds. 2023. *Inhabiting the Impossible: Dance and Experimentation in Puerto Rico*. Ann Arbor: University of Michigan Press.

Llenín-Figueroa, Beatriz. 2022. *Affect, Archive, Archipelago: Puerto Rico's Sovereign Caribbean Lives*. Lanham, Rowman & Littlefield.

Lugo, Rígel. 2012. The (un)United States of Tere. *80 grados*, January 20. https://www.80grados.net/the-ununited-states-of-tere/.

Martorell, Antonio. 2021. My Cry into the World. *Re-Vista: Harvard Review of Latin America* 20 (3). https://revista.drclas.harvard.edu/my-cry-into-the-world/.

Masters, Jeff. 2019. Fifth Straight Year of Central American Drought Helping Drive Migration. *Scientific American*, December 23. https://blogs.scientificamerican.com/eye-of-the-storm/fifth-straight-year-of-central-american-drought-helping-drive-migration/.

Meléndez, Priscilla. 2022. An Island in Crisis: Theater Groups and Social Change in Puerto Rico in the New Millennium. In *Performances that Change the Americas*, ed. Stuart Day, 131–153. New York: Routledge.

Schwartz, Stuart, and Matthew Mulcahy. 2022. Natural Disasters in the Caribbean to 1850. In *Sea and Land: An Environmental History of the Caribbean*, ed. Philp D. Morgan, J.R. McNeill, Matthew Mulcahy, and Stuart Schwartz, 187–252. Oxford: Oxford University Press.

Unruh, Vicky. 2006. Choreography with Words: Nellie Campobello's Search for A Writer's Pose. In *Performing Women and Modern Literary Culture in Latin America*, 92–114. Austin: University of Texas Press.

Vega, Ana Lydia. 1989. Cloud Covered Caribbean. Translated by Mark McCaffrey. In *Her True-True Name*, ed. Pamela Mordecai and Betty Wilson, 106–111. Portsmouth, NH: Heinemann.

Vega, Ana Lydia. 1983. Encancaranublado. In *Encancaranublado y otros cuentos de naufragio*, 11–20. Río Piedras, PR: Editorial Antillana.

CHAPTER 13

Catastrophe, Theater, Performance: Praxes of Re/Making the Caribbean With/Out Coloniality, A Conversation with Eliézer Guérismé, Judith G. Miller, Gaël Octavia, and Gina Athena Ulysse

Christian Flaugh

The present conversation—an electronic *krik krak*/call and response—brings together voices from the Caribbean, Europe, and North America to discuss the pressing questions the present volume highlights.[1] Each contributor has actively engaged in Caribbean theater and performance spaces over what would be, if spaced out according to "actual" time, an accumulation of over 80 years. In the current ensemble, these conversation-makers flesh out the following calls, made across the near past century, by prominent creatives and thinkers deeply committed

---

C. Flaugh (✉)
Department of Romance Languages and Literatures,
University at Buffalo, the State University of New York, Buffalo, NY, USA
e-mail: cflaugh@buffalo.edu

© The Author(s), under exclusive license to Springer Nature Switzerland AG 2025
C. Stevens and J. D. Rossini (eds.), *The Coloniality of Catastrophe in Caribbean Theater and Performance*,
https://doi.org/10.1007/978-3-031-85791-1_13

to thought and action on coloniality and disaster. They include: Léon Gontran Damas's poetic invitation, " Désastre / parlez-moi du désastre / parlez-m'en" (Damas 1937, 33) ["Disaster / tell me about the disaster / tell me about it" Damas 2011, 23][2] ; and Kasia Mika's urgent reminder that we do our intellectual work "for the sake of the living. And the dead." (Mika 2018, 6) ["Au nom des vivants. Et des morts."].

The participants remain committed to such work through various means and modalities: as playwright, performer, visual artist, translator, director (staged performance, artistic, or theater festival), and scholar. Every word they have written, mask they have worn, stage they have occupied has been to foster audience engagement with critical questions, creative potential, and the complex and rich experiences people *de la Caraïbe/des Caraïbes* have lived worldwide. I am grateful for the willingness and generosity of the *intervenant/e/s* to share their points of view, praxes, theorizing, skill, and knowledge in this conversational crossing, inspired by the collaboration and communion that theater and performance encourage.

Each question finds its inspiration in part in the work of the contributors as creatives who call, enliven, and engage audiences, in word and in body. Each question also arises from, of course, the central concerns of the book. This broader call helped us to focus our interaction on ideas and practices that the title for the conversation highlights: coloniality; catastrophe; performance (theater and more); the arts broadly practiced; lives broadly lived; self-making; world-re/making; and, of course, the Caribbean as space, project, and experience. I thank each of the four contributors for responding to the call, as it came to me, and as I passed it on to them, in the timeline that greeted us, and in the unintended challenge of 100-word responses. I also appreciate each participant, who has and always will help us to think, feel, and imagine what materializes when we attend to the crossings that find us.

Below you will find the original questions, and the contributors' responses in alphabetical order according to their last names. The questions were shared in both English and French (also listed in alphabetical order), because these two languages informed our previous interactions. The contributors have responded in English or French, based on their preference (the preferred is listed first). Adding Creole versions, to broaden access and interaction, was thoroughly considered. But given that each Caribbean region alone has at least one Creole language (or at least one version of the country's Creole language), this option has been noted in the sketch book for a future moment when more time and space are available for, among options, an in-person meeting.

1. Christian Flaugh (CF): How is your work as theater and/or performance practitioner, writer, performer, researcher, director (performance, festival, or artistic), translator, etc.—informed by your knowledge and experience of "the Caribbean"? [*Comment votre travail comme praticien/ne du théâtre et/ou de la performance— auteur/e, performeur/-euse, comédien/ne, chercheur/-euse, metteuse/ -eur en scène, directeur, traducteur/-trice, etc.—se voit informé de votre connaissance (savoir?) et expérience « de la Caraïbe » (ou plutôt, des Caraïbes)?*]

Eliézer Guérismé (EG): *Je suis un metteur en scène haïtien comme tel mon travail de créateur est largement influencé par l'histoire tragique des îles caribéennes. Mais, je dois l'avouer aussi mon inspiration me vient en grande partie de mon pays, Haïti (où il existe une méconnaissance du théâtre caribéen). Surtout qu'Haïti est la grande sœur, la première à se révolter contre la colonisation. Sinon je suis conscient que les acteurs et actrices de la culture, du théâtre en particulier, de la Caraïbe doivent se réseauter afin de sauvegarder par derrière ces barrières culturelles cette histoire commune.*

[I'm a Haitian theater director, and as such, my creative work is largely influenced by the tragic history of the Caribbean islands. But I must admit that my inspiration also comes in large part from my country, Haiti (where there is a misunderstanding of Caribbean theater). Especially because Haiti is "the Big Sister," the first to revolt against colonization. And yet I'm still conscious of the fact that Caribbean cultural organizations, especially theaters, must go beyond cultural barriers, and network among themselves to preserve this shared history.]

Judith G. Miller (JGM): I have taught theater, staged some twenty plays in French with students, and translated some thirty-five dramatic works of French and francophone authors (Caribbean, Québécois, and African)—the latter constituting my most recent creative focus. I have almost always chosen to work on plays from which we can learn something important and which prompt us to ask significant questions, but also which offer the pleasure of aesthetic discovery. Translating authors from the Caribbean, notably the Martinican Ina Césaire (*Island Memories*, 1991, with Christiane Makward; and *Fire's Daughters*, 1993) and Haitian Guy Régis Jr. (*And The Whole World Quakes: Chronicle of a Slaughter Foretold*, 2019; and *The Five Times I Saw my Father*, 2021), has taken me to very difficult emotional places. For in translating, I am simultaneously channeling the authors' words and their characters' emotions; and both of these authors, as is true, I feel, of so many francophone Caribbean playwrights, convey and impart historical and personal wounds from the multiple catastrophes that have beset Caribbean peoples.

[J'ai enseigné le théâtre, mis en scène une vingtaine de pièces avec mes étudiant/e/s et traduit environ trente-cinq œuvres dramatiques d'auteurs/rices français/es et francophones (caribéen/ne/s, québécois/es et africain/e/s), ces derniers constituent mon axe de créativité le plus récent. J'ai presque toujours choisi de travailler sur des œuvres à partir desquelles on pouvait apprendre quelque chose d'important et qui incitent à se poser des questions profondes mais qui en plus, offrent le plaisir d'une découverte esthétique. Traduire les auteurs/rices caribéen/ne/s, particulièrement la Martiniquaise Ina Césaire (<u>Mémoires d'Isles</u>*, 1991 [1984], avec Christiane Makward, et <u>Rosanie Soleil</u>, 1993 [1992]), et l'Haïtien Guy Régis Jr (<u>De toute la terre le grand effarement</u>, 2019 [2011]; et <u>Les cinq fois où j'ai vu mon père</u>, 2021 [2020]) m'a menée sur des chemins émotionnels difficiles. Car à travers la traduction, je transmets simultanément les mots des auteurs/rices et les émotions de leurs personnages; et chacun de ces auteurs/rices (et c'est aussi vrai je trouve pour un grand nombre de dramaturges caribéen/ne/s francophones) communique et transmet les blessures historiques et personnelles survenues à la suite des multiples catastrophes qui ont assailli les peuples caribéens.]*

Gaël Octavia (GO): *Je suis née et j'ai grandi en Martinique. Même si je vis à Paris depuis l'âge de 18 ans, toute ma famille habite encore en Martinique et j'y retourne régulièrement. La société martiniquaise m'a toujours intriguée, interpelée, questionnée, depuis l'enfance. Ce sont probablement ces questionnements (en plus de questionnements sur ma famille... et donc par extension sur la structure familiale en Martinique) qui ont motivé mon besoin d'écrire. Je pense que tout mon travail d'écrivaine s'inspire de la Martinique, de ses structures sociales, politiques, de ses hommes et de ses femmes.*

[I was born and raised in Martinique. Although I've lived in Paris since I was 18, my entire family still lives in Martinique and I visit often. Since my childhood, Martinican society has always intrigued me, engaged me, challenged me. It's probably this probing (and also about my family… about Martinican family structure), that fueled my need to write. My work as a writer finds its inspiration in Martinique, its social and political structures, and its men and women.]

Gina Athena Ulysse (GAU): The Caribbean as both a point of departure and a point from which to pivot lives in my projects. In that sense, everything concerning my knowledge and experience of the region is raw material to me. This is most evident in the concept of *rasanblaj* (gathering ideas, things, people, and spirits), which has been at the core of work I have been doing for the last thirty years. Concerned with the visceral in the structural, my approach to research questions engages geopolitics, historical representations, and aesthetics in the dailiness of Black diasporic conditions. As a result, I am in constant dialogue with activists, artists, scholars as well as the physical and immaterial.

[*La Caraïbe en tant que point de départ et lieu de détournement habite tous mes projets. De ce point de vue, tout ce qui a trait à mon savoir et mon expérience de la région est une matière première pour moi. Cela est particulièrement mis en évidence à travers le concept de rasanblaj (rassemblement des idées, des choses, des gens et des esprits) qui est au cœur du travail que j'ai fait ces trente dernières années. Préoccupée par ce qu'il y a de viscéral dans les structures, mon approche dans ma problématique de recherche cherche à questionner les représentations géopolitiques et historiques et l'esthétique de la condition diasporique des Noirs au quotidien. Par conséquence, je suis en dialogue permanent avec activistes, artistes et universitaires ainsi qu'avec ce qu'il y a de physique et immatériel.*]

2. CF: Based on the context of coloniality invoked by the title of this volume, how does your work explain or engage with (or without) coloniality of the Caribbean? [*Inspiré/e du concept de la colonialité dans l'appel pour ce volume, comment votre travail comme praticien/ ne explique- ou engage-t-il avec (ou sans) la colonialité des Caraïbes?*]

EG: *Comme héritage culturel, la colonialité a une franche influence sur mon travail, mais on doit se le dire aussi qu'Haïti reste et demeure un cas à part au milieu des îles anglophone, hispanophone et dutchophone qui constituent en grande partie la Caraïbe. J'entends par cas à part, qu'Haïti est la première république à se défaire du joug de la colonisation, deuxièmement c'est la plus grande communauté créolophone et francophone des Caraïbes, ce qui semble avoir condamné Haïti à se tourner davantage vers les métropoles que vers les autres îles de la Caraïbe.*

[As cultural heritage of the Caribbean, coloniality has a stark influence on my work. But you have to tell yourself as well that Haiti rests and remains unique amidst the anglophone, hispanophone, and dutchophone islands, which make up the majority of the Caribbean basin. What I mean by unique is that Haiti is the first republic to throw off the yoke of colonization. It's also the largest community to be creolophone and francophone in the Caribbean, which seems almost to have condemned Haiti to turn more and more toward metropolitan centers [where both languages live due to migration], than toward the other Caribbean islands which don't have that linguistic similarity.]

JGM: The wounds I describe above stem, in great part, from what I would call coloniality: or, as I see it, the project of dominating the world, extracting resources, including people, for economic benefit while imposing structures that guarantee the power of those who colonize. In the Caribbean, as we know, this takes the form of a long history of enslavement: of being torn away from a homeland, forced to work entirely for the benefit of others, and of being subjected to systemic violence that makes creating stable families and environments almost impossible. (Please see also my answers to questions 3 and 4.)

[*Les blessures que j'ai décrites plus haut proviennent en grande partie de ce que j'appellerais la colonialité: ou, comme je la conçois, ce projet de domination mondiale, d'extraction des richesses, la population y compris, pour générer un profit économique tout en imposant des structures qui assurent le pouvoir à ceux/celles qui colonisent. Dans la Caraïbe, comme nous le savons, cela prend la forme de la longue histoire de l'esclavage: d'être déraciné/e/s de sa terre natale, forcé/e/s de travailler entièrement pour le bénéfice des autres, et d'être assujetti/*

e/s à une violence systémique qui rend quasi impossible la création de familles et d'environnements stables. (Merci de voir aussi mes réponses aux questions 3 et 4.)]

GO: *La colonialité s'exprime de manière très particulière dans les îles de la Caraïbe d'expression française puisque, à l'exception d'Haïti, nous sommes toujours officiellement des régions françaises, nous ne sommes pas des pays indépendants. Ma pièce* Cette guerre que nous n'avons pas faite *est consacrée à cette question. J'essaie d'y retranscrire les sentiments paradoxaux des Martiniquais, entre désir d'émancipation et incapacité à se libérer de la dépendance française: un guerrier (dont on comprend au fil de la pièce qu'il n'a jamais fait la guerre) s'adresse avec acrimonie à sa mère, qui est une allégorie de la Martinique soumise.*

[Coloniality takes shape in a very particular way in the Caribbean islands where French is used because, with the exception of Haiti, we are still officially French regions, not independent countries. My play, *Cette guerre que nous n'avons pas faite* [Not Our War], takes up this very question. In it, I work to transcribe the paradox that Martinicans feel, caught between the desire for emancipation and the inability to break free from dependency on metropolitan France. A warrior (who we understand has never actually fought in war) speaks acrimoniously toward his mother, allegory of a disenfranchised Martinique.]

GAU: I often reference this quote from M. Jacqui Alexander's *Pedagogies of Crossing*: "Since colonization has produced fragmentation and dismemberment at both the material and psychic levels, the work of decolonization has to make room for the deep yearning for wholeness, often expressed as a yearning to belong that is both material and existential, both psychic and physical, and which, when satisfied, can subvert and ultimately displace the pain of dismemberment" (Alexander 2006, 281). My work in many ways is a response to Alexander's assertion in the ways that I build on and seek to continue the work of decolonization. It is there in any aspect of my multimedia practice, from the materials I use, the subjects I take or the chants and songs I deploy.

[*Je me réfère souvent à la citation tiré de* Pedagogies of Crossing *de M. Jacqui Alexander:* « *Étant donné que la colonisation a produit une fragmentation et un démembrement à la fois au niveau matériel et psychique, le travail de décolonisation se doit d'offrir un espace d'aspiration profonde à l'intégralité, souvent exprimé comme une aspiration à l'appartenance à ce qui est à la fois matériel et existentiel, à la fois psychique et physique et qui, quand il est pleinement accompli, a la possibilité de subvertir et à terme supplanter la douleur du démembrement »* (Alexander 2006, 281). *Puisque ce que je fais repose et cherche à continuer le processus de décolonisation, à bien des égards, mon travail se veut être une réponse à ce que soutient Alexander. C'est au cœur de toutes les facettes de ma pratique multi-médiatique, des matériaux que j'utilise, les sujets que je traite ou encore les chants et les chansons que j'emploie.]*

3. CF: How does the lived or documented experience of catastrophe in the Caribbean and diaspora—where catastrophe may be, for example, ecological, economic, artistic, metaphysical, political, technological, demographic, social—inform your work as practitioner? What is or are the catastrophe/s that inform your work the most, and why? [*Comment l'expérience vécue ou documentée de la catastrophe dans des espaces caribéens (du bassin, de la diaspora)—où le catastrophe est, par exemple, écologique, économique, artistique, métaphysique, spirituelle, politique, technologique, démographique, sociale—forme ou informe votre travail comme praticien/ne? Quel est la catastrophe (ou quelles sont les catastrophes) qui informe votre travail le plus, et pourquoi?]*

EG: *L'éclatement du tissu social haïtien influence profondément mon travail de création surtout que ce problème est lié aux héritages coloniaux qui par le passé avait stratifiée la société haïtienne. Du coup, je fais de mon œuvre un medium capable d'inviter à réfléchir sur ce point précis de notre histoire de peuple noir. Les grands thèmes qui constituent mon travail artistique sont: l'angoisse, les questions identitaires, la violence urbaine, les maladies, la condition féminine et les engagements féministes. Mon travail puise essentiellement dans les œuvres haïtiennes et francophones.*

[The ongoing erosion of Haiti's social fabric deeply influences my creative work, especially because this problem is linked directly to the colonial heritage that has, historically, stratified Haitian society. As a result, I make my work a means for inviting reflection on this aspect of our history as a Black people. The broader questions, then, that make up my artistic work are: fear, identity, urban violence, illness, the status of women, and feminist engagement. My work around such matters draws primarily from Haitian as well as francophone works.]

JGM: All the characters in the works I have translated live beyond catastrophe and beyond victimization—their energy and agency made even more palpable, of course, once communicated through onstage embodiment. In translating them, I hope to be making these works—what they make visible, what they query—available to non-French-speaking people, including other theater people who will, in turn, interpret them. (Please see also my answers to questions 2 and 4.)

[*Tous les personnages dans les œuvres que j'ai traduites vont bien au-delà de la catastrophe et la victimisation—bien sûr leur énergie et leur capacité d'agir deviennent d'autant plus évidentes une fois qu'elles sont incarnées sur scène. À travers la traduction, j'espère rendre ces œuvres—et notamment ce qu'elles rendent visible et ce qu'elles questionnent—accessibles à ceux/celles qui ne parlent pas le français, y compris aux autres gens du monde du théâtre qui pourront, à leur tour, les interpréter. (Merci de voir aussi mes réponses aux questions 2 et 4.)*]

GO: *Pour une Martiniquaise (et si bien sûr on cherche au-delà de la catastrophe originelle bien connue qu'est la traite négrière, l'esclavage), la catastrophe est ce qui n'a pas eu lieu. Notre problème, c'est l'absence de catastrophe. Nous appelons de nos vœux la catastrophe (au sens mathématique de la théorie des catastrophes): c'est-à-dire la rupture de continuité. Nous voudrions qu'il se passe quelque chose et avons le sentiment que rien ne se passe. La catastrophe qui irrigue mon travail est donc la catastrophe qui n'a pas eu lieu, comme dans* <u>Cette guerre que nous n'avons pas faite</u>, *et que je dois inventer, imaginer comme dans* <u>La belle drive</u>, *pièce inédite où la Martinique se détache du fond de l'océan et part en errance.*

[For myself as a Martinican (and obviously when you look beyond the well-known origin catastrophe, the slave trade, slavery) catastrophe is what did not happen. For Martinique, our problem is the absence of a large-scale catastrophe. We long for a catastrophe (from the mathematical sense of catastrophe theory) that breaks with continuity. We wish something would happen, but we feel as if nothing did. The catastrophe which runs throughout my work is the catastrophe that didn't come to pass, as in *Cette guerre que nous n'avons pas faite* [Not Our War]. It's a catastrophe I have to invent and imagine, like in *La belle drive* [Great Drive], an unpublished work in which Martinique detaches itself from the ocean floor and wanders free.]

GAU: History is always there and is my primary influence. Colonialism is the first catastrophe and its concomitant geopolitical warfare has been as crucial. I understand the various dimensions of these, especially in the ways we recognize them as areas of study and or indices that are used to measure their impact on populations. Because I begin with the premise that no subject lives life along disciplinary lines, my approach is purposefully holistic. I don't divide the natural disasters from man-made ones. I am more interested in capturing what is revealed in particular moments. For example, the January 12, 2010, earthquake affected everything. Yet, the scope of its impact can be traced back to that colonial encounter and its aftermath.

[*L'histoire est toujours présente et reste mon influence principale. Le colonialisme est la toute première catastrophe, et la lutte géopolitique qui l'accompagne est toute aussi décisive. Je comprends leurs différentes composantes, surtout dans la manière dont on les conçoit comme champs d'investigation ou significateurs utilisés pour mesurer leur impact sur la population. Dans la mesure où je pars du préambule que personne ne demeure entièrement dans des cadres disciplinaires bien définis, mon approche est volontairement holistique. Je ne sépare pas les désastres naturels de ceux créés par l'homme. Ce qui m'intéresse davantage, c'est de capturer ce que chacun de ces moments révèlent. Par exemple, le tremblement de terre du 12 janvier 2010 a tout touché. Et pourtant, l'ampleur de son impact peut être attribuée à cette initiale confrontation coloniale et ses répercussions.]*

4. CF: In such a context of catastrophe, coloniality, and the Caribbean, whose work in theater and performance has informed yours? How?
[*Dans ce contexte de la catastrophe, de la colonialité, et des Caraïbes, le travail de qui informe le vôtre? Comment?*]

EG: *Les œuvres de certains auteur/res contemporains, tels Guy Régis Jr, Jean-René Lemoine, Samuel Beckett, Bernard-Marie Koltès, Jean*

Genet, Céline Delbecq, Franca Rame, Dario Fo, Jean-Luc Lagarce, et Andrise Pierre exercent une réelle influence sur mon travail de metteur en scène. Parce que je pense sincèrement que leurs œuvres traduisent au mieux l'ampleur de la catastrophe a laquelle fait face le monde d'aujourd'hui.

[The oeuvre of certain contemporary authors —like Guy Régis Jr., Jean-René Lemoine, Samuel Beckett, Bernard-Marie Koltès, Jean Genet, Céline Delbecq, Franca Rame, Dario Fo, Jean-Luc Lagarce, and Adrise Pierre—exert a great influence on my work as director of theatrical performance. And that's because I believe sincerely that their contributions convey as fully as possible the depths of catastrophe that the world faces today.]

JGM: In the four Caribbean works I have translated [as, indeed, in the three I have staged, Aimé Césaire's *Une tempête* (in 1990), Ina Césaire's *l'Enfant des Passages* (in 1992) and her *La Lettre d'Affranchissement* (in 1995)], what courses through these works, and what makes them powerful, are resilience and inventiveness. They are all "songs" (and they *are* very lyrical) to the spirit of people capable of surmounting terrible odds and imagining a better future. In other words, we are not in the realm of tragedy. To be more specific: Ina Césaire (like her father, Aimé Césaire) tells history from a perspective disallowed under colonialism, unearthing heroines (unlike her father), and thus foregrounding women's roles. She also rehearses the hierarchy of color, the better to dispense with it as central to what gives meaning to life.

[*Dans les quatre œuvres que j'ai traduites [tout comme, d'ailleurs, les trois que j'ai mises en scène,* Une tempête *d'Aimé Césaire (en 1990), et* L'Enfant des Passages *(en 1992) et* La Lettre d'Affranchissement *d'Ina Césaire (en 1995)], ce qui parcourt ces œuvres, ce qui les rend fortes, c'est avant tout la résilience et l'inventivité. Toutes ces œuvres sont des « chants » (et elles sont très lyriques) qui célèbrent l'esprit de tout un peuple capable de surmonter de terribles difficultés et d'imaginer un avenir meilleur. En d'autres termes, nous ne sommes pas dans le domaine de la tragédie. Pour être plus spécifique: Ina Césaire (tout comme son père Aimé Césaire) raconte l'histoire à partir d'une perspective rejetée par le colonialisme, révélant des héroïnes peu ou pas connues (contrairement à son père), lui permettant ainsi de mettre en valeur le rôle des femmes. Elle réitère aussi la hiérarchie de la couleur pour se débarrasser de sa centralité afin de faire place à ce qui donne vraiment du sens à la vie.]*

GO: Le travail du Nigérian Wole Soyinka, et en particulier la pièce La mort et l'écuyer du roi, qui se situe pourtant dans un univers très différent de celui dont je parle, mais où des personnages situés de part et d'autre de la ligne coloniale affirment leurs valeurs et se confrontent, a nourri ma réflexion sur comment aborder les thématiques qui me tenaient à cœur. Plus récemment, j'ai été très intéressée par le travail de Rébecca Chaillon mais malheureusement je n'ai pas encore eu l'opportunité de le voir. Mais je pense que son approche très frontale de la colonialité (d'après ce que j'en ai lu) devrait être enrichissante pour ma propre réflexion.

[The oeuvre of the Nigerian, Wole Soyinka—especially his play, *Death and the King's Horseman*, set in a universe very different from the one I describe, but where characters are dotted all along the colonial line, shoring up their values as they confront each other— has enriched my practice for approaching matters close to the heart. Recently, I've been intrigued by the work of Rébecca Chaillon, but unfortunately I've not had the opportunity to see it performed. But I think that her very head-on approach to coloniality (based on what I've read) could very much enrich my own.]

GAU: I have been informed by North American theater artists as well as visual artists who have been concerned with the same or similar question from a broader Black diaspora perspective. Suzanne Césaire's work remains a constant presence as inspiration and influence, also because of the surrealist undercurrent in my work. Suzan-Lori Parks, Kaneza Schaal, Anna Deavere Smith have approached and staged work in ways that continue to push my own imagination. Of course, I am particularly interested in the oeuvre of Guy Régis Jr. for the ways his works insist on exploring the interstices in which agency can be found from bits of humanity whether these are the highest or lowest forms. He is adept with humor and tragedy and allows us to see and recognize that Haiti has much to offer and teach the world.

[J'ai été influencée par les artistes du monde du théâtre nord-américain et les artistes visuels qui s'intéressent aux mêmes questions

ou aux questions similaires aux miennes et ce à partir d'une perspective assez large de la diaspora noire. L'œuvre de Suzanne Césaire demeure une présence constante en termes d'inspiration et d'influence, d'autant plus de par les courants surréalistes sous-jacents dans mon travail. Suzan-Lori Parks, Kaneza Schaal, Anna Deavere Smith conçoivent et mettent en scène des œuvres qui continuent de me pousser à dépasser ma propre imagination. Bien évidemment, je m'intéresse particulièrement à l'œuvre de Guy Régis Jr, pour la manière dont ses travaux persistent à explorer les interstices à partir desquelles on trouve sa capacité d'agir à travers les tout petits morceaux d'humanité, qu'ils soient dans leurs plus grandes ou plus petites formes. Il est aussi habile avec l'humour et la tragédie, et nous permet de voir et de reconnaître qu'Haïti a beaucoup à offrir et à enseigner au monde.]

5. CF: If theater and performance engage publics in the act of witnessing in order to re/make the world, how does your work encourage theater publics to think beyond the "same old tragic even catastrophic" story (trope?) of Caribbean spaces? In other words, how does your work re/make or invite the public to participate in the re/making of the Caribbean, with/out catastrophe and coloniality? Is this possible? [*Si le théâtre et la performance engage le public dans un acte de témoignage afin de re/faire le monde, comment votre travail motive le public à penser hors l'histoire (la trope?) « tragique voire catastrophique » des Caraïbes? C'est-à-dire, comment votre travail lui-même re/fait ou invite le public à participer dans l'acte de re/faire les Caraïbes, avec ou sans catastrophe et colonialité? Est-ce possible?*]

EG: *Si la reconstruction de l'être haïtien contribue à refaire les Caraïbes, je pense que toute œuvre qui s'engage à redresser la dignité d'un peuple caribéen participe du coup à ces rationalités qui forcent les Caraïbes vers un destin uni. Cela dit, si cet élan porte ses fruits on pourrait passer de l'appellation des Caraïbes à la Caraïbe, un peuple multiculturel avec un projet diversifié mais commun. Scindé mais toujours uni.*

[If reconceptualizing the Haitian way of being contributes to remaking the Caribbean, I think that any work which strives to redress the dignity of a Caribbean people participates from the get-go in a reasoning that ushers the Caribbean toward a shared destiny. In other words, if this momentum continues and comes to fruition, we could move from being a divided Caribbean to a united Caribbean, a multicultural people with a shared but diversified project. Separate but still united.]

JGM: Were loss and trauma the main affective valences of the works I have translated and staged, they would not, to my mind, be as consequential as they are, nor would they "remake," or reposition, the catastrophes of coloniality. At this stage of my career, I have understood that "What is theater?" and "What can theater do?" are questions that have motivated my work from the beginning. Within the vastness of these interrogations, I have settled on a doubled notion of theater as a creative and critical engagement with the world and theater as a ritualized coming together that forms a community, however momentary, of thinkers—whose thoughts are triggered by all the languages of the stage. I think theater can help heal a wounded psyche. I think theater can also provoke action, accompanying movements for social justice. I also think theater can project theater-makers and theater publics into a space of wonder, a safe space where one can discover other possible selves.

[*Si le malheur et le traumatisme étaient les valences affectives principales des œuvres que j'ai traduites et mises en scène, elles ne seraient pas, pour moi, aussi substantielles qu'elles le sont; elles ne participeraient pas non plus à « réinventer » ou repositionner les catastrophes de la colonialité. À ce stade de ma carrière, je comprends maintenant que « Qu'est-ce que le théâtre? » et « Que peut faire le théâtre? » sont les questions qui ont motivé mon travail depuis le début. Devant l'immensité de ces interrogations, je me suis arrêtée sur la double notion de théâtre comme engagement créatif et critique avec le monde ainsi que le théâtre comme rendez-vous ritualisé permettant la création d'une communauté, même temporaire, de penseurs—dont les pensées sont suscitées par les multiples langages sur scène. Je pense que le théâtre peut aider à cicatriser les blessures psychiques. Je pense que le théâtre peut aussi provoquer une réaction, et ainsi accompagner les mouvements en faveur de la justice sociale. Je pense aussi que le théâtre peut offrir aux créateurs de théâtre et au public un espace d'émerveillement, un espace sûr où il est possible de se découvrir d'autres existences possibles.*]

GO: *Dans mon travail, je pose des questions, je n'apporte pas de réponses (si j'avais les réponses, je suppose que je ferais de la politique, pas de l'art). J'aime surtout confronter le public à ses propres paradoxes. Le confronter au mensonge, d'une certaine manière. Là où le monde politique a tendance à créer le mensonge ou à l'entretenir, je préfère dissiper l'écran de fumée, déchirer le rideau, dire « quand nous affirmons cela, est-ce que nous nous mentons à nous-mêmes? » ou bien « quand nous affirmons ceci et agissons comme cela, que voulons-nous vraiment? ». Mes pièces parlent de l'ici et du maintenant (peut-être un peu du futur) et assez peu du passé.*

[In my work, I ask questions, I don't offer answers (if I had answers, I'd be in politics, not art). I especially love making audiences confront their own paradoxes. Confront them with a lie, in one way or another. Where the political realm tends to create and foster lies, I prefer to clear the air, tear down the curtain, and say, "when we affirm something, are we lying to ourselves?" or "when we affirm this and act like that, what do we really want?" My plays speak of the here and now (and perhaps a little in the future), very little of the past.]

GAU: Even when I focus on catastrophe and coloniality, my work has consistently sought to reorient and, at times, reverse the gaze, if you will, to recognize that the human condition is shaped by more than external and or geopolitical factors. My approach seeks to look inward to explore the hidden depths of the imagination as source of connectivity primarily with the unseen. That concern, which is also often materialized in the natural world, and the minutia, could allow the public to experience some element of conscientization, if they are primed at the very least to find allure in the aesthetics and poetry of the work.

[*Même quand je mets l'accent sur la catastrophe et la colonialité, mon travail a toujours cherché, d'une certaine manière, à réorienter et parfois même à renverser le regard porté, afin de reconnaître que la condition humaine n'est pas seulement façonnée par les facteurs externes et géopolitiques. Mon approche cherche à se tourner vers l'intérieur pour sonder les profondeurs cachées de l'imagination en tant que source de connectivité majoritairement avec l'invisible. Cette préoccupation, qui se matérialise souvent aussi dans le monde naturel, et la minutie, pourraient permettre au public de faire l'expérience de certains éléments de conscientisation, si ce public est prêt à trouver un certain charme dans l'esthétique et la poésie des œuvres.*]

6. CF: How might we discuss, even theorize, the re/making of the Caribbean through theater and performance—with/out coloniality and catastrophe—as an ethos and/or an aesthetic? Or has the long history of Caribbean theater and performance always and already created an ethos and/or aesthetic of coloniality, catastrophe, and the re/making of the Caribbean? [*Comment discuter, ou même théoriser, l'acte de re/faire les Caraïbes au traves le théâtre et la performance—avec/sans colonialité et catastrophe—comme un éthos et/ou une esthétique? Ou la longue histoire du théâtre et de la performance des Caraïbes a-t-elle déjà et toujours créé un éthos et/ou une esthétique de la colonialité, la catastrophe, et l'acte de re/faire des Caraïbes?*]

EG: *Avant d'avoir lu cette question je n'avais jamais pensé à cette possibilité de construire un théâtre identitaire intimement lié au destin des peuples caribéens. Aussi, il sera toujours difficile d'arriver à cela, si l'art et les théories sociales n'essaient pas de concevoir une identité caribéenne excluant toute tentative de suprématie culturelle.*

[Before having read this question, I had never thought of the possibility of building a theater of identity, intimately woven to the future of Caribbean people. Also, it will always be difficult to attain that goal, if art and social theory don't both try to conceive of a Caribbean identity without any temptation of establishing one culture's supremacy over another.]

JGM: (Please see my answers to questions 5 and 7.)

[(*Merci de voir mes réponses aux questions 5 et 7.*)]

GO: *La colonialité/catastrophe est le contexte de nos récits, mais pas forcément son sujet central—sauf dans quelques cas spécifiques. Peut-être que, de manière impressionniste, nous avons créé une esthétique de la colonialité, mais selon la génération à laquelle on appartient, ce que nous voulons montrer ou dire de la Caraïbe diffère. Aujourd'hui, une partie du travail des jeunes créateurs, et surtout des créatrices, est justement de déconstruire certains mythes caribéens. Personnellement, je m'attaque (et je ne suis pas la seule), au poto mitan, cette figure de mère courage sacrificielle et surpuissante révérée aux Antilles. Une partie des Caribéens continuent de revendiquer et de célébrer le poto mitan. D'autres, dont je fais partie, le dénoncent et cherchent à le déconstruire.*

[Coloniality/catastrophe is the context for our story, but not its focus—except in some specific cases. Maybe, in an impressionist way, we writers and theater makers have created an aesthetics of coloniality that aligns with our respective generation, and so what we show or say about the Caribbean differs. Today, part of the work of young creatives, and especially of female creatives, is in fact to deconstruct certain Caribbean myths. Personally (and I'm not the only one), I focus on the *poto mitan*, that fabled mother figure of self-sacrificing, endless courage revered throughout the French Caribbean. Some people continue to reclaim and celebrate the *poto mitan*. Others, and I'm one of them, denounce it, work to deconstruct it.]

GAU: We are and have been making work that has been pushing us beyond some of these tropes and thematics, precisely because they can be limiting. What else are we if not subjects and actors of our histories? My proposal of *rasanblaj*, for example, is an attempt to eschew coloniality and catastrophe as ethos and aesthetics. Whether as an approach, method, or theory, the aim of *rasanblaj* is to recenter the impulses and strategies we deploy as agents, in the ways we both live and express our connection to our environment and unequitable world.

[*Nous avons et nous continuons de créer des œuvres qui nous poussent au-delà de ces tropes et thématiques, précisément parce qu'elles peuvent être restrictives. Que sommes-nous sinon les sujets et les acteurs de notre propre histoire? Ma proposition de rasanblaj, par exemple, est une tentative d'éviter de concevoir la colonialité et la catastrophe comme un éthos et une esthétique. Qu'on l'utilise comme approche, méthodologie ou théorie, le rasanblaj a pour but de remettre au centre les impulsions et les stratégies que nous déployons en tant qu'individu, et ce à travers la manière dont nous vivons et exprimons notre connexion à notre environnement et un monde inéquitable.*]

7. CF: What do you consider to be the future of Caribbean theater and performance, as regards coloniality, catastrophe, and re/making the world? What pressing ethical and aesthetic matters are on the horizon that theater and performance makers are engaging? And who, of younger generations of theater and performance makers, leads the charge in engagement of publics in such matters?

[*Que pensez-vous être l'avenir du théâtre et de la performance caribéens, au sujet de la colonialité, la catastrophe, et l'acte de re/faire le monde? Quelles questions urgentes éthiques et esthétiques sont immédiatement devant nous que les praticien/n/es du théâtre et de la performance engagent? Et qui, de la génération plus jeune des praticien/n/es, prennent en charge l'engagement des publics dans de telle questions?*]

EG: *Le théâtre caribéen doit se donner les moyens de dépasser leur confinement insulaire. Deuxièmement les questions esthétiques ou étiques reviennent à la création d'une identité caribéenne. Sans cela parler de la caraïbe comme étant un tout est faussé.*

[Caribbean theater must allow itself to go beyond insular confinement. In doing so, the aesthetic and ethical practices of theater will then come back to imagining and creating a Caribbean identity. Without that, talking about the Caribbean as a whole is flawed.]

JGM: Guy Régis Jr. draws a parallel between natural disasters and the disaster of contemporary coloniality, making his accusation all the more salient and startling. Régis Jr. also chronicles through activating memory, as does Ina Césaire, the possibility of working through tremendous loss, finding humor, and accepting paradox as part of life.

[*Le parallèle que fait Guy Régis Jr entre les désastres naturels et le désastre de la colonialité contemporaine rend son accusation d'autant plus saillante et extraordinaire. Tout comme Ina Césaire, Régis Jr relate aussi comment à travers l'activation de la mémoire, on peut surmonter une perte colossale, trouver une part d'humour et accepter le paradoxe comme une partie intégrale de la vie.*]

GO: *Il me semble qu'aujourd'hui, plutôt que de traiter directement de la colonialité ou même de la caribéanité, nous interrogeons et déconstruisons des concepts, idées, mythes ou constructions sociales qui, évidemment, sont chez nous marqués par la colonialité ou l'identité caribéenne. La violence sociale, la condition féminine, la mère poto mitan, la famille, notamment, occupent une grande place dans nos créations—je pense aux travaux d'Adeline Flaun ou encore Magali Solignat et Charlotte Boimare, par exemple.*

[It seems to me that today, more than directly addressing coloniality or even Caribbeanness, we probe and deconstruct concepts, ideas, myths, or social constructions which are, obviously, in our part of the world marked by coloniality or Caribbean identity. Social violence, the status of women, the *poto mitan* mother figure, and family, all occupy a large part of our creative activity. This makes me think of the work of Adeline Flaun, and also Magali Solignat and Charlotte Boimare, among others.]

GAU: I consider work that redirects our gazes and interests toward self-actualization of fuller selves, and maneuvers toward such integration, is most pressing and exemplary of our futurities. The conditions of the so-called New World remain characterized by its past. Work that recognizes this intersection demands that our expressions are not determined by our conditions no matter how damning and limiting. Nicolás Dumit Estévez and Josefina Baez are not of younger generations. From the Dominican Republic, they have been at the forefront of work that engages the spiritual for decades.

[*Je considère que les œuvres qui réorientent nos regards et nos intérêts vers une réalisation de soi plus complète, et les procédures qui mènent à une telle intégration, sont les plus urgentes et les plus représentatives de notre avenir. Les conditions du soi-disant Nouveau Monde restent définies par son passé. Les travaux et les pratiques capables de concevoir cette intersection se doivent de faire en sorte que nos expressions ne soient pas déterminées par nos conditions, aussi accablantes et limitantes soient-elles. Nicolás Dumit Estévez et Josefina Baez ne font pas partie des jeunes générations. Depuis la République dominicaine, ils ont été et restent les précurseurs d'un travail qui engage le spirituel depuis des décennies.*]

Conclusion

This conversation sheds much-needed light on ways in which we, as publics and performers amidst coloniality and catastrophe, can continue to attend to the roles we perform in theaters of artistic creation, intellectual engagement, and local and global relation.

Without hesitation, the artists and scholars agree that colonial contact, its *longue durée* impact, and the discursive and material modes by which the colonial takes form, remain the recurring cause and effect of catastrophe. They also illustrate, earnestly and evocatively, the means by which theater and performance respond to such wide-reaching systems through the recrossing of histories, modes, and audiences.

Miller reminds us of the very systemic, even systematic framework of the colonial, when she emphasizes the reach of "coloniality [...] [that] project of dominating [...] while imposing structures that guarantee the power of those who colonize." She and fellow contributors underscore repeatedly the link between the colonial and the catastrophe, irrevocably connected, with an oft-destructive reach. Earthquakes and hurricanes become, sadly but surely, opportunities for all sorts of interference in the Caribbean.

Encroachments range from recent and ongoing interventions to the first points of colonial contact in Caribbean spaces. Recalling Aimé Césaire's dialectically and thereby intentionally hyphenated "Toi-Moi! Moi-Toi!" [You-Me! Me-You!] from *Une tempête* (1969), as well as Anne McClintock's query about pitfalls of the "post-colonial" (1992), the colonial and the catastrophe are, thus, "colonial-catastrophe." Ulysse draws an indisputably synonymous line between the two: "I don't divide the natural disasters from man-made ones. [...] Colonialism is the first catastrophe, and its concomitant geopolitical warfare has been as crucial."

Catastrophe—whether seismically or volcanically upending, or void of said materially blatant peril—is, as the conversation helps us to understand, impossible to isolate from overlapping social, political, and inextricably colonial catastrophes. Indeed, we learn of efforts to define and navigate said catastrophes—as cataclysmic "events" with tailwinds for those who lived amidst the storms said to have already passed. But we also come to understand how the generations who live well after said events navigate, resist, or even attempt to clean up and carry on. *Kenbe la*, hang in there, as many Haitians say.

Take as one example of colonial-catastrophe the imperial language silos across Caribbean spaces. They have often been bridged through diverse practices like creoles and pidgins forged for generations by enslaved and maroon communities, and multilingualism learned and lived in fields, ports, schools, streets, and scholarly publications. But Guérismé's reflection on Haiti's linguistic experience—Haitian Creole (Kreyòl) and French (for some but not all)—reminds us of limits. It reveals ways in which some Haitian artists in the Caribbean find themselves or their work "apart." Guérismé states that, as a result, some Haitians "turn more and more toward metropolitan centers" (e.g., Montreal, New York City, Paris) for sustainable collaboration, where communities use French and Kreyòl.

While colonial-catastrophe ripples across multiple Caribbean environments at times without any evidentiary, or seemingly seismic devastation, it still brings to lived experience a limiting and imprinting weight. As Octavia explains for islands like Martinique, an overseas department of France where the "same" colonial has persisted in daily life and governmental institutions for centuries: the "problem is the absence of a large-scale catastrophe. We long for a catastrophe [...] that breaks with continuity. We wish something would happen, but we feel as if nothing did." In a separate interview, Octavia drives home this point when she explains what she considers one of the great, long-standing conflicts for Martinicans: "We haven't fought our war of decolonization and we are perpetually fantasizing about this decolonization" (Octavia et al. 2020).

Certainly Martinique—as *longue durée* colony of France from as early as 1635 (with a handful of *courte durée* changes of European imperial occupation), labor colony with France's second abolition of slavery in 1848, and then as overseas department of France since 1946 (and putative equal with France's metropolitan departments)—has weathered its natural catastrophes and political storms. As one example: the 1902 eruption of Montagne Pelée. It destroyed the cultural capital and central port of Saint-Pierre, killed instantly nearly all of the over 30,000 city occupants at the time, and resulted in the largely southward displacement of ports and government to Fort-de-France, the official capital and since then major city.

Such colonial-catastrophe resonates through the ruins in today's active but calmer Saint-Pierre, like the Théâtre Saint-Pierre (1786). They fossilize in the residual detail of the central foyer and staircases, as they publicly record in material performance form, the *longue durée* racialization of colonial-catastrophe that the theater's seating segregation had enacted. One might argue similarly for the mediatized archive of the 2009 embodied and thereby performative demonstrations in Martinique over inequitable costs of living and higher unemployment rates in overseas France. And how records of the swift, and for many, unsatisfactory ensuing formal referendum, reenacts anew the dialectical, post-colonial *Moi-Toi Toi-Moi* of "Martinique-France."

Certainly, Octavia's observations about Martinique draw attention to differences in form, duration, and the "newness" of colonial-catastrophe as compared to Haiti, also noted by Guérismé and Ulysse. The Haitian experience has been foundational and characterized as "large-scale," from as early as its time as the French colony of Saint-Domingue. French colonial presence became palpable on the island of Hispaniola as early as 1659. It then became formal for the western third in 1697, leading eventually to large-scale colonial-catastrophe via further disregard for the enslaved and colonized of Saint-Domingue. The colony would become the French empire's most profitable, with equally record-breaking death tolls of enslaved people in the Caribbean due to the French slavery machine until Haiti's independence in 1804.

Throughout the twentieth century, Haitians have lived repeated "large scale" experiences. It is as if a colonial-catastrophe series has unfolded, with an international exchange of global flows and even "modern" powers. Haitians have weathered exploitative, invasive military occupations (by the United States, 1915–34/47; 1994). They have also endured brutal internal dictatorships (by the Duvaliers, 1957–86), internationally supported and silenced from the outside. Such external repetition with/out difference becomes—to borrow again from the powerful hyphens of Césaire and McClintock—a new-but-old colonial-catastrophe. Haitians in Haiti and the diaspora work tirelessly to live and thrive within and beyond it, pulling from networks to survive as best possible unpredictable storms of chaos.

As the conversation unveils, artists and scholars have a shared goal in response to colonial-catastrophe: rerouting, rewiring, and recrossing colonial-catastrophe. Their praxes involve resisting, reclaiming or, as this contribution's title underscores, re/making beyond it. *On refait, on croise* [we remake, we cross], to paraphrase their practices of weaving together forms fromvaried performance traditions and bringing together people of diverse backgrounds. This happens in performance and performance spaces, as the contributors share in the conversation and in their repertoire. Ulysse directs us to Alexander's work (2006), for considering how the intersections and crossings are revealed and reclaimed, as Ulysse herself does through her praxis of *rasanblaj*.

Such modes, as the conversation highlights, convey struggles and successes of those who dare to devise said modes. Specifically invoking the "palpable" power of theater, of "onstage embodiment" in this process, Miller brings us to the same page and stage when talking of her work as translator. She achieves her goal powerfully when she discusses how characters convey both imagined and real means for navigating colonial-catastrophe: "All the characters in the works I have translated live beyond catastrophe and victimization."

The work of many Caribbean creatives alone also re/makes local myths born of colonial-catastrophe, myths which some embrace and others reject. As one example, the tradition of the *poto mitan*: the Martinican (and also Haitian) Creole term for the mother-savior figure, the (moral) pillar of society. Octavia underscores how the discourse and even practice inscribed for the *poto mitan* is far from salvatory. It is instead to be redressed, as she and many theater makers do: "Today, part of the work of young creatives, and especially of female creatives, is in fact to deconstruct [such] Caribbean myths."

Scholars, too, make significant contributions to re/making of myths like the *poto mitan*, as a taking on of colonial-catastrophe. Emily Sahakian (2017) addresses the ways in which women theater makers of the French Caribbean, like Ina Césaire and Gerty Dambury, regularly carve out space on the page and stage to shed light on such gendered power relations, especially on the *poto mitan*. Vanessa Lee (2021) returns to the work of the same women theater makers, to ask and answer questions about how their theater is decisively postcolonial and thereby contribute to postcolonial discourse, in theory and in practice. In Haitian contexts, Sabine Lamour (2021) dives deep into the intersectional and colonial history of the *poto-mitan* (as also spelled), to sift through contemporary uses of the term in Haiti for women who either choose or must work outside of the home.

At the same time that the conversation emphasizes how artists and scholars strive to reconsider and even reclaim the colonial-catastrophe of such "tradition," artists and scholars in Haitian spaces remind us of the spiritual context of re/making to which an overlapping meaning and practice of the *poto mitan* is literally central. In Vodou practice, the *poto mitan* is the central, wooden pillar in the *ounfò* (temple), directly in the center of the temple's sacred space—much as the *poto mitan* is the central pillar to many Haitian structures built of spirit-imbued wood. But for Vodou, the *poto mitan* is the physical site through which the *lwa* (spirits) pass during possession ceremonies. The *poto mitan* plays, then, a vital role in Vodou spiritual performance as it has in Haitian theater and performance. In this light, we can understand the *poto mitan* for its critical role in artistic creation, akin to the way that Franck Fouché (2008) re-theorized Vodou as *the* pre-theater of Haitian popular theater, Haitian life, and Haiti.

Such broad reaches of re/making remind us, as Guérismé states, that "the depths of catastrophe" are ever-present in today's world. We encounter the magnitude in countless works of artistic creation. Recent memory includes the most-referenced event in Haiti, the 2010 earthquake, with: the death of over 300,000 people; the fracturing and shattering of infrastructures in the capital city, Port-au-Prince, and in Léogâne and Jacmel (Mika 2018); the over 15-year displacement of residents; the concomitant colonial-catastrophe of fake international aid; and the aspiration to inspire movement away from such future colonial-catastrophe.

Plays like Guy Régis Jr.'s *De toute la terre le grand effarement* (2011) put colonial-catastrophe on new international stages. In harmony with Ulysse's call (2015) for new narratives, Régis Jr. brings attention to often overlooked aspects of the post-2010 experience. *De toute la terre* transmits the centuries-old Haitian, and thereby transatlantic knowledge of dying and living, practices of navigating such experiences, and stoic and satirical critique of the states of power which perpetually reactivate colonial-catastrophe. Gaëlle Bien-Aimé (2023) also turns audience attention to the trauma Haitians (including herself) have been forced to live due to internationally fueled colonial-catastrophe since 2018. Residents of some (not all) sections of Port-au-Prince dodge bullets from the guns of externally funded gangs (while some loved ones have not been so fortunate). Or they find their homes destroyed from the fires of conflict, displaced within, or seeking exile without. Based on Bien-Aimé's experience, her play *Port-au-Prince et sa douce nuit* (2022) humanizes, powerfully yet tenderly, a couple's struggle over staying or leaving. It spotlights the deep fear and insecurity (*insekerite*) that makes one of them wish to flee, and the love for city, fellow citizens, and especially each other that makes them stay.

Earlier theater makers, like *feue* (recently passed) Maryse Condé, retell and thereby propose how to build bridges across Caribbean experiences of colonial-catastrophe. Condé's *An tan révolisyon* (1989; 2015) rehashes the French revolution (1789–1794) at the time of its bicentennial (1989). More important, it underscores the French revolution's temporal and geographical intersections with overlapping *and* separate movements in Saint-Domingue (Haiti), and Guadeloupe. *An tan* highlights multiple voices (including through the 2015 translations), bodies, and stages of revolution*s* and/as resistance movements: the often silenced Haitian revolution (1791–1804); and the militarily-arrested but forever-revered 1802 Guadeloupean resistance, led in part by the formidable Louis Delgrès.

Theater and performance as alternative—as re/making—burn in the hearts of many Caribbean theater and performance creatives, who have not forgotten but will not be branded by the broad, brutal reach of colonial-catastrophe. Such is the case with Ulysse's "recenter[ing]" through *rasanblaj*. She "eschew[s] coloniality and catastrophe as ethos and aesthetics" and offers an expansive model for thinking through and with our environmental connections in an "unequitable world." As Ulysse, Octavia, Guérismé, Miller, and many artists and scholars like them reveal, one cannot shake off colonial-catastrophe, in part or in whole, from one's self or one's work. But one must not remain controlled by it. One must eschew, recenter, deploy, live and work to thrive—even in moments—beyond colonial-catastrophe. One must turn toward and with a collaborative strategy of re/making, particularly relevant within the theatrical space, and in our world today. And that is precisely what the above conversation achieves and inspires, if we allow it, for performers and audiences of Caribbean theater and performance.

Notes

1. All translations from French to English are mine, unless otherwise noted. I also offer heartfelt thanks to Linda Brindeau, specialist in Caribbean studies, for her life-giving translations from English to French, her expertise in editing format and style, and her generosity and good humor. Much appreciation is owed to The Melodia E. Jones Chair of French at SUNY-University at Buffalo, for the sponsorship of Linda's translation. I remain forever inspired by *feue* [the late] Maryse Condé (1934–2024), for her decades of bringing attention to *les traversées* [the crossings], which make and re/make all lived experience. I am grateful to my sister, Jennifer, and the circle of friends alongside me, for their strength, encouragement, and good will. And as always, I thank Mark.
2. Translated by Alexandra Lillehei.

Works Cited

Alexander, M. Jacqui. 2006. *Pedagogies of Crossing: Meditations on Feminism, Sexual Politics, Memory, and the Sacred*. Durham: Duke University Press. https://doi.org/10.1515/9780822386988.

Bien-Aimé, Gaëlle. 2023. Gaëlle Bien-Aimé sur son texte 'Port-au-Prince et sa douce nuit': 'J'écrivais d'un lieu de chaos.' Interview with Julia Wahl. *TouteLaCulture.com*, May 4. https://toutelaculture.com/spectacles/theater/gaelle-bien-aime-sur-son-texte-port-au-prince-et-sa-douce-nuit-jecrivais-dun-lieu-de-chaos/.

Césaire, Aimé. 1969. *Une tempête*. Paris: Seuil.

Condé, Maryse. 2015. *An tan révolisyon: elle court, elle court la liberté*; with translations: *An tan révolisyon: libèté, sékouriika*; *In the Time of the Revolution: run, liberty, run*; *Tiempos de revolución: corre, corre, la libertad*. Paris: l'Amandier.

Damas, Léon Gontran. 1937. *Pigments*. Paris: G.L.M.

Damas, Léon Gontran. 2011. *Pigments in Translation*. Translated by Alexandra Lillehei. Wesleyan U, Undergraduate honors thesis. https://digitalcollections.wesleyan.edu/object/ir-391.

Fouché, Frank. 2008. *Vodou et théâtre: pour un théâtre populaire*. Montreal: Nouvelle optique, 1976. Montreal: Mémoire d'encrier.

Lamour, Sabine. 2021. Between Intersectionality and Coloniality: Rereading the Figure of the *Poto-Mitan* Woman in Haiti. *Women, Gender, and Families of Color* 9 (2): 136–151.

Lee, Vanessa. 2021. *Four Caribbean Women Playwrights: Ina Césaire, Maryse Condé, Gerty Dambury and Suzanne Dracius*. New York: Palgrave Macmillan.

McClintock, Anne. 1992. The Angel of Progress: Pitfalls of the Term 'Post-Colonialism.' *Social Text* 31–32: 84–98. https://doi.org/10.2307/466219.

Mika, Kasia. 2018. *Disasters, Vulnerability, and Narratives: Writing Haiti's Futures*. London: Routledge.

Octavia, Gaël, Daniely Francisque, and Fabrice Théodose. 2020. "Cette guerre que nous n'avons pas faite", "Le Monologue du Gwo Pwèl" and "Ladjablès, femme sauvage": plays about "us." Interviewed by Gladys Dubois. Trans. Evelyne Chaville. KariCulture.net. 19 August. http://www.kariculture.net/en/cette-guerre-navons-faite-monologue-gwo-pwel-and-ladjables-femme-sauvage-plays-about-us/.

Régis Jr., Guy. 2011. *De toute la terre le grand effarement*. Paris: Solitaires Intempestifs.

Sahakian, Emily. 2017. *Staging Creolization: Women's Theater and Performance from the French Caribbean*. Charlottesville: University Press of Virginia.

Ulysse, Gina Athena. 2015. *Why Haiti Needs New Narratives: A Post-Quake Chronicle. Sa k fè Ayiti bezwen istwa tou nèf; Pourquoi Haïti a besoin de nouveaux discours*; trans. Nadève Ménard and Evelyne Trouillot. Middletown: Wesleyan University Press.

Index

A
adaptation, 1, 14, 15, 19, 51, 55, 58, 60–62, 67, 89, 122, 151
Afro-Caribbean, 3, 10, 19, 20, 147, 158
Alexander, Anjellina, 123
All Our Monsters, 123
All Our Monsters: Witches, 123
American Shakespeare Center, 68, 80
anglophone, 9, 10, 25, 81, 147, 246
apocalyptic narratives, 20, 171
archipelago, 2, 11, 22, 76, 109, 186, 188, 199, 203
Ariel, 17, 74–78, 81, 82, 89, 94–97, 110
Aristide, Jean-Bertrand, 14, 51, 57–60
Artaud, Antonin, 72, 89
assemblage, 8, 11, 12

B
The Bahamas, 2, 12, 18, 108–110, 114, 121, 128, 130, 136, 141
Bahamian theater, 120, 121
Bethel, Nicolette, 1, 17, 18, 110, 118, 129, 135, 137–140
Bien-Aimé, Gaëlle, 264
The Black Jacobins, 14–16, 50–55, 58–62, 64
body, 5, 10, 22, 40, 41, 43, 61, 72, 82, 87, 96, 100, 127, 128, 130, 133, 134, 137, 141, 156, 173, 190, 222, 223, 226, 231, 235, 237, 242, 264
Bonilla, Yarimar, 4, 6, 21, 167, 180, 181, 199, 222
Burnett, Sarah, 123
Burrows, Philip A., 112, 117–119

C
Caliban, 16, 68, 72, 76–81, 92, 110
camp, 21, 37, 45, 198, 207
Canboulay, 148, 150–155, 159, 160
capitalism, 2–4, 19, 34, 108–110, 149, 171, 182, 184, 188, 200, 207, 212

Caribbean, 1, 6, 10, 15, 24, 25, 54, 62, 76, 91, 107, 119, 129, 147, 158, 164, 180, 186, 194, 212, 223, 242, 246, 257, 263, 265
Caribbean Literature in Transition, 12
Caribbean theater, 4, 8–11, 16, 24, 148, 265
Carrió, Raquel, 16, 86, 94, 97
catastrophe, 1, 4, 18, 23, 25, 29, 42, 46, 50, 56, 85, 108, 121, 146–148, 160, 161, 180, 181, 184, 213, 248, 250, 255, 260, 265
catastrophic reality, 21, 181, 192
Centre for Creative and Festival Arts (CCFA), 55
Césaire, Aimé, 9, 23, 67, 68, 71, 73, 78, 80, 134, 260
Césaire, Suzanne, 16, 68–71, 252
The Children's Teeth: A Play in Two Acts, 18, 123, 129, 135, 140, 141
Class of 2020, 123
colonialism, 1, 3, 13, 14, 17, 25, 49, 56, 63, 87, 88, 98, 134, 148, 181, 203, 260
coloniality, 4, 15, 18, 22, 23, 34, 37, 40, 45, 88, 90, 97, 113, 121, 128, 134, 177, 242, 246, 257, 259, 265
coloniality of power, 89, 99, 128
communion, 189, 242
community, 6, 20, 34, 42, 55, 56, 70, 79, 116, 122, 129, 156, 176, 220, 233, 235, 236, 254
Competent Authority, 117, 119
crises, 2, 9, 20, 131, 149, 180, 186, 204, 235, 236
cross-cultural, 9, 11, 15, 25
crossing, 71, 242, 262, 265
Cuba, 87, 97, 166, 187, 193, 220
cultural catastrophe, 137, 153, 159

D
decolonial aesthetics, 5, 165
decolonization, 9, 56, 67, 202, 247, 261
De toute la terre le grand effarement, 29, 264
Diary of Souls, 18, 129, 132, 133, 136, 137, 141
diaspora, 10, 22, 24, 94, 120, 212, 252
Díaz-Quiñones, Arcadio, 7, 222
disaster, 2, 6, 25, 34, 74, 128, 130, 137, 149, 153, 160, 165, 170, 199, 242, 258
Disla, Frank, 20, 164, 165, 172, 174–176
Dominican Republic, 19, 163, 164, 167, 170, 176, 177, 259
drag, 21, 173, 198, 199, 206–210, 212

E
earthquake, Haiti 2010, 2
ecopoetics, 68, 74
Eggs for Breakfast, 123
Elegguá, 88, 93, 94, 97, 101
empathy, 18, 119, 121
errancy, 92
Ezili, 32, 38–40, 42, 44, 45

F
flood, 13, 163, 166
Francis, Patrice A., 117–119
francophone, 10, 22, 23, 38, 243, 244, 246, 249

G

García-Cartagena, Manuel, 20, 164, 165, 167–170, 176
gender, 3, 42, 64, 92, 198, 205, 228
Gibbons, Rawle, 14–16, 19, 51, 55, 56, 58, 60, 62, 155, 158, 160
Glissant, Édouard, 6, 11, 80, 89, 92, 186, 192
Guadeloupe, 23, 264
Guérismé, Eliézer, 9, 23, 24, 260, 265
Gun Boys Rhapsody, 113, 114

H

Haiti, 14, 23, 32, 35, 40, 49, 56, 58, 59, 122, 130, 243, 252, 263
Haitian migration, 19, 141, 220
Haitian Revolution, 14, 30, 50, 51, 57, 63, 265
Hanna, S.A., 123
healing, 18, 61, 108, 119–121, 161
Hernández, Teresa, 22, 222–229, 231, 233–235
Hill, Errol, 9
hispanophone, 9, 246
Hudes, Quiara Alegría, 20, 179, 184, 189, 190
hurricane, 2, 25, 93, 115, 116, 122, 222
Hurricane Dorian, 18, 115, 116, 131, 132
Hurricane Maria, 4, 7, 19, 180, 181

I

identity, 9, 11, 23, 69, 71, 146, 150, 174, 206, 219, 225, 235, 237, 249, 256, 259
I Lawah, 19, 147, 148, 150, 159, 160
insurrection, 77, 79
Iwa, 32

J

James, C.L.R., 14, 50–53, 55, 60, 62, 141

L

language, 8, 16, 86, 128, 175, 184, 207, 242, 254, 260
La otra orilla, 20, 179, 180, 183, 184, 186, 188, 192
Lauten, Flora, 89, 90, 96, 97, 99
Lebrón, Lolita, 21, 167, 199, 203–205, 207
LGBTQ, 199, 206
l'homme-plante, 70, 71, 78
Louverture, Toussaint, 51, 52, 60
Love Trilogy, 19, 148, 155

M

Maldonado-Torres, Nelson, 3, 34, 50, 57, 150, 165, 181, 192
marginality, 235
Martinique, 2, 16, 25, 68, 70, 247, 261
Miller, Judith G., 23, 46
Mimeologías, 22, 222, 224, 225, 231, 232, 235
multi-sensory aesthetics, 20, 181
multi-sensory theater, 180
Music Box, 123

N

naufragio, 17, 193
neoliberal, 2, 6, 20, 165, 180
neoliberal sensorium, 182, 190
New York, 20, 198, 208, 209, 213
Notes on Killing Seven Oversight, Management and Economic Stability Board Members, 21, 197, 201, 208, 212

O

obliteration, 148
Octavia, Gaël, 23, 244, 261
Ogun Ayan- As in Pan, 147, 148, 155
Oshún, 88, 91–93, 97, 101
Otra tempestad, 17, 86–92, 95, 103
Oyá, 88, 91, 93, 97, 98, 100, 185

P

païdeuma, 16, 68–71, 76
pan-Caribbean, 9, 10, 12, 184
politics, 50, 59, 81, 128, 176, 201, 205, 210, 228, 255
post-colony, 128, 139, 141, 142
poto mitan, 256–258, 263
Puerto Rico, 2, 4, 8, 21, 171, 180, 185, 193, 197, 201, 203, 209, 220, 227
Puerto Rico Oversight, Management and Economic Stability (PROMESA), 21, 197, 198, 201, 202, 212–214, 235

Q

queer, 21, 39, 198, 200, 204, 205, 207, 212
Quijano, Aníbal, 3, 53, 90, 109

R

rasanblaj, 12, 245, 257, 265
Régis Jr., Guy, 13, 29–37, 39–41, 43–46, 244, 250–253, 258, 264
relation, 122, 192, 193
resilience, 19, 30, 148, 251
revolution, 22, 52, 57, 205, 264
rhizome, 11
Rolle, Valicia, 112
Rossini, Jon D., 8, 205, 213

S

Saunders, Winston, 111–113
Senior, Olive, 2
Shakespeare in Paradise, 17, 108, 110, 114, 117, 120, 121
Shakespeare, William, 1, 3, 16, 18, 68, 79, 81, 88, 89, 91, 92, 98, 108, 121, 122
Sheller, Mimi, 4, 6, 109
Sheperd, 19
Short Tales (4 volumes), 115, 116
Shouters Prohibition Ordinance, 156, 157
Siete días antes del Tsunami, 20, 164, 165, 171
slow violence, 19, 131, 181
Small Axe, 110
Soho Rep, 198, 201, 202, 208
solo performance, 22, 172, 223
spatial injustice, 19
Stevens, Camilla, 9, 192, 211
Strachan, Ian, 18, 19, 109, 113, 114, 133–136, 140, 141
structural violence, 4, 18, 128, 129, 133, 135, 138
Sunk in Love, 123
surrealism, 69, 71, 252

T

Teatro Buendía, 16, 17, 86, 91
Teatro Guloya, 167
Teatro Pregones, 20, 179, 186
The Tempest, 1, 15, 16, 67, 71, 74, 75, 79, 80, 86, 88, 109, 110
temporality, 19, 182, 187, 192
theater, Cuba, 12
theater, Dominican Republic, 12
theater, Martinique, 12
theater, New York City, 212
theater of migration, 20
theater, Puerto Rico, 12

theater, Trinidad and Tobago, 12
third theatre, 16, 19, 55, 149, 159
Toussaint Louverture: The Story of the Only Successful Slave Revolt in History, 50
tradition, 6, 9, 15, 19, 23, 25, 82, 155, 160, 198, 206, 263
transdisciplinarity, 22
transgender, 21, 198–200, 206
trauma, 31, 36, 42, 116, 134, 173, 254
Trinidad and Tobago, 58
Tropiques, 68, 69, 71
Turner, Telcine, 123

U

Ulysse, Gina Athena, 12, 14, 24, 35, 49, 50, 260, 262, 265
Une tempête, 16, 67, 68, 71, 74, 75, 80, 89, 260
Un romance andaluz, 20, 164, 174, 176

V

Vélez Meléndez, Mara, 21, 23, 197–200, 202, 205, 207, 209–213

vigil, 13, 30–32, 37, 43, 45
violence, 3, 14, 17, 32, 40, 51, 52, 59, 61, 79, 87, 91, 99, 108, 111, 113, 120, 128, 132, 134, 136, 138–140, 152, 164, 171, 209, 223, 246, 249, 259
voice, 22, 60, 95, 128, 157, 223, 231, 264

W

wake, 8, 14, 18, 30–32, 34, 37, 44, 46, 52, 116, 138, 180
Walcott, Derek, 9–11, 15, 127, 142
Wall Street, 198, 206, 212
warfare, 145, 250, 260
Woman Take Two: A Play in Three Acts, 123
women's experience, 39

Y

Yemaya's Belly, 20, 179, 180, 184, 191
Yoruba cosmology, 20, 181, 192
You Can Lead a Horse to Water, 111–115